ORTHOPAEDIC NURSING

Anne Footner RGN, ONC(Hons), Dip.N(Lond), F.E.T.C. Cert Ed.(F.E) RCNT

Course Tutor, the Nuffield Orthopaedic Centre, Oxford;
Member of the ENB Specialist Panel for Orthopaedic Nursing; and
Chairman of the Orthopaedic Nursing Forum of the Royal College of Nursing.

Baillière Tindall
London Philadelphia Toronto Sydney Tokyo

Baillière Tindall   24–28 Oval Road
  WB Saunders   London NW1 7DX

The Curtis Center
Independence Square West
Philadelphia, PA 19106-3399, USA

1 Goldthorne Avenue
Toronto, Ontario M8Z 5T9, Canada

Harcourt Brace Jovanovich Group (Australia) Pty Ltd.
32–52 Smidmore Street
Marrickville, NSW 2204, Australia

Harcourt Brace Jovanovich (Japan) Inc
Ichibancho Central Building, 22-1 Ichibancho
Chiyoda-ku, Tokyo 102, Japan

First published 1987
Reprinted 1989

Typeset by MC Typeset Ltd, Chatham
Printed in Great Britain at The Alden Press, Oxford

British Library Cataloguing in Publication Data

Footner, Anne
  Orthopaedic nursing.
  1. Orthopaedic nursing
  I. Title
  617′.3′0024613   RD753

ISBN 0-7020-1255-6

ORTHOPAEDIC NURSING

3.92

)

i

0702012556

CONTENTS

PREFACE

It has given me much pleasure to write this book on orthopaedic nursing. I am proud to follow in the footsteps of Beth Stone and Ted Pinney in writing for Baillière Tindall about a branch of nursing which has changed so much during my own career.

The book has been written for those students about to take the orthopaedic nursing courses run by the National Boards. It is hoped that it will be useful to students in general training, those taking the RSCN Course and any nurse who is engaged in caring for patients with orthopaedic conditions.

As a member of the English National Board orthopaedic specialist panel which planned the English National Board courses, I have tried to follow the philosophy of the board in taking a nursing model on which to base the book. Past orthopaedic courses have concentrated on a biomedical model. Knowledge of the anatomy and medical condition is important when planning the management of an orthopaedic patient, but the emphasis in this book is nursing care.

Nursing practice itself has changed and I have taken this into account. Care is now planned with an holistic approach, looking at the patient as a whole. The book is planned around Roper, Logan and Teirney's model of nursing and the nursing process. Nursing research is gaining momentum and wherever possible this has been used as the rationale behind the nursing actions which have been planned. The roles of all members of the team have been included whenever appropriate.

Like the previous authors of this book I have retained the nursing related to patients with tuberculosis and poliomyelitis. These diseases have not been a major problem for the UK for some years, but there is evidence to suggest that they may be seen more frequently in the future, and these diseases do present a major problem in some countries where this book will be read.

Many of the areas of concern in orthopaedic nursing need further reading by the student. Sections such as trauma and the application of plaster casts are specialist areas which require in-depth knowledge. Suggested further reading is found at the end of each chapter.

The students undertaking these courses are adult learners and the book has been written with this in mind. The references to research and suggested further reading should provide the student with a guide to help them increase and expand their knowledge by self-directed study.

Orthopaedic nursing has entered a new phase in its history. My hope is that this book will enable those nurses already in this specialty, and those about to enter into it, to nurse their patients with the care and dedication of those who pioneered this branch of nursing in the past.

ANNE FOOTNER

ACKNOWLEDGEMENTS

I would like to record my thanks to Miss Sue Ponting and Mrs Jan Simons for typing the manuscript of this book and for deciphering my often illegible handwriting and notes.

My thanks to my teaching and clinical colleagues who have given me valuable advice and guidance throughout the book. In particular I would like to thank Peter Davis, Tutor, Bloomfield College of Nurse Education for the time and help he has given me in producing the final manuscript. I am indebted to Messrs Matthew Thomas and Paul Cooper for their help with the photography.

Also my thanks for the invaluable help and advice given by Baillière Tindall in their careful production of this textbook.

Last, but by no means least, I would like to thank my husband, Laurence, for his patience, tolerance, support and the innumerable cups of coffee he has supplied me with during the writing of this book.

1

ORTHOPAEDIC NURSING: YESTERDAY AND TODAY

The past forty years have seen a rapid change in the field of orthopaedics and orthopaedic nursing. Common conditions treated in those early days were tuberculosis of bone and joint, poliomyelitis, osteomyelitis and many deformities due to the low standard of living and hygiene. Today many of these conditions have virtually disappeared with the discovery and use of new drugs, improvements in hygiene and living standards, and the advent of the National Health Service. However, the old type of problems have been replaced by a new set of problems.

Many advances in our society today have extended the life expectancy of man, resulting in an increase in degenerative conditions of bones and joints. At the same time advances in methods of transport have made the world a smaller place, but it has also increased the number of injuries associated with travel, and the accident and emergency departments are frequently overflowing with the resultant casualties. These departments are also kept busy with new types of injuries from the violent society in which we now live. Many orthopaedic problems have not changed. Rheumatoid arthritis has long been the scourge of many of our patients. New techniques and drugs directed towards the relief of this crippling condition, early detection to prevent the onset of complications, and research into the cause of the disease, are all helping to alleviate some of the problems for patients.

The year of the disabled in 1982 was aimed at educating the general public towards the handicapped person, to change attitudes and to bring about an awareness of the problems encountered by disabled persons. Rehabilitation of the handicapped is now established practice and takes place in recognized centres under the direction of a consultant in physical medicine. Many new buildings are at last beginning to reflect the need to accommodate the disabled.

Together with these changes, orthopaedic surgical procedures have developed and patient management has been adapted to meet a new set of needs and circumstances.

WHAT IS AN ORTHOPAEDIC NURSE AND WHAT IS SO SPECIAL ABOUT ORTHOPAEDIC NURSING?

Of necessity, hand in hand with everything else, orthopaedic nursing has had to change, and is presently still undergoing changes and accepting new challenges. The preparation of the orthopaedic nurse to enter this speciality has also changed. It is important for any nurse to realize, before she embarks upon a course of training for orthopaedic nursing, that this branch of nursing is continuously changing to meet the needs of the patient and the expectations of the medical profession.

Orthopaedic nursing is essentially a branch of the nursing profession which demands a considerable amount of basic nursing skills based on a careful assessment of the individual patient's needs (see Figure 1.1). The care planned to meet these needs is then evaluated, which may lead the nurse to review the care she has given and either continue or change the plan accordingly. Her ultimate goal is the reinstatement of the patient in society, ready to accept the limitations of his mobility or loss of body image, if this is necessary.

The first essential for any orthopaedic nurse is a good understanding of the musculo-skeletal system and how it works in health. The ability to observe, recognize and report the abnormal is of the greatest importance.

An understanding of the musculo-skeletal system will also enable the orthopaedic nurse to understand her own body. She needs to be strong and healthy and her knowledge of anatomy should enable her to maintain her own body in a healthy condition. The orthopaedic nurse is very much part of a team headed by the

DAILY ACTIVITIES

Nutrition Weight	Breathing	Recreational activities
Dentures /braces (specify)	Sleeping pattern	
Elimination	SENSES Sight: Hearing: Speech:	Religious activities/helpful beliefs
Hygiene and skin condition Norton Score	HOME CONDITIONS AND SOCIAL ARRANGEMENTS	Mental/emotional state Reaction to hospital admission
Mobility		Other relevant information

Fig. 1.1 Sample of an assessment and care plan sheet.

Ward: Admission date:	House Officer:	Consultant:

Tel. No.

STICKY

Reason for admission

GP: ....

Age: ____ Marital status:
d.o.b. ____ Occupation:

Social
worker ....

Religion: Baptised:

Surgery/Treatment

Relatives staying:

Likes to be referred to as:

....

Dependants/Siblings

NEXT OF KIN   Tel Nos.

Name: ....
            ....

Patient's understanding of admission

Discharge arrangements

Address: ....
....

                                          Needed   Ordered

....

Out-Patients   ....

MEANINGFUL OTHERS

Family's understanding of admission

District Nurse   ....

....

Convalescence   ....

Health Visitor   ....

....

Relevant Past Medical History

Home Help   ....

TYPE OF ADMISSION

Transport   ....

Emergency/Waiting List

Discharge advice ....

Provisional Medical Diagnosis

TTOs   ....

DRUGS taken   Allergies/Infection

Others   ....

Actual Medical Diagnosis

at home   Diseases

Discharge date: ....

DATE	PROBLEMS (ACTUAL (A) AND POTENTIAL (P))	DESIRED OUTCOME	REVIEW DATE	NURSING ACTION

orthopaedic consultant; a team which consists of many disciplines, each contributing to the patient's care. Members of this team include the physiotherapist, occupational therapist, dentist, speech therapist, chiropodist, disablement resettlement officer, dietitian, pharmacist, medical social worker, and many others. The patient and his family or friends are an important part of this team. Each has his own part to play, but the nurse has the special role of coordinator.

The nurse is the only one to provide a 24 hour service to meet the changing needs of the patient. Many orthopaedic conditions have a bearing on the patient's daily life and his fears and worries have a need to be expressed and the nurse needs to show a willingness to listen. This means that, wherever possible, she needs to have a very balanced and stable outlook in her own life and to be able to approach the patient's problems with patience and understanding.

Teaching plays an essential part of the nurse's role. The patient needs to be made aware of the complications of immobility. Careful planning with the nurse will enable the patient to set his own goals to minimize these risks. Preparation for postoperative regimes and the correct use of equipment and appliances is equally important to allow the patient to familiarize himself with these. This will help to allay anxiety in both the pre- and postoperative phases of the patient's time in hospital. The nurse must be prepared to take time to teach the patient how to use each item.

A knowledge of psychology will enable the nurse to appreciate the fears and apprehensions of the orthopaedic patient. The reaction of the family, relatives and friends of the patient to deformity or alterations in his social and daily life is very relevant. This is particularly so when the patient is a child. The involvement of parents and siblings in the care of the child is important. Children with orthopaedic conditions need preparation for the reaction of peers to their appearance, particularly if orthoses are used. Some parents feel guilty over their child's deformity, some do not. Many have the need to talk through their feelings with the nurse. The orthopaedic ward sister must not only be a good manager, but she must be an expert in her chosen field, an educator to both students and patients, and be ready to increase her own knowledge and keep abreast of research in nursing and in orthopaedics. The clinical aspect of her work is constantly changing as new

methods of dealing with orthopaedic conditions are introduced. New equipment and practices quickly become established and the ward sister has to be willing to change and to be aware of the reasons behind the change. As the trainer in the clinical area she has to be aware of the new needs of the student, while at the same time keeping her patients' care at the necessary standard to maintain an excellent service.

The orthopaedic ward needs to provide a safe environment in which to nurse the patients. Sufficient space between the beds and furniture to accommodate nursing equipment is essential. Traction equipment, unwieldy splints and plasters may all constitute a hazard to both the patient and the nurse, if space is restricted.

All orthopaedic beds should have a firm base on which to nurse the patient. This will provide full support for the musculo-skeletal frame. The beds should be adjustable for height, not only to facilitate nursing actions, but to enable the disabled patient to get in and out of bed with ease.

Patients in traction or with heavy plaster casts need to be wheeled to various departments in the hospital. Beds with large wheels will enable this to be done. Constant servicing of the beds is essential by the engineering department. Easily wheeled beds will also enable the patients to be wheeled out into garden spaces, if available.

Bed-making is often unconventional. It should primarily provide comfort for the patient. However, it must also allow the nurse easy access to carry out observations of the necessary area of the patient's body.

Admission of the orthopaedic patient gives the nurse the opportunity to start forming a professional relationship with the patient and his family. Assessment of the patient's problems is undertaken once the patient has been formally admitted to the ward (see Figure 1.2). Some patients may like a relative to be present during this time, and this may help to make the patient feel relaxed and to know he is providing all the information required of him.

Assessment is an ongoing process. As the patient's condition changes, so re-assessment must be carried out. During the initial interview with the patient most information will be obtained, but it may take several days before all relevant data is completed. Once the assessment is complete the nurse will plan, with the patient, the care she is going to give the patient. Setting patient-orientated goals is important. The patient is then able to identify exactly what he

Fig. 1.2   Nurse assessing the patient's individual needs with a relative present.

hopes to achieve, aided by the nurse. Goals need to be realistic and easily achievable. This will motivate the patient to progress, but at his own rate.

Implementation of the care plan is carried out by the nurse following the plans set by the patient and herself. The patient is able to assist the nurse whenever possible as he has the knowledge of what the nurse is going to do for him.

Evaluation of the care plan (see page 1) is a means of seeing whether the care has enabled the patient to reach his own goals. It is made at regular intervals throughout the patient's stay in hospital. It should invoive the patient, who is then able to help replan his own care when it is necessary.

Whenever possible, total independence for the patient is the aim of the whole orthopaedic team. This may be unrealistic for those patients who were dependent on others prior to their admission to hospital. In these cases maximum independence, within the individual's own capabilities, is the aim of the team.

2

OUTLINE OF THE ANATOMY RELATED TO THE MUSCULO-SKELETAL SYSTEM

A good general knowledge and understanding of anatomy is essential to the orthopaedic nurse in order that she may apply it to the individual patient's care. However, this book is not an anatomy book and therefore only an outline of the basic anatomy is included. Living anatomy is far more relevant for the learner studying orthopaedic nursing and the nurse should be able to locate, on the human body, particular bony points to identify landmarks for the application of orthoses. Practice on her own body will aid this.

BONE TISSUE

Bone is classified as connective tissue. It is composed of both organic and inorganic substances; because of this, living bones are springy and resilient, have a nerve supply and a rich blood supply. Live bones can also adapt their shape to their function by being shaped by pressure. This is particularly so in young bones. Poor posture or unsuitable footwear may result in permanent distortion of the bony skeleton of the feet (see Figure 2.1)

THE SKELETON

The skeleton itself has several major functions:

1. It provides the main supporting structure of the body and provides attachment for muscles, ligaments and fascia.
2. The bones are linked together by joints, and this enables them to act as levers for the muscles.
3. The skeleton provides protection for many organs of the body.
4. It acts as a manufacturing and storing

agent. Red blood cells are manufactured in the red bone marrow of bones, and calcium is stored which is essential for the daily activity of tissues.

Nursing care

- Careful position of the orthopaedic patient in bed, and of the patient's limbs in the optimum and well-supported position, will prevent further complications of fixed deformities for the patient.
- Nursing the patient in a firm-based bed will provide good support for the bony framework of the body.
- Knowledge of the bony skeleton will aid the nurse in the application of splints, traction, plasters and orthoses without creating problems for the patient.

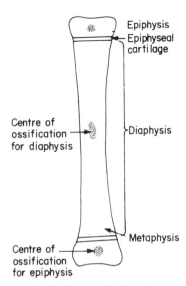

Fig. 2.1 Schematic diagram showing the parts of a long bone.

- Nursing observations of orthopaedic patients' extremities for colour and capillary return, sensation and movement will indicate any interference with major blood and nerve supply.
- Patient teaching as to correct posture and footwear, particularly to parents, may prevent further complications.
- Re-education of the patient following surgery with regard to posture and movement.
- Nutrition—an adequate intake of protein and calcium during a 24 hour period—is essential for good bone formation. Milk is a particularly good source of these components and also helps with the fluid intake to maintain a correct electrolyte balance.

JOINTS

A joint is formed where two or more skeletal structures meet. There are three major classifications of joints:

1. *Fibrous joints* are formed where fibrous tissue holds the bones together, e.g., the sutures of the skull. Very little movement, if any, occurs at these joints (see Figure 2.2).
2. *Cartilaginous joints.* In these joints the bone ends are covered in hyaline cartilage and the bone ends are then separated by a pad or disc of fibrocartilage. A typical example of these joints is the symphisis pubis and the joints between the vertebral bodies. Some limited movement is permissable at these joints (see Figure 2.3).
3. *Synovial joints.* These are the most freely moveable joints in the body and a considerable amount of orthopaedic nurses' work will consist of caring for patients who have problems with these types of joints. A

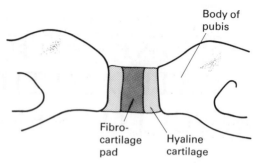

Fig. 2.3 Schematic diagram showing the parts of a cartilaginous joint.

typical synovial joint has certain common characteristics:

(i) The bony articular surfaces are covered with hyaline cartilage which forms a smooth, shiny mass on the surface.

(ii) Continuous with the periosteum of the bones is the joint capsule. It forms a sleeve of dense, fibrous tissue which supports the joint. The capsule varies in thickness and in some areas is deficient. It may be reinforced by bands of fibrous tissue called ligaments. It is perforated to allow the passage of nerves and blood vessels.

(iii) Synovial membrane (see Figure 2.4). This is a thin, highly vascular tissue which lines the joint capsule and covers any structures within the joint not covered by hyaline cartilage. Its principal function is to secrete synovial fluid which fills the joint cavity. The func-

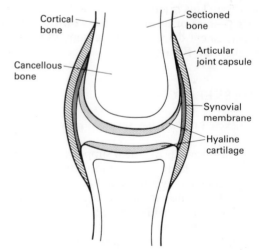

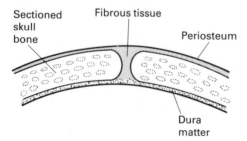

Fig. 2.2 Schematic diagram showing the parts of a fibrous joint.

Fig. 2.4 Schematic diagram showing the parts of a synovial joint.

tion of the synovial fluid is to lubricate the joint and nourish the hyaline cartilage. The fluid also contains phagocytic cells which aid absorption of microscopic foreign bodies, such as bacteria and broken down blood cells.

There are a variety of types of synovial joints to be found in the body:

1. Ball and socket.
2. Hinge.
3. Double hinge.
4. Condyloid.
5. Pivot.
6. Saddle.

Nursing care

When nursing patients with joint problems, the following considerations should be taken:

- Position of the patient's joints to enable free movement within the confines of surgery, traction, orthoses and plasters.
- Support to the joint. If joints are not supported in the correct position, stretched ligaments and capsules may occur and result in an unstable joint. Secondary soft tissue contractures may occur if the joint is permanently held in an abnormal position.
- Care to prevent pain when handling the patient's joints is essential. Careful handling will result in less pain and trauma to both the patient and the joint.
- Observations of joints both before and following surgery is desirable if possible. Both the skin temperature and appearance over the joint and the size of the joint should be

observed. A rise in skin temperature, swelling of the joint and tautness of the skin may indicate either the onset of a haemarthrosis, synovitis or septic arthritis. At the same time the patient will have an increase in the level of pain. Medical intervention should be sought.

The movements at joints (see Figure 2.5) are governed by the shape of the bones, but there are six movements which joints are capable of:

1. Flexion.
2. Extension.
3. Abduction—movement away from the midline of the body.
4. Adduction—movement towards the midline of the body.
5. External or lateral rotation, and internal or medial rotation.
6. Circumduction—combination of all of the above movements moving through a circle.
7. Special movements of the radio-ulnar joints, providing the movements of pronation when the palm of the hand points downwards and backwards, and supination when the palm of the hand points upwards and forwards.
8. Special movements at the ankle joint are: dorsiflexion—bringing the sole of the foot upwards; plantar flexion—taking the sole of the foot downwards.
9. Special movements at the tarsal joints are: inversion—turning the sole of the foot towards the midline; eversion—turning the sole of the foot outwards.

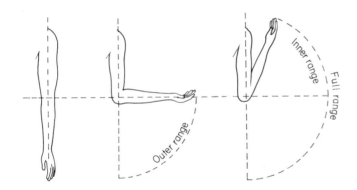

Fig. 8.17   Range of muscle movements.

MUSCLES

Muscles are the general stabilizing factors of joints. A joint cannot work if the muscles controlling it are not active. Skeletal muscles are striped voluntary muscles and must pass over a joint to enable the joint to move. These muscles are composed of bundles of muscle fibres which shorten or contract to their fullest when stimulated by a nerve impulse. Muscle fibres can only actively contract, they passively extend. Due to the continuous discharge of impulses from the central nervous system, some of these muscle fibres are continuously in a state of contraction, even when the muscle is in a state of rest. This is known as muscle tone and is vital in maintaining body posture.

Muscles may be attached to bone themselves or may be anchored by bands of fibrous tissue called tendons. At the wrist and ankle these tendons are enclosed in synovial sheaths, which serve to provide a smooth tunnel in which the tendons can move. The tendons' smooth, pulley-like action ensures that effort is concentrated in the right direction.

The attachment of muscles to bone is known as the origin and insertion. When a muscle contracts, the insertion moves closer to the origin. The origins are generally fixed points, and are often the areas where muscle tissue is directly attached to bone.

Muscles work in groups. Those muscles which initiate movement are called the prime movers and always have another group of muscles opposing them known as antagonists. The two opposing groups are known as:

1. Flexors—extensors.
2. Abductors—adductors.
3. External rotators—internal rotators.
4. Pronators—supinators.
5. Dorsiflexors—plantar flexors.

Muscles are said to contract statically when they contract without moving a joint. Muscle tissue is a highly specialized tissue and is not easily able to regenerate. A small area of damage in a muscle may be repaired by regeneration of the muscle fibres themselves, but a large area can only be repaired by means of scar tissue. If a whole muscle is lost as a result of mechanical damage, or as a result of loss of blood or nerve supply, other muscles may need to be trained to take over the original muscle function.

Nursing care

- Muscle tone must be maintained. A trained physiotherapist will teach both the patient and the nurse the means for maintaining muscle tone. However, it is the orthopaedic nurse's responsibility to assist and to supervise the patient in his exercise programme when the physiotherapist is off duty. The exercises may include:

  (i)   Static movement of muscles when a joint is immobilized;
  (ii) Passive movements when a muscle and joint are put through a range of movements initiated by the nurse;
  (iii) Active movements when the patient is actively encouraged to move a joint and its muscles.

- When splinting injured or paralysed muscles, they should be splinted in the middle range of movement to prevent over stretching or contracting of the affected muscle.

THE NERVOUS SYSTEM AND THE CIRCULATORY SYSTEM

To undertake a brief description of the nervous system or the circulatory system in an orthopaedic nursing text book is a difficult task and, therefore, the areas of the nervous system pertaining to the care of patients with individual problems will be discussed at relevant points throughout the book.

SUGGESTED FURTHER READING

Moffat, D.B., and Mottram, R.F. (1983) *Anatomy and Physiology for Physiotherapists*, 1st edn. Oxford: Blackwell Scientific.

Rowett, H.C.Q. (1983) *Basic Anatomy and Physiology*, 2nd edn. London: John Murray.

Platzer, W. (1986) *Color Atlas and Textbook of Human Anatomy*, vol. 1. *The Locomotor System*, 3rd edn. Stuttgart: Springer-Verlag.

3

NURSING CARE OF PATIENTS WITH ORTHOPAEDIC CONDITIONS

The use of the nursing process, as briefly outlined in Chapter 1, allows nurses to assess, plan, implement and carry out the care of their patients in conjunction with the patients themselves. Care is then evaluated and either continued or adjusted in the light of the evaluation.

A further aid to enabling nursing to be carried out is the use of a nursing model. A nursing model is a framework on which to plan the care to be given to the patient.

The model should reflect the philosophy of nursing held by the team of nurses on the ward. This will provide a basis for consistency of care.

Orthopaedic patients are, on the whole, active people waiting for their bones and joints to heal once corrective measures have been taken by the medical team. Roper, Logan and Tierney's model reflects twelve activities of daily living (see Table 3.1). The nursing of orthopaedic patients relates very well to these activities. The major aim of nursing care is for the patient to be independent in these activities, or as independent as is realistic. In this book an attempt has been made to base suggested care on Roper, Logan and Tierney's model of care.

The other model for nursing which has particular relevance for orthopaedic nursing is

Table 3.1 Activities of daily living as described by Roper, Logan and Teirney.

1.	Maintaining a safe environment
2.	Breathing
3.	Communicating
4.	Eating and drinking
5.	Eliminating
6.	Personal cleansing and dressing
7.	Controlling body temperature
8.	Mobilizing
9.	Working and playing
10.	Expressing sexuality
11.	Sleeping
12.	Dying

Dorothea Orem's Self-Care Model. In this model the patient starts with having the self-care abilities present in all of us. During ill health and disablement, the patient's self-care demands outweigh his self-care abilities. Nursing intervenes to support the patient.

If the patient is never able to be fully independent or be self-caring, then significant 'others', such as relatives or friends, take the caring role.

The elements in this chapter, however, have been looked at under the needs of the patient, without specifically relating it to a model of care. They have been written looking at the problems which would be elicited during the assessment part of the nursing process, the goal or aim of care, the possible cause of the problem and the care needed to solve it.

This chapter deals with the general orthopaedic nursing considerations which the majority of patients with orthopaedic conditions will require whilst in hospital. Guidelines to specific care are included in chapters dealing with the orthopaedic condition being described.

The first essential part of any orthopaedic nursing plan is to take an accurate history of the patient on admission on which to base an assessment of the patient's needs from a physical, emotional, spiritual and cultural viewpoint. Assessment should be an ongoing process and, as a close relationship is formed between the orthopaedic patient and nurse, further information is often devolved. This needs to be acted upon and the care plan adjusted as necessary to meet the new, emerging needs. Careful assessment is essential in dealing with orthopaedic patients as the condition affecting the patient may be long-standing and long-term, having an effect on the patient, his family, friends, future employment and reintegration into society.

Once the assessment has started, then the

nurse is in a position to set realistic goals in partnership with her patient. She is then able to plan care to meet the needs of her patient, deliver the care and use continual evaluation to ensure she and the patient are meeting the targets set. It is essential that the care is planned using current nursing research and the patient and his family are involved with each step taken.

PROBLEMS RELATED TO LOSS OF MOBILITY

Problem 1:   Inability to maintain personal hygiene

Aim: To assist the patient to maintain cleanliness of skin, hair, nails and mouth.

Causes: Inability to perform tasks related to normal hygiene by loss of use of limbs, loss of sensation, use of various tractions and orthoses, and surgery.

Nursing intervention

- Assist patient to wash and dry skin as required, paying particular attention to finger and toe nails. A chiropodist may be employed to enable professional care to be given to the patient's feet.
- Give mouth care, if necessary, or assist the patient to maintain a clean, moist mouth by providing the necessary equipment. This includes positioning the patient to enable him to use the mouth care equipment.
- Assisting the patient to comb and to wash and dry his hair as required. A hairdressing service is often employed in an orthopaedic hospital to aid the patients in this function.
- Assist male patients to shave daily, if required.

Problem 2:   Susceptibility to pressure sores

Aim: To prevent the formation of pressure sores. To maintain the integrity of the skin.

Causes: *In all age groups*
Immobility.
Use of traction, plasters and orthoses.

Incorrect diet and reduced or poor fluid intake.

In the elderly
Loss of skin resilience.
Incontinence.
Arteriosclerosis.
Confusion.

In the hemiplegic, paraplegic or quadriplegic patient
Loss of sensation.
Incontinence.

In the unconscious patient
Incontinence.

In the obese patient
Perspiration.

Communication
The inability to communicate instructions to the patient.

In patients with rheumatoid arthritis the skin, due to the disease process, may become very friable, and drugs such as steroids may also predispose these patients to pressure sores. Any part of the body which is subjected to abnormal pressure unrelieved over a period of time may succumb to pressure sores. Careful application of tractions, plasters and orthoses is essential to avoid either friction or constriction. Bony prominences are particularly susceptible, especially the sacral area, hips, knees, the malleoli, heels, dorsum of the toes, shoulders, elbows, vertebral column and back of the head.

If the pressure load is maintained, then the following series of events will take place which will result in the formation of a sore:

1. The skin blanches and then blisters.
2. The skin breaks.
3. Superficial necrosis and ulcer formation.
4. Gangrene.
5. Sloughing.

The 'at risk' scoring system as shown in Table 3.1 may be used to determine which patients are most susceptible to the formation of pressure sores. Much research has taken place into the use of scoring systems and the care of patients' pressure areas: Versluysen (2), Isles (3), Deacon (4) and Livesley (5), to mention a few. The orthopaedic nurse must base her care of pressure areas on the current research.

Table 3.2 'At risk' scoring system for pressure sores: patients who score a total of fourteen or less on this scale are considered to be 'at risk' of developing a pressure sore.

		Score 1	Score 2	Score 3	Score 4
A	General physical condition	Very bad	Poor	Fair	Good
B	Mental state	Stuporous	Confused	Apathetic	Alert
C	Activity	Bedfast	Chairbound	Walks with help	Ambulant
D	Mobility	Immobile	Very limited	Slightly limited	Full
E	Incontinence	Double	Usually urinary	Occasionally	Never

From Norton, D., McLaren, R. and Exton-Smith, A.N. (1)

Nursing intervention

- Change the position of the patient at least two hourly.
- Ensure the bed clothes are smooth, taut and free from crumbs. Change soiled sheets.
- Ensure all tractions, plasters and orthoses are fitting correctly; not too tight or too loose.
- Wash and dry skin and apply a barrier cream if incontinence occurs.
- Avoid trauma to patient's skin by correct lifting and positioning. Encourage patient to lift himself by supplying aids such as an overhead trapeze.
- Encourage patient to move skin gently under appliances.
- Use aids to relieve or redistribute pressure, for example water pillows, foam pads and troughs, ripple mattress, water bed, low-loss airbed, cradles, and sheepskins.
- Encourage a well balanced diet and fluid intake.

If a pressure sore does occur, it should be treated as an open wound and dressed aseptically. If infection is present, the patient may need medical intervention in the form of systemic antibiotics. Various solutions may be used to clean the wound when necessary. A deep cavity may need to be packed with ribbon gauze or Debrisan granules to allow granulation to take place from the base upwards.

Occlusive dressings, such as Opsite, can be applied to superficial wounds to promote healing.

Problem 3:   Stiff joints, contractures, muscle wasting, foot drop and venous thrombosis

Aim: To prevent complications of immobility.

Nursing intervention

- Encourage static muscle exercises of the immobilized part, at least every four hours.
- Encourage patient to exercise actively all other joints at least twice daily.
- Work with physiotherapist and continue regimes when the physiotherapist is off duty.
- Encourage use of weights, when appropriate, to maintain muscle tone.
- Apply anti-embolic stockings to those patients who are particularly at risk, e.g., those with a history of previous venous thrombosis.
- Remove pillows from under calf of leg and encourage exercises of the ankle joint, every hour, in the immobile patient.
- Prevent any pressure from appliances on to this area.
- Remove bandages, if possible, from lower leg and inspect calf at least twice a day.

Problem 4:   Renal calculi

Aims: To prevent formation of renal calculi.
          To maintain normal kidney function.

Causes: Urinary stasis.
          Immobility of skeletal system.

Immobilization of all, or part, of the skeleton over a period of time may lead to withdrawal of calcium from the bones, leaving an osteoporotic bone. This may be seen particularly in very young children who are prone to fractures following immobilization of the hip, for example, following treatment for congenital hip dislocation.

Nursing intervention

- Maintain a fluid intake of at least two litres every 24 hours.
- Maintain an accurate fluid balance chart. Encourage movement of patient as much as possible.

PROBLEMS RELATED TO NUTRITION

Problem 1:   Inability to maintain normal nutrition

Aim: To assist the patient to achieve a good, nutritional intake.

Causes: Inability to use fingers, wrist and arms, due to painful joints.
Unpleasant taste in mouth.
No teeth, or poor fitting dentures.
Painful jaw joints.
Unappetizing, poorly presented food.
Loss of appetite due to a febrile illness.
Anxiety.
Cultural and religious differences making hospital food unacceptable, for example: Hinduism; Islam; Orthodox Judaism; Sikhism.
Immobilization: arms, legs, and lying flat.

Nursing intervention

- Relieve pain, adjust patient's position. Provide aids such as large handled cutlery and non-slip mats to hold plates, or an overhead mirror to enable the patient to see his food properly; firm, specially adapted drinking cups.
- Assist patient to cut up his food.
- Ensure the patient is wearing his dentures.
- Offer a soft diet in small, attractive quantities, every two to three hours.

- Relieve anxiety by talking to patient and allowing him to express his fears.

Problem 2:   Dehydration

Aim: To maintain a correct fluid balance.

Causes: Insufficient fluid intake.
Loss of fluid by sweating, diarrhoea, vomiting, haemorrhage, excessive urinary output, and rapid respirations.

Nursing intervention

- Assist medical staff in treating the cause.
- Increase fluid intake by:
  Encouraging the patient to increase his oral fluid intake;
  Ensuring patient can reach fluids without discomfort;
  Giving aids, such as a feeding cup, to encourage independence;
  Giving fluid by a nasogastric tube;
  Administering intravenous fluids;
  Selecting fluids the patient enjoys;
  Giving frequent mouth care to prevent dryness of the mouth;
  Maintaining accurate fluid intake and output charts;
  Giving pressure area care at least two hourly.

Severe dehydration does not occur very frequently in orthopaedic patients, but may be seen in patients with osteomyelitis, septic arthritis and in complications following spinal surgery.

PROBLEM ASSOCIATED WITH ELIMINATION

Problem: Constipation

Aim: To achieve a normal bowel action.

Causes: Immobility;
Diet deficient in roughage;
Dehydration;
Pain;
Stress, embarrassment;
Drugs, for example analgesics and sedatives;
Gastrointestinal disease;

Loss of bowel habit through over use of aperients.

Nursing intervention

- Assist medical staff in treating the cause.
- Ensure privacy for the patient when using a bedpan.
- If possible, allow patient to use lavatory or commode instead of bedpan.
- Increase roughage content of diet by adding bran and cereals, vegetables and wholemeal bread.
- Encourage fruit in the patient's diet.
- Increase fluid intake, if possible.
- Give aperients, suppositories or enemas as prescribed.

PROBLEMS RELATED TO LOSS OF BODY IMAGE

Recent research into the development of a nursing assessment tool to diagnose altered body image of immobilized patients in the USA, by Sue Baird (6), states that a great deal more research is required regarding this topic. The following is based on one aspect of need of the orthopaedic patient.

Problem: Psychological problems

Aims: To prevent patient from becoming apprehensive, bored and depressed. To maintain the patient's morale.

Causes: The 'why me?' syndrome. This may also be seen in the parents of children, in particular those children with a congenital condition.
Fear of loss of place in the family, with peers and in society.
Pain.

Orthopaedic patients are often confined to bed for long periods when they feel constitutionally well, but the need for immobilization of part of their skeleton is an essential part of treatment. It is at these times that the patient may become apprehensive and sometimes depressed about his future in relation to his family and employment. It is also during this time the patient may become bored. This may reveal itself in aggression towards staff, family and friends. It is also a time when patients may have to come to terms with disability.

Nursing intervention

- Allow the patient time to express fears and to talk. These fears will frequently only be expressed once a relationship has been established between the nurse and the patient. It is up to the nurse to help the patient overcome his problems. However, she may need to seek professional advice, but must be granted the patient's permission before proceeding with this.
- Sexual worries often form part of these fears, and the nurse must learn to encourage the patient to discuss such matters without embarrassment. There will be times when, in the present climate, there is little which can be undertaken to help, but talking and listening can often be a large step towards finding a solution.
- Provide facilities for patient to be afforded privacy to talk to family.
- Candid, open discussions with patient and family on potential problems.
- Ensure patient has access to means of entertainment, e.g., television and radio earphones.
- Employ the services of the occupational therapist and medical social worker.
- Be available to talk to relatives. Ensure family are kept fully informed of patient's progress.
- Provide constant reassurance for the patient in the form of truthful explanations of progress and procedures.
- Allow patient the opportunity to fulfil his spiritual needs, if required, by informing the relevant spiritual leader.
- Introduction to someone with similar problems who is now fully rehabilitated.
- Control of pain (7), (8) by:
  Reducing the patient's levels of anxiety by allowing him to express his fears.
  Allowing the patient to express his feelings over pain.
  Monitoring the level of pain and the effect of analgesia using a pain chart.
  Assisting patient to achieve a comfortable position.
  Applying warmth or cold to area.
  Administering analgesia before pain returns and adjusting dosage to enable patient to be pain free.

- Start the rehabilitation programme as soon as possible following the patient's admission to the ward.

NURSING CARE OF PATIENTS DURING THE PRE-OPERATIVE PHASE

The majority of orthopaedic patients have a planned admission to hospital and there is therefore time to allow the patient to come to terms with the forthcoming events and to arrange his work, domestic and social events accordingly. There is also time to allow the nurse to provide a considerable amount of patient teaching.

If at all possible, the patient should attend the hospital one to two weeks prior to admission where a nursing assessment can be made of the patient and a full teaching programme of the pre-operative and postoperative phases can be undertaken. This is presently unrealistic in National Health Service hospitals, but is widely used in many Canadian and American clinics. Prepared booklets with explanations of the staff, procedures, equipment and patient's role can be prepared and handed to the patient to take home with him. This gives the patient and his family an opportunity to prepare any questions or queries they may have when the patient is finally admitted to the ward. A quick review of the initial nursing assessment is made and, if there is no change, then the patient's needs are identified and a care plan made accordingly. If no such programme exists, then the following needs must be identified and met.

Problem 1:   Anxiety on admission to hospital
(9), (10)

Aim: To alleviate fear and apprehension on admission to hospital.

Causes: Lack of knowledge of staff and ward layout.
Lack of information of procedures.
Fear of being unpopular (11).
Bad experience during past admissions to hospital.
Cultural differences.

Nursing intervention

- Introduce yourself to patient and make

patient and relatives welcome to the ward in a friendly manner.
- Explain different uniforms and personnel.
- Show patient layout of ward and introduce fellow patients.
- Answer both the patient's and relatives' questions or queries. These must be answered honestly and should reinforce any literature previously sent to the patient.
- Ensure relatives know the visiting hours and telephone number of the hospital and ward. It is also important for the relatives to know the approximate time of surgery and when they should first be able to telephone and visit following surgery.
- Valuables should be removed from hospital, if possible, but if they are to remain, then the procedure for locking them away and the reasons why should be explained to the patient.
- Inform the patient of mealtimes, doctors' rounds, other personnel and the time-table of events planned for him as an individual.

Problem 2:   Risk of postoperative complications

Aim: To reduce the risk of complications following surgery, such as:
Infection—wound and chest.
Deep vein thrombosis.
Stiff joints and muscle wastage.
Pressure sores.
Urinary problems.
Bowel problems.
Vomiting.

Cause: Lack of knowledge by the patient to complete the nursing assessment.

Nursing intervention

- Skin hygiene. A total body bath, with attention being paid to the umbilicus, nails and genital area. Antiseptic solutions added to the bath are of little value unless a strict regime of three baths over a period of time is followed pre-operatively and the bath re-cleaned between each bath. Ayliffe (12) states that one bath is of little use, but three or more are useful in reducing the bacterial count on the skin.
- Hair should be washed prior to surgery.
- The skin near to the site of the proposed

incision should be inspected for abrasions. Shaving (13) is seldom undertaken as this tends to release many bacteria from the skin and may also lead to abrasions.

- The physiotherapist visits the patient to teach exercises:
  - (i) deep breathing to help prevent chest infections;
  - (ii) dorsi and plantar flexion of the ankle joint to prevent deep vein thrombosis, to aid venous return and hence reduce the risk of venous thrombosis;
  - (iii) exercises to remaining joints to prevent joint stiffness and muscle wastage.
- Teach the patient to lift himself and explain the importance of movement in preventing the formation of sores. The patient may be shown various aids which can be used to relieve pressure. It is helpful to explain any drains which may be used, and to tell the patient the importance of not touching any dressings, and why. The patient may wish to discuss his apprehension about pain at this point. Reassurance of how the pain will be dealt with should be given.
- A full urinalysis must be performed to detect any abnormalities in the patient's urine and, if ordered, a mid-stream specimen of urine sent to the laboratory for microscopy and culture. A bedpan or urinal should be shown to the patient and relevant explanations given.
- Bowel care is carried out to ensure the patient has an empty rectum prior to surgery. The patient's normal bowel activity must be recorded. The use of aperients, suppositories or small enemas may ensure the patient's rectum is empty.
- Food and fluids are restricted for at least four to six hours before the premedication is given if a general anaesthetic is to be used. If a local anaesthetic is used, then a light meal, such as tea and toast, may be given up to two hours before surgery.

Flexibility is the key word and in the RCN Research Project 'Nil by Mouth', Stephanie Hamilton Smith concludes 'Routines should be flexible, a guide to practice rather than something to be carried out to the letter, without further thought. After all they should be tools not masters'. At this time it is essential the patient be allowed to express his fears over vomiting, and reassurance given as to how this will be dealt with if it occurs. If an intravenous infusion is likely to be used then an explanation of the equipment and procedure is given to the patient. A pre-operative 'check-list' may be employed to ensure all essential points have been covered.

NURSING CARE OF PATIENTS DURING THE POSTOPERATIVE PHASE

General postoperative nursing care of orthopaedic patients has few variations to the general postoperative care of any surgical patient. Tractions and appliances can cause a problem for the nurse and the fact that many patients are unable to be nursed in the recovery position may lead to further problems. However, careful assessment of the individual patients needs must be systematically carried out and the care planned accordingly. The need will be, at first, of a totally dependent patient gradually decreasing to independence.

Specific care will be given in the chapters relating to specific conditions.

Postoperative stress (14) in a patient demands accurate assessment by the nurse before she is able to modify the effects of stress.

Problem 1:   Patient's inability to maintain own airway

Aim: To maintain a clear airway.

Cause: Administration of general anaesthetic

Nursing intervention

- Until the patient has regained consciousness and a cough reflex is present, he should not be left unattended.
- If the patient is unable to be nursed semiprone, the head should be positioned in such a way as to prevent the patient's tongue falling back and occluding the airway. (A word of warning here, as patients with rheumatoid arthritis frequently have cervical spine involvement, tilting the patient's head in this case is not always possible and medical advice should be sought.)
- As soon as possible, the patient should be encouraged to breathe deeply.
- Maintain oxygen therapy if ordered by the

anaesthetist. This may be ordered to relieve hypoxia. The patient may need constant reassurance while a mask is in place because he may feel frightened and anxious.

Problem 2: Inability to maintain own temperature, pulse and blood pressure

Aim: To monitor vital signs: pulse, blood pressure and temperature and respirations.

Causes: Orthopaedic surgery is often protracted and may be carried out in a laminar flow theatre. This may have an adverse effect on the patient's temperature by causing it to be subnormal.
Shock.
Haemorrhage.

(Pulse rate, volume and rhythm may need to be compared to the opposite limb to ensure an accurate reading is obtained.)

A raised respiratory rate may be due to pain or a chest infection. Accurate pre-operative assessment of vital signs is essential to ensure a good base line for postoperative observations.

Nursing intervention

- Take radial pulse rate every 15 minutes, usually for the first hour then half-hourly, reducing to hourly until the pulse rate is constant and stable. Providing the rate remains stable and satisfactory during this time, the observations may be reduced to four hourly.
- The blood pressure is recorded at the same time as the pulse.
- Wound dressings and drainage systems should be observed and assessed for the amount of blood loss. A sudden rise in pulse rate, accompanied by a drop in the blood pressure, may indicate haemorrhage. Assessment of wound dressings and drainage systems may show an increase in blood loss. The patient may feel cold and clammy and be restless. Medical advice must be sought immediately.
- Pain may reduce the blood pressure. Measures to relieve the pain should be dealt with, as mentioned on page 15.

- The temperature should be recorded initially and, if within normal limits, may then be recorded four hourly. If, however, it is low, measures should be taken to restore the temperature to within normal limits. A device, such as a 'space blanket', may be employed. This is a foil-backed sheet which is placed foil side to the patient until the temperature improves.
- Observations must be charted to be of value. Accurate, careful charting is important.

Problem 3: Postoperative pain

Aim: To alleviate and control pain.

Causes: Operative surgery.
Application of splints, traction, plasters.
Abnormal position of body.

Nursing intervention

See page 15.

Postoperative pain is variable and therefore accurate assessment of the individual patient's pain must be undertaken. Pain, other than that at the wound site, should be investigated and, if necessary, reported to the surgeon, as should severe pain at the wound site.

Problem 4: Inability to maintain own fluid intake

Aims: To monitor fluid balance.
To maintain electrolyte balance.

Causes: Administration of anaesthesia.
Postoperative vomiting.
Abnormal position of body or limbs due to application of plasters and appliances.

Nursing intervention

- Careful observations of any intravenous infusion in progress for the following points:
  (i) Safety. Ensure the correct fluid is being administered at the correct rate.
  (ii) The site of the cannula to ensure it is safely held in place and that fluid is not entering the surrounding tissues indicating the cannula has been displaced.

- If a blood transfusion is in progress, the temperature should be monitored every 30 minutes with the pulse and blood pressure. Reactions which may occur:
  (i)   rise in temperature;
  (ii) increased pulse or respiratory rate;
  (iii) change in blood pressure;
  (iv) low back pain or loin pain;
  (v)   any rash on face or body.
  If any of these signs occur, the transfusion must be stopped immediately and medical advice sought.
- Any additives to the infusion must be administered according to hospital policy.
- A careful fluid intake and output chart recorded.
- Monitor urinary output carefully. Orthopaedic patients having had a prolonged anaesthesia, spinal surgery, hip surgery, or are immobilized in traction, or have large plasters, may experience difficulty in passing urine postoperatively. Catheterization should be used as a last resort, although some children undergoing spinal surgery may be catheterized as a routine procedure pre-operatively to prevent complications during surgery and in preparation for the postoperative phase.

Problem 5: Neurovascular occlusion

Aim: To prevent neurovascular problems arising in limbs which have been operated on.

Causes: Surgery.
Restricting bandages or plasters.
Pressure from traction or orthoses.
Poor positioning of limbs.

Nursing intervention

- A diligent observation of extremities every 15 minutes for the first hour, then every hour for the following eight hours. Providing these remain satisfactory, they may be carried out every four hours. The extremities are examined for (see Figure 3.1):
  (i)   Colour of skin of the extremity which should be normal flesh colour, to ensure that both arterial supply and venous return are satisfactory.
  (ii) Capillary return—the blanching test is used where the nail of the extremity

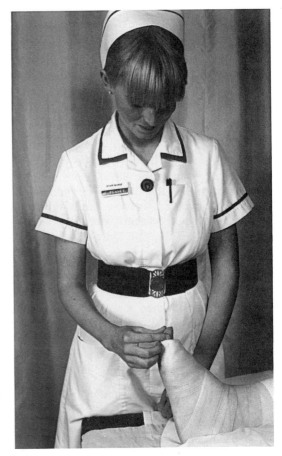

Fig. 3.1   Examination of the patient's toes.

  is gently compressed between the fingers: upon release, the colour should change from pale to normal.
  (iii) Mobility—asking the patient to move his fingers or toes and assessing the success of this procedure.
  (iv) Feeling the extremities to determine the temperature.
  (v)   Ascertaining the amount of sensation present, as indicated by the patient's complaint of lack of feeling as each toe or finger is lightly pinched. (If a local anaesthetic or nerve block has been used, then this must be taken into consideration.) Each finger and toe must be assessed individually. Factors which may prevent these examinations taking place, other than use of nerve blocks, include the use of immobilization techniques.
- Elevation of the limb to aid venous return

and prevent oedema. This may be achieved by elevating the foot of the bed for operations on the lower limb and elevating the arm, following surgery, to wrist and hand. The arm may be suspended in a roller towel or in Netalast from an intravenous infusion stand, close to the patient. Care must be taken when elevating the arm to ensure that the shoulder joint is not hyperextended and that pressure is relieved under the elbow joint. If possible, the patient's arm should be taken down from the elevated position four hourly. At this time the shoulder and elbow, if not involved in the immobilization method, should be gently exercised.

PROBLEMS RELATED TO THE WOUND

One of the most threatening times in orthopaedic nursing is when a wound has become infected, as this may eventually lead to the condition of chronic osteomyelitis, rejection of a new prosthesis and, at the very worst, amputation of a limb. These, in turn, may lead to the following:

1. Increased discomfort for the patient.
2. Prolonged hospitalization.
3. Loss of employment or earnings.
4. Domestic upsets.
5. Long-term psychological effects on the patient.

It is therefore in the orthopaedic nurse's best interest to reduce the risk of infection in surgical incisions, and to promote healing of wounds. A 'nontouch' technique must be used when handling any incision, however small, as all incisions carry the same risk.

Problem: Infection of wound incision or drainage sites

Aim: To prevent infection occurring in the wound and to promote healing.

Causes: An unsafe ward environment.
Lack of knowledge by patient.
Lack of care towards the surgical incision.
Poor nutritional status of patient.
Poor circulatory status of tissues.
Drug therapy.
Poor aseptic technique.

Nursing intervention

- General factors of cleanliness in the ward environment must be observed and, although the nurse is no longer fully responsible for this, she must be aware of the standards necessary to reduce the risk of infection occurring.
- Bed linen must be changed daily; more frequently if the patient is pyrexial, or the wound is discharging an exudate.
- The patient's own clothes need to be changed daily. This may present a problem in having an adequate supply of clean clothes, particularly if the patient has no visitors able to undertake this task. It is sometimes possible to employ the services of the hospital volunteers to undertake this for the patient or, in some hospitals, the laundry provides a facility for patient's own clothes to be washed.
- The patient should be told quite simply how he can help to prevent infection forming in his wound by:
  (i)   maintaining careful hygiene;
  (ii)   by resisting the temptation to look at the wound under the dresing;
  (iii) reporting any discomfort, such as irritation or heat at, or around, the wound site;
  (iv)   any undue exudate, such as blood or serous fluid staining the dressing, should also be reported;
  (v)   any undue pain at the site of the incision.
- In spite of these precautions, many elderly patients will attempt to alleviate discomfort from the wound by 'picking' under the dressing. It is therefore the nurse's duty to inspect the wound dressing and ensure it is intact at least once on each shift, and more often if the patient is elderly and confused.
- The majority of orthopaedic surgical measures are covered with a dressing and then a pressure dressing may be applied to prevent the formation of a haematoma. Pressure dressings are generally removed after 24 hours, but the dressing covering the wound should never be touched unless contraindicated by a rise in the temperature, inflammation arising around the dressing, undue pain or irritation under the dressing, and an exudate appears on the dressing.
- Swelling of the affected limb may be reduced

by elevation or by the application of ice packs. This may also help to reduce pain.

- A high protein diet should be encouraged and this can be supplemented by milk drinks. The diet should also contain vitamins A and C to promote collagen synthesis.
- Undue pressure on the wound should be relieved by the use of bed aids such as bed cradles.
- Movement, whenever and wherever possible, should be encouraged. Any specific exercises will have been taught pre-operatively to the patient by the physiotherapist, and the nurse will need to surpervise these in her absence.
- The wound must be free from pressure from resting splints, traction or orthoses, if used.
- Patients having received steroid therapy as treatment for their condition, have poor healing capabilities and inflammatory responses may not reveal themselves. The orthopaedic nurse has a need to observe these wounds with added care.
- A strict non-touch technique is used when dealing with any wound, and the principles of asepsis adhered to.
- The wound should be kept dry at all times, cleaning the incision is usually unnecessary, but if it has been carried out, the suture line must be carefully dried before a clean dressing is applied.
- When vacuum drains are removed, the remaining incision should be covered with a dry dressing.
- The dressing must be adequate to protect fully the incision without being bulky.
- As a general rule, most lower limb wounds will have their sutures removed at between 10–14 days postoperatively; upper limb and abdominal wounds between 7–10 days. Facial sutures, areas which have a good blood supply and areas which are not subjected to physical stress are removed about three days after operation.

Problems related to the application of traction and plaster casts will be dealt with in the relevant chapters.

PROBLEMS RELATED TO REHABILITATION

Rehabilitation is the whole process of restoring a person to normal life following illness or injury. Many orthopaedic patients make a full recovery without special arrangements for rehabilitation, but their recovery is often speeded up by the setting of realistic short-term and long-term goals aimed at maintaining their motivation. To this end, rehabilitation starts immediately the patient is admitted and is an ongoing process. Full rehabilitation practices are discussed in Chapter 16, but the nurse's role is important from the outset and it is with this in mind, as a general orthopaedic nursing principle, that the following plans are included in this chapter.

Problem 1:   Loss of the patient's independence

Aim: To enable the patient to move towards total self-care if possible.

Cause: Admission to hospital.

Nursing intervention

- Encourage the patient to undertake as much of his own care in relation to hygiene, nutritional needs and elimination as possible. It is important never to ask the patient to do too much for himself, and realistic goals must be set with the nurse maintaining close observation of the patient and being ready to assist, when necessary.
- Encourage and supervise exercise therapy for nonaffected limbs. This will ensure the patient is able to conserve the function of joints and muscles during periods of immobilization in bed.
- Encourage and supervise exercises for affected limbs within the limits set by the medical and physiotherapy teams.
- Involve the patient's relatives and friends in encouraging the patient towards independence.

Problem 2:   Inability to accept patient's change in his role

Aim: To act as counsellor for the patient and his family.

Causes: Patient's orthopaedic condition and surgery.

Nursing intervention

- Allow time for the patient to express his worries and to talk. This is an important part of the orthopaedic nurse's role. Once a relationship has been established between the patient and his nurse, it becomes important to build on this relationship so the patient learns to trust his nurse to deal with his worries. Confidences should never be divulged without the patient's permission.
- Be available to talk with the patient's family when they have the need.
- Be aware of the other members of the orthopaedic team who may be contacted as necessary. For example, medical social worker, occupational therapist, disablement resettlement officer, sexual counsellor.

Problem 3:   Same as problem 2

Aim: To teach the patient and his family to meet and adjust to the new needs of the patient.

Causes: Lack of knowledge by the patient and his family.

Nursing intervention

Teaching is not confined to passing on new knowledge and skills, although these are obviously important. It also includes changing attitudes and helping the patient and his family adjust to a new way of life.

- Assist the patient to use new pieces of equipment or aids to daily living.
- Give the patient's family the opportunity to watch and then help with new pieces of equipment or aids.
- The nurse must be aware of health education and accident prevention, and include this as part of her teaching.
- Advise the patient and his family about the various societies and statutory and voluntary organizations available to help them.
- Take the opportunity to educate the general public in their reaction and attitude to the disabled in society by example and teaching.

Problem 4:   Lack of communication

Aim: To act as communicator between various members of the team, the patient and his family.

Causes: Not all team members are able to attend ward meeting.
Care plans not written in realistic terms.
Care plans not devised with the patient and/or his family.

Nursing intervention

- Provide both formal and informal methods of communication between the various parties.
- Maintain an accurate assessment, ongoing care plan and evaluation of the care plan, and make it available to the various members of the team.
- Act as the patient's advocate when he is unable to do so.
- Record all observations clearly and accurately.

PROBLEMS RELATED TO CARE OF THE DYING PATIENT AND THE BEREAVED

Death is an infrequent visitor to the elective orthopaedic ward, but may be a frequent occurrence when dealing with the trauma aspect of orthopaedic nursing.

It is therefore not the intention of this book to deal at any length with the dying patient, but an outline of the role of the nurse in this respect will be given.

If at all possible the dying patient should be cared for at home. The nearness of familiar faces who know, intimately, the needs and preferences of the patient, help to allay the fears experienced by the patient. If this is not possible, then the hospital surroundings should be as accommodating as possible and the family given free, private access to the patient and be as involved in his care as much as they wish to be.

E. Day, in an article entitled, 'The Patient with Cancer and the Family' (15) states: 'Death cannot be denied but its dignity can be—by thoughtless, underfeeling and overscientific care. Everything that is done for the dying patient should be based on the constant awareness that, although death may be postponed—sometimes dramatically—the master plan cannot be altered'.

Caring for the dying patient can bring its own rewards, as the true caring nature of nursing can be reflected. It is the final nursing consideration which can be performed for any patient and, as such, should be given as much time as possible.

Problem: Patient's distress and nonacceptance of dying

Aim: To alleviate discomfort and to help the patient to die with dignity.

Causes: Lack of knowledge.
Acute anxiety and distress.
Loss of ability to maintain activities of daily living.
Loss of patient's independence.
Pain.

Nursing intervention

The needs of the patient can be identified under three broad headings:

1. Spiritual care.
2. Physical care.
3. Psychological care.

- Ensure the relevant religious authority is informed of the patient's wishes to meet his needs.
- Provide the necessary facilities, including privacy, for both the patient and his family to partake in any service as requested by the patient.
- Ask for advice and guidance, if necessary, in order that nursing considerations conform to the patient's beliefs. Nursing considerations for many of the physical needs have already been dealt with in this chapter. These include hygiene, nutrition, elimination, oral toilet, pain, pressure sores.
- Pain in the dying needs special consideration. It must be dealt with sympathetically and swiftly and controlled at all costs.
- Ask the patient to describe any pain in its severity, character and location. Chart the frequency of pain with the above characteristics.
- Note the effectiveness of any analgesia administered.
- If possible encourage the patient to chart his own pain levels.
- Use all nursing considerations described in

this chapter to alleviate pain.
- Provide positive help in all aspects of care.
- Allow the patient and his family the opportunity to express their feelings. Often these are of anger, and this must never be taken personally.
- Sit with the patient whenever time allows, and use nonverbal communications such as holding the patient's hands. Never leave the patient in a corner of the ward or in a side-room where they may feel rejected.
- Allow all members of the orthopaedic team, especially nursing staff, to express their feelings following the death of the patient. Counselling groups, following the death of a patient, may be set up to allow this to happen.
- Ensure the bereaved relatives have all the relevant information and help to enable them to finalize arrangements for the burial.

REFERENCES

1 Norton D., McLaren R. & Exton-Smith A.N. (1975) *An Investigation of Geriatric Nursing Problems in Hospital.*

2 Versluysen M. (1985) Pressure sores in elderly patients. *Journal of Bone and Joint Surgery*, Vol. 67B No. 1.

3 Isles J. (1986) An eradication campaign. *Nursing Times*, August.

4 Deacon L. (1986) Does anyone read research? *Nursing Times*, August.

5 Livesley B. (1986) Airwaves take the pressure. *Nursing Times*, August.

6 Baird S. (1985) The development of a nursing assessment tool to diagnose altered body image in immobilised patients. *Orthopaedic Nursing*, Vol. 4 No. 1, America: National Association of Orthopaedic Nurse.

7 Franklin B.L. (1974) *Patient Anxiety on Admission to Hospital.* London: Royal College of Nursing.

8 Hayward J. (1979) *Pain, Nursing Series 1*, Oxford University Press.

9 Munday A. (1973) *Physiological Measures of Anxiety in Hospital Patients.* London: Royal College of Nursing.

10 Wilson-Barnet R. (1983) *Stress in Hospital Patients*, Nursing. Reprint. Edinburgh: Churchill Livingstone.

11 Stockwell F. (1973) *The Unpopular Patient.* London: Royal College of Nursing.

12 Ayliffe G.A.J. (1983) Comparison of preoperative bathing with chlorhexidine detergent and non medical soap in the prevention of wound infection. *Journal of Hospital Infection* No. 4.

13 Winfield U. (1986) Too close a shave? Journal of infection control. *Nursing Times*, 5th March.
14 Macdonald Ross S.E. & Mackay R.C. (1986) Postoperative stress. *Journal of Psychiatric Nursing and Health Services*, Vol. 24, No. 4; Slack Inc.
15 Day E. (1966) The patient with cancer and the family. *New England Journal of Medicine*, 274, 883–886.

SUGGESTED FURTHER READING

Kratz C.R. (1979) *The Nursing Process*. London: Baillière Tindall.

Long R. (1981) *Systematic Nursing Care*. London: Faber & Faber.
Pearson A. & Vaughan B. (1986) *Nursing Models for Practice*. London: Heinemann.
Kershaw B. & Salvage J. (1986) *Models for Nursing*. Chichester: John Wiley & Sons.
Powell M. (1986) *Orthopaedic Nursing & Rehabilitation*. 9th Edn. Edinburgh: Churchill Livingstone.
Twycross R.G. (1975) *The Dying Patient*. London: Christian Medical Fellowship.
Roper N., Logan W.W. & Tierney A.J. (1984) *Using a Model for Nursing*. Edinburgh: Churchill Livingstone.
Orem D.E. (1980) *Nursing: Concepts of Practice*, 2nd Edn. Basingstoke: McGraw-Hill.

4

NURSING CARE OF PATIENTS IN TRACTION

If any part of the bony framework of the body is broken, that part becomes unstable and the pull of muscles may cause deformity and consequent shortening of a limb.

If a joint is damaged or infected, the muscles controlling the joint immediately go into spasm, thus holding the joint in the position of greatest comfort and preventing friction of joint surfaces which would otherwise occur in movement. This is a useful action in that it rests the joint but, if prolonged, may lead to fixed deformities.

Traction is used to overcome the pull of muscles on the joint or fracture and, therefore, to reduce or prevent deformity occurring, to maintain or to gain correct bony alignment, to secure immobilization of an inflamed or injured joint and to relieve pain. It may be used postoperatively to hold joint surfaces apart and to ensure soft tissues heal without contracting.

PRINCIPLES OF TRACTION

Newton's Third Law of Motion states, 'For every action there must be an equal and opposite reaction'. For example, a horse is unable to pull a loaded cart up a slippery slope when its hooves are unable to grip the ground for the counter-thrust (see Figure 4.1). In order to pull an object in one direction there must be an equal counter-thrust in the opposite direction.

When traction is applied to a limb, the necessary counter-traction may be achieved in two major ways:

1. When the weight of all or part of the body, acting under the influence of gravity, is utilized to provide counter traction (1). This is called balanced or sliding traction.
2. By using a splint to obtain a counter purchase on a fixed bony point on the skeleton. This is termed 'fixed traction'.

In order to apply traction to a limb it is necessary to obtain a satisfactory grip on the part. This may be done by two means:

1. Skin traction.
2. Skeletal traction.

SKIN TRACTION

A large area of adhesive or nonadhesive extension tape is applied to the skin area. It has a tendency to slip when a large traction force is applied. This may act as a safety device, as excessive force is seldom necessary and is always dangerous. The pull is transmitted from the material used and the skin to the underlying tissue and bone.

Indications for use

When a light pull or temporary immobilization of a limb is necessary, or when the traction force required need not be a continual one.

Fig. 4.1 In order to pull an object in one direction there must be an equal counter thrust in the opposite direction.

Nursing care

Prior to application of traction

- There are very few extension tapes which are not prepared prior to application by the manufacturer. Some skin extension packs include a plastic spreader and prepared padding for the patient's ankles.
- It is vital during the assessment period to identify the patient's allergies as these could cause complications where the tapes are applied. This is particularly important in children.
- The skin to which traction is to be applied must be checked thoroughly for abrasions.
- If desired the skin may be shaved to prevent hairs being pulled when traction is removed. This may cause abrasions to the skin so shaving must be performed with great care. The skin may further be prepared by painting it with compound tincture of benzoin. This acts as a protective covering to the skin and aids the adhesion of the strapping. However, some modern extension tapes react to the application of this tincture and the manufacturers' instructions must be read carefully before embarking on this procedure.
- The limb should be held gently but firmly by one nurse while a second nurse applies the strapping smoothly, allowing it to conform to the limb. Wrinkles in the strapping may cause sores. Bony points such as the patella, tibial crest and malleoli should be left uncovered. The extensions are held in place by a bandage applied in a spiral fashion. The extensions should end above and behind the malleoli to allow for full free movement of the ankle joint. If a ready prepared pack is used, the spreader is positioned first, then the foam padding. Lastly, the skin extensions are applied, observing all the points mentioned above. Traction should be maintained for 24 hours each day unless ordered otherwise by the surgeon.
- Observations must be made by the nurse to prevent skin and neurovascular problems. There may be a late onset of an allergic reaction to either the strapping or bandages.
- The nurse must ensure that all members of the ward team, i.e., nursing, medical and ancillary, are aware of the traction and they must be taught to avoid knocking the weights or lifting them as this may cause pain

to the patient. A wooden block called a 'spreader' is then attached to the extension tapes to maintain the distance between them. This should be placed to allow for full dorsi and plantar flexion of the ankle. Crepe or domette bandages are then applied to the limb over the extensions in a figure-of-eight, starting from above the ankle to below the head of the fibula. It is important when applying the bandage to (i) avoid pressure on the tendon of Achilles which may become irritated if covered, and (ii) the head of the fibula must be left uncovered. It is advisable to bandage the leg to within two inches of the fibular head as there is a danger of causing pressure on the common peroneal (lateral popliteal) nerve which may result in a drop foot palsy. Weights are then gently applied to the extensions from a cord passed over a pulley mechanism attached to the bed. The foot of the bed is elevated to provide counter-traction. If a ready prepared extension pack is used, an elasticated bandage is included in the pack. This is applied observing all the points mentioned above.

Following application of skin traction

Approximately one hour following the application of skin traction the following should be checked:

1. Skin reactions to extensions and bandages.
2. Extremities for signs of neurological or circulatory complications.
3. The traction to ensure it is safe and working as required.

SKELETAL TRACTION (see Figure 4.2)

A metal pin or wire is inserted through a suitable bony point of the skeleton. This is an efficient method of applying traction. The force is transmitted directly through the bony skeleton and must therefore be used with care.

The common types of skeletal pins employed are as follows:

1. *Steinmann's pin* is a rigid steel pin which is generally attached to a special hoop or stirrup (Bohler Hoop or Nissen Stirrup).
2. *Denham pin* is similar to Steinmann's pin

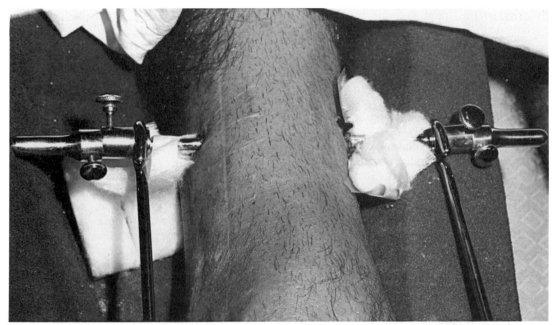

Fig. 4.2 Insertion of a metal pin through a bony point.

but has a screw thread in its centre. This makes it a very stable pin as it is unable to move without being deliberately turned.
3. *Kirschner's wire* is a narrow steel wire which is not rigid until it is pulled taut by the use of a spreader stirrup (Gissane Stirrup).

The most common sites for introducing pins are femoral condyles, tibial tubercle, and calcaneum.

Specific nursing care
- Before the pin is introduced, the skin is carefully prepared aseptically. Once introduced the pin should be observed twice daily for the onset of infection. The pin is a foreign body and reactions such as rashes on the overlying skin may occur.
- The area of skin around where the pin has been introduced should be kept clean and dry. There are different methods used to achieve this. An occlusive dressing may be applied and left until the pin is removed, or dressings such as normal wound dressings may be carried out. Sometimes the skin around the pin is sprayed or painted with iodine or an iodine preparation.
- The points of the pin must be covered at all

times either by the metal caps provided by the manufacturers, or with corks. This is to protect the patient and the nurse from injury.

General nursing care of the patient in traction

Maintaining a safe environment

The nurse must understand the principles of the type of traction in use in order to make an accurate assessment prior to formulating a care plan.

- The patient should be nursed on a firm-based bed to fully support the bony framework.
- To maintain the efficiency of the traction, the patient should be nursed as flat as possible or in a semi-recumbent position unless the splint is used purely as a resting splint. Most patients are nursed in a semi-recumbent position to prevent complications of the chest occurring. The patient is only recumbent when asleep. They are unable to lie on their side.
- Bed aids such as a bed cradle should be used to keep the bedclothes away from the patient's feet and to ensure free running of the traction cord. The alternative is to nurse the patient in a bed with the bedclothes divided

to allow the splint and the traction to be outside the bed. This is known as a 'split' or divided bed.

- The necessary pull and counter pull must be maintained in the correct position. This means the nurse must check the patient's position at least three hourly to ensure the patient is not being pulled against the end of the bed.
- It is essential to explain to the patient, in terms that he can understand, the principles of the traction being used. Inclusion of the patient in his own care will gain cooperation.
- The weights on the traction must be checked to ensure they are hanging free and not resting on the floor.
- The cords and knots must be checked for fraying and looseness to ensure safety of the traction. Cords must run freely over the pulleys or the effectiveness of the traction will be lost.
- The pulleys must be silent. A squeaky pulley may be a great source of irritation to both the patient and his neighbours. A small application of oil will help to maintain a silent pulley.

Breathing

- The nurse must check that the patient is able to breathe freely and deeply. Encouragement must be given to cough at least every four hours.

Eating and drinking

- It is often difficult for the patient to eat once traction has been applied because of their position in bed. Meals should be served in a way which the patient can handle easily, i.e., the food should be cut up and small helpings should be given to enable digestion to take place. An overhead mirror fixed to the head end of the bed may help the patient to feed himself. Bran or some form or fibre should, if possible, be included in the diet to help prophylactically against constipation.
- Fluid intake must be encouraged. The use of flexible straws or a beaker rather than a cup may help the patient towards independence and, where practical, the drinks should be enjoyable. This will also aid urinary output and help to maintain good kidney function. An accurate fluid balance chart must be

maintained. Prevention of such potential problems as cystitis, retention of urine and the formation of renal calculi must be undertaken. An adequate amount of daily fluid intake should prevent these problems. Regular urinalysis to check the content of the urine should be carried out. The patient may need help washing the genital area.

Eliminating

- Elimination may present problems for the patient restricted by traction. Privacy, and being given enough time, may help the patient to adjust to some of the unusual positions he may find himself in. With the foot end of the bed elevated, the patient often has a fear of soiling the bed. This should be dealt with by careful positioning of the bedpan and a sympathetic approach to the problem. After seeking advice from the medical staff, the end of the bed may in some types of traction be lowered to assist in elimination. Constipation may be a complication for patients in traction, particularly in the elderly patient. It is important at the outset to establish patterns of normal bowel habits. The means by which the patient maintains effective elimination by diet, or the type of laxative he is used to, may help in solving this problem. Added fibre in the diet may be acceptable.

Personal cleansing and dressing

- Personal hygiene must be maintained and the patient must be encouraged to be as independent as possible within the constraints of the traction. The patient's hair should be washed at least once a week and more frequently if desired or possible. This is not an easy task, but aids such as the bedfast rinser may help. Oral hygiene is essential and should be encouraged after each meal. Again the use of flexible straws and carefully supported equipment will ensure that the patient feels safe while cleaning his teeth. If possible, the affected limb should be washed and thoroughly dried at the same time as the bathing is taking place.
- Pressure area care should be carried out once the patient has been assessed using a suitable scale. As these patients are bed bound they are obviously patients 'at risk' and need

preventative care. Areas other than normal pressure areas present pressure problems as a result of splints being in contact with the skin. Areas such as the skin under the ring of a Thomas' splint must be checked every three to four hours. It is desirable to involve the patient in his own care by teaching him how to inspect and move skin in contact with splints, but the nurse remains accountable. Other areas particularly at risk are those in contact with splint material and appropriate care should be taken to relieve this pressure. The application of pads under rings or against splint bars does not relieve pressure, it adds to it. The use of an overhead trapeze device may enable the patient to move independently.

- During the initial assessment, enquiries about allergies to adhesive tape should be made and appropriate preventative action taken.
- Skin extensions must be checked twice daily for the occurrence of dermatitis or 'traction' blisters. These occur when skin traction starts to slip, causing friction.
- Bandages must be checked twice daily for staining which may indicate sores under the strapping. They should not be too tight or too loose. The limb should be re-bandaged daily if this is possible. If pads have been placed against the limb, e.g., in a fractured shaft of femur to correct alignment, then these bandages should be left undisturbed.

Controlling body temperature

- Clean bed linen and night clothes should, if possible, be given daily. Patients immobile in bed often sweat profusely, which in turn may add complications of sores in between skin folds. When bedcradles are used it may be necessary to supplement the patient's clothes with a warm flanellette sheet or light blanket placed next to the patient. Bed socks also help to maintain body temperature and provide comfort.
- Four-hourly observations of the extremities for colour, temperature, sensation and mobility will avoid the onset of neurological or circulatory problems. Each toe or finger must be observed individually.

Mobilizing

- The patient should be encouraged to put all unaffected limbs through a full range of active movements each day. Instructions from the physiotherapist concerning the affected limb should be followed and maintained by the nurse. This will help to avoid potential problems of venous thrombosis, stiff joints, muscle wastage and osteoporosis.

Expressing sexuality

- The nurse may need to deal with problems over expressing sexuality by the patient.
- Traction may confine the patient to bed for some time and affectionate contact with a partner is limited. Most orthopaedic beds are easily wheeled about and pushing the patient's bed out into the surrounding grounds, when possible, may not only allow the patient to talk privately with his family but will also give the patient the benefit of fresh air.
- The patient is encouraged to retain his or her sexual identity. Facilities to enable a man to shave or a woman to apply cosmetics if they wish should be available.

Working and playing

- The nurse must make sure the patient has access to radio and television headphones that work and that they are in a position to see the television. Again an overhead mirror may be of value, and this will also aid the patient to see what is going on in the ward. The occupational therapist must be employed to help the patient during his immobilization. Aids to daily living such as a helping hand, which is a device to enable the patient to reach and pick up small objects, may help the patient to retain some independence.

Sleeping

- Sleep is vital for the patient and a good ward environment, a peaceful mind and quietness will help. Sleeping may be difficult in the positions of traction. The orthopaedic nurse must be aware of this, particularly on night duty. If the patient is only sleeping for short periods the nurse should take the opportunity to move the patient when he is awake. She may also take the opportunity to straighten his sheets, treat pressure areas, turn pillows and generally ensure the patient is as comfortable as possible.

CARE OF PATIENTS IN FIXED TRACTION

With fixed traction (see Figure 4.3) some form of splint is used in order to obtain a hold on a part of the patient's body which is used as a point of counter thrust when the traction is applied.

The Thomas' splint is usually the splint of choice. This splint should be measured accurately to ensure a good fit for the patient. It may be necessary to measure the patient's unaffected leg instead of the affected one as this may cause pain to the patient. Measurements should be taken around the thigh at its highest point. Nowadays most Thomas' splints have a strap and buckle device at the ring which allows for swelling and, therefore, adjustment at a later stage. The length of the limb from the greater trochanter to the lateral malleolus, plus 15–17 centimetres to allow for foot movements, will give the length of the splint. The correct right or left splint must be selected. This is done by ensuring that the long bar lies on the lateral side and the largest part of the ring is uppermost. The splint is prepared by attaching a firm sling, either made of canvas or nylon, to it to support the limb. Skin extensions are applied to the limb. The tapes attached to the ends of the extensions on the limb are pulled taut and tied over the end of the splint. The splint ring should be in contact with the patient's ischial tuberosity, which provides a point of counter pressure, so that the counter thrust travels from the tied cords, through the side bars of the splint to the padded ring.

Specific nursing care

- A small pad is placed under the knee to prevent hyperextension occurring and to retain approximately five degrees of flexion.
- A pillow is placed under the splint to support the limb and a block is placed under the end of the splint to ensure that the heel is kept free from the bed.
- The skin area under the Thomas' splint must always be kept clean and dry. The patient should be taught how to move the skin under the ring every hour and encouraged to do this himself. The area may be lightly powdered but excessive talcum powder may form small hard lumps under the ring which, in turn, may cause pressure. It is essential that this practice is not only carried out for the skin on the top of the thigh, but should continue all round the ring.
- The ring of the splint should be kept supple; application of arachis oil or saddle soap may help this.
- It is essential that when the patient uses a bedpan the ring of the splint is protected from contamination by the use of nonabsorbable cotton wool which is placed over the ring of the splint.
- Prior to and following application of traction as for skin traction.
- General nursing considerations (see page 27) are continued.

CARE OF PATIENTS IN HAMILTON-RUSSELL TRACTION

Hamilton-Russell traction is a type of balanced skin traction which can be used for a patient following an arthroplasty operation of the hip or following a fracture of neck of femur in the elderly patient.

The bed has to have an overhead beam and

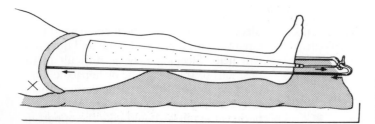

Fig. 4.3   Fixed traction. Extension tapes are tied to the end of a Thomas's splint and the ring of the splint presses against the ischial tuberosity.

bar and also a bar at the foot of the bed. The limb is supported on a pillow to prevent backward sagging. Skin extensions are applied to the lower leg and a canvas sling applied under the knee. The sling may need to be lined with 'gamgee' to prevent sores occurring.

From the knee sling a cord is taken to a pulley fixed to the beam (A). From this pulley the cord is taken to another pulley on a frame at the bottom of the bed (B) and then to a third pulley which is attached to a spreader separating the skin extensions (C). It is essential that this spreader is wide enough to ensure that the skin extensions do not exert pressure on the malleoli. The cord then finally passes to a second pulley at the foot of the bed (B). Weights are then attached to its end. The resultant pull should be in a direct line with the femur, as seen in Figures 4.4 and 4.5 showing the parallel force.

Specific nursing care

This is the same as for any patient in skin traction.

- Daily checks of the pulley and cord alignment with the leg are essential as medial or lateral pull can cause deformity.
- Four-hourly checks of the condition of the skin under the sling are important to prevent the formation of sores.

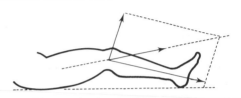

Fig. 4.5   Diagram showing parallel forces.

CARE OF PATIENTS IN GALLOWS TRACTION

This traction (see Figure 4.6) is used for the very young child with a fractured shaft of femur, or it may be used to aid reduction in congenital dislocation of hip in a child. The traction itself is thought in some cases to be responsible for avascular necrosis of one or more of the tarsal bones and therefore it is now less popular.

The child should be admitted with the mother and father if possible. In a planned admission, this should happen at least thirty-six hours before application of the traction. This will give both parents and child time to adjust to the hospital environment.

Skin extensions are applied to the child's limbs from the greater trochanter to lateral malleolus and lesser trochanter to medial malleolus on each leg taking into account the usual nursing considerations.

The child's parents should be present to

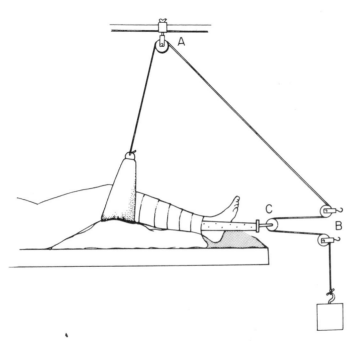

Fig. 4.4   Hamilton-Russell traction.

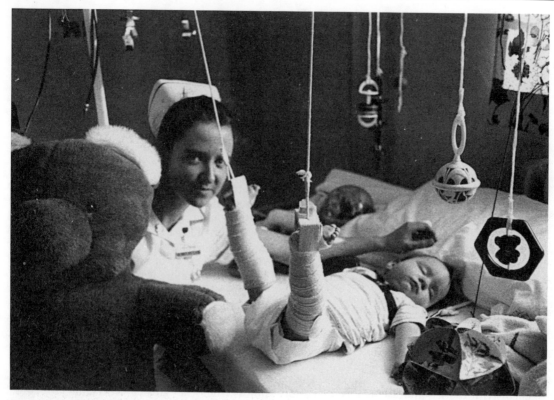

Fig. 4.6 Child with gallows traction on her legs.

comfort the child, having received appropriate explanations from the medical and nursing staff.

In a planned admission the extensions should be applied for twenty-four hours and left in position before traction is commenced.

With the aid of the child's mother/father and an assistant, the child is placed in the supine position and the hips flexed at 90 degrees; cords from the extensions are passed through overhead pulleys and the relevant weights as ordered by the physician applied gently. The child's buttocks should be raised clear of the bed. A light plastic splint may be bandaged to the back of the child's legs to maintain them in good alignment.

Specific nursing care

- Feeding may present special problems. Food and drink should be offered in small quantities and the child must be encouraged to eat and drink slowly.
- Special attention should be given to the occiput and shoulders as pressure may cause sores to form.
- If abduction is to be carried out this must be

done according to the surgeon's wishes. Care must be taken to ensure that the skin in the groin does not become taut and cause pain. Lanolin gently applied to this area is a preventative measure.

- Elimination of urine and faeces may cause problems and care must be taken to ensure that urine does not track back down the child's back.
- General nursing considerations as set out on page 27.

CARE OF PATIENTS IN PUGH'S TRACTION

This type of skin traction (see Figure 4.7) may be used to reduce a congenital dislocation of the hip in a young child.

It is a straightforward bilateral skin traction applied to the child's legs as for gallows traction. The cords are then passed over a bar attached at the end of the cot. A board is inserted under the mattress to maintain the child's legs at an angle of 45 degrees to the bed.

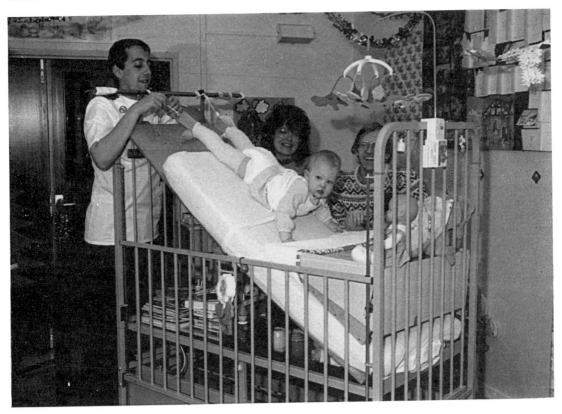

Fig. 4.7 Child with Pugh's traction on her legs.

Specific nursing care

The nursing care is as for gallows traction, but there are two major differences:

- These children are frequently nursed lying prone. They adapt easily to this position; it enables them to have a clear view of the ward and its occupants and leaves the child's hands free to be able to feed and play.
- The child's limbs can safely be taken down from the traction for an hour each day. This enables the mother and child to maintain a close relationship and to have a cuddle! If the extensions are not adhesive at this time they can be removed, the skin inspected, washed and dried thoroughly and the extensions reapplied.

CARE OF PATIENTS IN DUNLOP TRACTION

This type of traction is used in the management of supracondylar fractures of humerus in child-ren. The patient lies recumbent in bed and skin extensions are applied to the forearm. The shoulder joint is abducted to about 45 degrees from the trunk.

A cord is attached to the skin extensions and passed over a pulley suspended from an over-head beam so that the elbow is flexed to 45 degrees.

A padded sling is placed over the distal end of the humerus above the elbow joint. A weight is attached by a cord to the sling. The weight will be decided by the doctor according to the size of the patient.

A pad is placed under the mattress of the bed the side of the affected arm to provide counter traction.

Specific nursing care

- Hourly observations of the neurovascular state of the limb are carried out. The patient is asked to extend his fingers. If the patient is unable to do this actively then the nurse must passively extend the patient's fingers.

If this exercise is painful then ischaemia should be suspected and the doctor informed immediately. The traction should be discontinued at once.

CARE OF PATIENTS IN TYPES OF SKELETAL TRACTION

- Balanced skeletal traction using a Thomas' splint with a Pearson knee flexion piece.
- This type of traction can adapt to two systems. One is the traction system using a pin through a point in the skeleton, and the other is the balanced suspension of the limb.
- There are various methods for achieving the balance but, providing that counter traction is achieved and that the lower limb is suspended, the end result will be the same.

Indications for use

This type of traction may be used for patients with fractures of the shaft of femur or to correct a deformity.

The bed is prepared with an overhead beam. A Thomas' splint is selected, meeting the measurements of the patient and a Pearson knee flexion piece attached under the splint at the position of the knee joint. The splint and the knee piece are then prepared with splint material and cords.

The crossbars and pulleys are arranged as shown in Figure 4.8 and 4.9.

The pin may be inserted into the patient under a general or local anaesthetic and the patient will need routine preparation for this procedure. If the patient is conscious, sufficient explanation should be given by the nurse to support and comfort the patient. Once the pin has been inserted the patient's limb is gently lifted onto a splint. A pad is placed under the knee to prevent hyperextension of the joint occurring.

A hoop or stirrup is attached to the pin, a cord is tied onto the hoop which is then passed over a pulley attached to the bar at the foot of the bed. Weights are attached to this cord, as directed by the surgeon.

The splint is then suspended so that the lower limb is clear of the mattress and the foot of the bed is elevated to provide counter traction.

Specific nursing care

- General nursing care for patients in traction (see page 27).
- The skin under the Thomas' splint requires care and, once the patient is well enough, they should be taught to carry out these measures every hour.

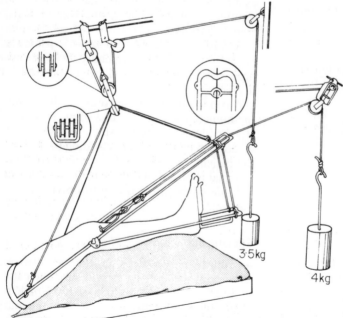

3·5kg

4kg   **Fig. 4.8**   Balanced traction using Steinmann's pin (skeletal traction) through the tibial tubercle. The leg is supported in a Thomas's splint with a Pearson knee flexion piece attached.

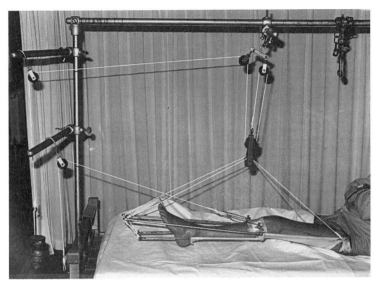

Fig. 4.9   Pulley arrangement for elevating Thomas's splint.

- Daily observations of the pin must be made to ensure that it is not bending as this may indicate that too much weight is being applied to the skeleton. Nurses must never reduce the pin weight until medical instructions have been given.
- Care of the pin sites as directed above. Recent research carried out in the USA suggests that different types of pin require different types of care. To prevent a pin reaction, each patient needs to be assessed individually for the amount of time the pin is to be in and whether there are two or more existing physical disorders which may be correlated to pin reaction (2).
- Skin care for the limb in traction is important. The skin may not need washing every day but should be washed every second day. The toes and the heel should be inspected daily, washed and gently but firmly massaged, to avoid tickling.

CARE OF A PATIENT IN TULLOCH-BROWN TRACTION

This type of traction is used for patients having undergone an excision arthroplasty of the hip joint (Girdlestone pseudarthrosis), for patients with an unstable total hip replacement or for patients following a reduction of a dislocated total hip replacement.

A Tulloch-Brown U-shaped splint is selected to fit the patient and is prepared by putting a piece of tubigrip in position over the splint. A foot piece is attached to the splint to support the patient's foot in the optimum position. A Denham pin or Steinmann pin is inserted through the patient's tibia by the medical staff. The limb is placed on the splint, the pin being inserted through the holes at the top of the splint. A Nissen stirrup is attached to the skeletal pin. A cord is attached to the stirrup and run through a series of pulleys as shown in Figures 4.8 and 4.9. Protective corks or metal caps are attached to cover the ends of the pin. The patient's leg is placed on a pillow, ensuring that the heel is free from the press of the bed. Weights are attached to the cord, according to the surgeon's wishes.

Specific nursing care

- The pin site dressings are checked at least twice a day and dressed as necessary or according to the regime used on the nursing unit.
- Specific exercises are taught to the patient by the physiotherapist and are reinforced by the nurse.
- Four-hourly observations of the position of the top of the U-splint are important. Pressure from this part of the splint on the common peroneal (lateral popliteal) nerve may result in drop foot.
- The pillow under the patient's leg may

present a possible complication of deep venous thrombosis. The pillow should be removed four-hourly with care, the patient's calf gently massaged and the pillow plumped up and replaced ensuring the patient's heel is free. The foot piece is removed at the same time and ankle exercises encouraged. The patient should be encouraged to breathe deeply every few hours to give additional aid to venous return.

CARE OF PATIENTS IN PERKIN'S TRACTION

Perkin's traction may be used in the treatment of fractures of the tibia and the femur. It is a form of skeletal traction without the use of any external splintage. This allows active movements of the leg to take place at an early stage, thus preventing a variety of complications. A 'split bed' in which the distal one-third of the mattress and the base of the bed can be removed is necessary. This allows for flexion of the patient's knee joint when fractures of the femur are being treated. Patients with a fracture of the tibia are nursed in a standard bed.

A skeletal pin is inserted through a variety of sites depending on the fracture site. Denham collars to which the traction cords are attached are fitted onto the ends of the pin.

New swivels have been developed to overcome the problems experienced by attaching the cords to Denham collars. These are termed 'Simon's low friction swivels'. A cord is attached to each side of the pin using whichever attachment is thought suitable. The traction cords are kept parallel and passed over separate pulleys at the foot of the bed. A weight is attached to each cord according to the surgeon's wishes. The foot of the bed is elevated. In fractures of the femur one or more pillows are placed under the patient's thigh to maintain the natural anterior bowing of the femur. Active quadricep exercises are commenced immediately if the patient's general condition permits this and if there are no other injuries which may lead to complications. Knee flexion can be commenced approximately one week following admission under the supervision of a physiotherapist. In fractures of the tibia, the traction is applied in a similar way with the leg resting on a pillow. Active ankle exercises are commenced straight away and knee flexion exercises started as soon as the patient is able to do so.

Specific nursing care

- Routine nursing care and observations are maintained as for any patient in skeletal traction.
- Care when handling the patient's limb is essential and the pillows supporting it only removed following medical advice. This means the nurse needs to be extra vigilant when observing pressure points.
- Careful explanations concerning the reasons for no external splintage and encouragement to the patient are important.
- The patient is encouraged to maintain the exercise programme.

OS CALCIS TRACTION

This type of skeletal traction is frequently used for those patients who have sustained either a complicated or compound fracture of the lower limb. The traction is commonly applied using a Kirschner wire inserted through the calcaneum, with a Gissane stirrup applied to the wire to tighten it. The limb may be encased in a plaster of paris to prevent rotation of the bony fragments. A Braun's frame is used to support the limb and this is prepared by covering the frame in flannel bandage or tubigrip. The traction is normally applied in the operating theatre following manipulation of the fracture and insertion of the wire, and therefore, general preparation of a patient for anaesthesia may be necessary. Local cleansing and preparation of the patient's limb may not be possible in the presence of an exposed piece of bone.

Specific nursing care

- Routine care for patients in skeletal traction is maintained.
- As the patient's limb is elevated on a Braun's frame it is important that the patient is kept warm and comfortable.
- Safety of the patient's injured limb on the frame is necessary and also the safety of the frame on the bed. It is sometimes necessary to tie the frame to the bottom of the bed to prevent it from being dislodged from the bed.
- If a cast is applied it must be dried (see Chapter 6).
- The extremities of the patient's injured limb

must be observed for the onset of neuro-vascular complications and appropriate action taken as necessary.

CARE OF PATIENTS IN PELVIC BELT TRACTION

Pelvic belt traction is used in the conservative or nonoperative management of patients with 'back pain'. Back pain is a common complaint dealt with in orthopaedic hospitals. Much research has been carried out into the causes and treatments of this condition and many opinions, both informed and not so well informed, are proffered as to the effectiveness of various forms of management.

The traction provides a degree of immobilization and gives some relief of pain, although this is variable, and the patient also feels something is actively being done to help them.

A ready-made belt is used to fit the patient. Measurements are taken of the patient's waist and the circumference of the patient's hips five centimetres below the level of the anterior superior iliac spines. The appropriate belt is selected. It should be checked before application to ensure that all the buckles are present. There are a variety of disposable belts available which are secured in place by surfaces which adhere to each other.

The patient is nursed, as are all orthopaedic patients, on a firm-based bed with one pillow only under their head.

It is advisable to administer an analgesic prior to application of the belt to ensure that the procedure is a comfortable one for the patient and causes minimal distress. The belt is placed under the patient by rolling the patient from side-to-side, ensuring that the spine is kept in a straight line. This action is termed 'log rolling' as the patient's body is kept in line like a log.

When the buckles are fastened there should be a small gap between them. The waist buckle is fastened as tightly as is comfortable for the patient; the bottom buckle may be left slightly loose to allow for movement and possible bladder distension. The shaped hip sections of the belt should rest on the patient's iliac crests.

The two long adjustable side straps lie longitudinally down each side of the patient, the apex of the V level with the patient's knees. These straps attach to weights to exert a downward pull on the lower back. There are two ways in which these straps may be used. They may be threaded through a long spreader, ensuring that there is sufficient room for the patient's feet to move and that the straps are of equal length on both sides. A cord is then run from the spreader so that the spreader lies approximately five centimetres higher than the patient's toes to ensure an accurate pull on the lower back. Weights are then attached as ordered by the doctor and the foot of the bed elevated to provide counter traction. The second method of attaching the side straps to the weights is by attaching a traction cord to each of the straps, threading each cord through a pulley secured to a crossbar at the foot of the bed and then attaching weights equally to each side.

The foot of the bed is then elevated. In both cases it is essential to ensure that the bedclothes do not interfere with the smooth running of the traction. A bed cradle should be used to prevent this happening (see Figure 4.10).

Specific nursing care

- The nurse must monitor the patient's pain levels accurately and frequently, or help the patient to do this himself by use of a chart. The exact location of the pain, the type and intensity should be assessed by the nurse in the initial stages, therefore allowing the nurse an accurate baseline from which to work. The nurse monitors the effect of analgesia and informs the medical staff if medication is not reducing pain.
- Elimination may cause problems for the patient. In consultation with the medical staff, the foot of the bed may be lowered to aid successful use of bedpans. A slipper bedpan protected by non-absorbent wool may be more comfortable for the patient. The use of female urinals may be helpful. The patient should be 'log rolled' onto the bedpan, which requires careful positioning. The belt should be inspected for soiling once the procedure is complete, pressure areas should be checked and treated as necessary, and bed sheets are pulled taut at the same time to prevent unnecessary movement for the patient.
- Routine nursing care is carried out according to the patient's individual needs.
- Teaching the patient simple measures of fluid intake and nutrition may prevent the problem of constipation.

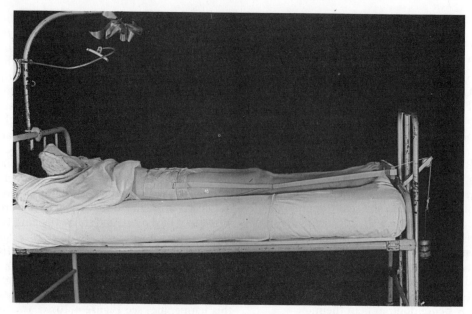

Fig. 4.10   Pelvic belt traction.

- Feeding needs may be met by the use of an adjustable angled bed mirror. This will further help the patient to see what is happening in the ward and also enable him to watch television. In consultation with the medical staff, the traction may be removed totally to enable personal hygiene to be carried out.
- The patient's bedside locker must be placed within easy reach of the patient.
- An understanding of the patient's feelings may aid recovery. Chronic back pain is disheartening and depressing. Acute back pain may lead the patient to have feelings of guilt about the length of time spent away from work and he may be depressed about the future both in terms of employment, his family and social life. The nurse must be willing to listen and enlist the help of an appropriate member of the team if the patient's needs cannot be met with her own counselling skills. The patient can be encouraged to talk while the nurse is actively nursing. This need not take up extra time.

There are numerous other types of traction and splints and some of these are described when the nursing care of patients with the appropriate specific conditions is considered.

REFERENCES

1   Stewart J.D.M. & Hallett J.P. (1983) *Traction and Orthopaedic Appliances*, 2nd Edn. Edinburgh: Churchill Livingstone.
2   Sproles K.J. (1985) Nursing Care of Skeletal Pins. *Orthopaedic Nursing*, January/February, Vol. 4. No. 1.

SUGGESTED FURTHER READING

Powell M. (1986) *Orthopaedic Nursing and Rehabilitation*, 9th Edn. Edinburgh: Churchill Livingstone.
Stewart J.D.M. & Hallett J.P. (1985) *Traction and Orthopaedic Appliances*, 2nd Edn. Edinburgh: Churchill Livingstone.

5

CARE OF THE PATIENT USING AN ORTHOSIS

An orthosis is 'a force system that is designed to control, to correct or to compensate for a deformity, deforming forces or absent forces' (1).

The term 'orthosis' is gradually replacing words such as 'appliance', 'splint' and 'brace'.

The prescription for such a device is written by the orthopaedic consultant and the construction of the orthosis by an orthotist who is a specialist in the construction of such devices and skilled in the application of orthoses.

In general, orthopaedic nurses are seldom required to measure patients for splints, except those kept in stock by the hospital such as the Thomas' bed-splint, but it is important that the nurse knows how to care for patients in these devices and to reinforce instructions given to the patients during the fitting of their appliances.

Orthoses are fitted for several purposes:

1. To provide immobilization and local rest for a part of the body by limiting the amount of movement.
2. As a means of applying traction to the skeletal system.
3. To prevent deformity, correct mild deformity or to retain correction when this has been achieved.
4. To stabilize joints, as seen in Charcot's joints, and to protect weak muscles.
5. To maintain extension of the spine.
6. To relieve weight bearing, as in a Thomas' patten-ended caliper used to relieve weight in a patient's hip affected by Perthes' disease.
7. To relieve pain and pressure on nerves, as in a prolapsed cervical disc lesion.
8. To give support postoperatively, e.g., following a spinal fusion.

In the past, orthoses were made mainly of leather and metal, or a combination of both. These days the majority of splints are made in many modern materials, often a form of plastic which makes them lightweight, durable, easily cared for and far less obvious than those of the past. They have however also brought their own problems such as skin reactions from allergic reactions to the materials and the fact that the materials are often nonporous, causing sweat to collect beneath the splint. They also break more readily. Expense is a consideration not to be overlooked and the orthopaedic nurse must be conscious of the cost of these devices and take the appropriate measures to care for the splint as well as for the patient. She must also take time to teach the patient how to care for his orthosis.

General nursing care

Maintaining a safe environment

- The orthosis must fit accurately otherwise it will be ineffective and uncomfortable for the patient.
- It may take time for the patient to become accustomed to the device and this must not be mistaken for the orthosis not fitting correctly. If it is obvious the device is not fitting accurately then the orthotist should be contacted as soon as possible. An ill-fitting splint may cause sores from pressure if too tight or sores from friction if too loose.
- The orthosis must perform the function for which it has been ordered. It must be worn according to the doctor's advice and only discarded when the doctor advises this.

Communicating

- Teaching the patient about the care, use and management of the splint must be carried out carefully and repeated often. It is necessary to include the patient's family in this teaching particularly if the splint has to be removed and reapplied by a second person.
- Clear instructions are given as to how long the splint is to be worn each day and whether it can be worn under or over clothing.

- The splint must be maintained in good order. Many of the materials used today are spongeable and washable. It is important to stress that, unless otherwise instructed, the patient should remain in bed while the splint is not being worn. The orthosis must be inspected daily for signs of wear and tear. Any deterioration in the splint must be dealt with expertly and immediately or its effectiveness will be lost.
- It is important to realize that orthoses applied to children may need constant reappraisal as a child may soon outgrow the original size provided. Children's splints may also require careful inspection for damage as a lively child may inadvertantly cause damage to the splint.

Breathing

- It is important to ensure that devices which enclose the trunk do not impair respiration.

Eating and drinking

- Nutrition and fluid intake should present few problems. Some upper limb and cervical splints may create difficulties from the position they hold the head in or prevent normal use of the arm, but the patient should be encouraged to maintain his independence. Some discomfort may be experienced by the patient following a large meal. The patient should be advised to take time to eat the meal slowly and to ensure only small portions are taken.

Eliminating

- Elimination may prove difficult in the early stages of using an orthosis such as a Milwaukee brace, which is used for the treatment of idiopathic scoliosis. The patient should soon learn to adapt with patience and understanding on the part of the family.

Personal cleansing and dressing

- Skin hygiene is imperative. General personal hygiene should be encouraged. The skin under the orthosis should be kept clean and dry. The use of talcum powder should be kept to a minimum as this may form small balls and create abnormal pressure under the

splint, thus predisposing the patient's skin to sores.
- The splint itself must be kept clean and dry.
- Circulation to the skin under the splint must be carefully observed. Skin areas which are in contact with the splint material along with underlying soft tissue should, if possible, be gently moved under the splint to relieve pressure. Patients should be taught to perform this task themselves or, if not able to do so, a member of the family taught how to do this for the patient. At first this should be performed every two hours but as the skin becomes accustomed to the splint the regime of moving the skin may be reduced to three times a day. The patient and his family are instructed how to observe the skin for adverse signs such as increased redness and heat and to seek advice if such a problem arises.
- The patient's skin should be observed for reaction to the splint material or for heat rashes occurring as a result of sweat gathering under the splint. Small, light, thin body vests can be supplied to be worn under some of the spinal braces, and this will alleviate these problems.
- Frequent changing of these vests is desirable on a daily basis. Instruction to the patient in this procedure is given. The skin should be observed for the onset of a splint sore. If the skin appears red when the splint is removed then observations of the skin are increased. The splint should be inspected to ensure it is not at fault in the fitting or cleanliness of the device. If it is pressure alone which is the cause of the redness, then there is no point in increasing pressure by placing a pad over the area of the impending sore. The orthosis should be adjusted. If this is not possible then protective material such as felt should be placed on either side or all round the pressure point. Should the skin break down it must be treated as any open wound, dressing it with an aseptic technique and sterile dressings.
- Dressing may cause problems if the patient is wearing a spinal support such as a Boston or Cotrel brace for the control of scoliosis. Although clothing may cover these devices, the patient (who is often a young adolescent girl) may be very conscious of the fact that she is wearing a brace. Today's fashions change rapidly and it is difficult for a young teenage girl to accept the problems related to

her condition. Sympathy, with support and tactful suggestions over fashionable clothes to wear, may help these patients to accept this difficult period of their development.

- Buckles and straps on the splints create their own problems and patients need to be warned about the possibility of tearing their own clothes and bedclothes on such apparatus.

Working and playing

- The patient should be taught the purpose of the orthosis so they may cope with the tasks of daily living within the confines of the device. Encouragement to live a normal life is important and to maintain as much independence as possible. This includes such activities as working and playing.
- The patient may have problems in accepting the orthosis. This is particularly difficult for children as they feel different and often isolated from their peer group. It is essential that the orthopaedic nurse allows the patient the time and space to adjust to his orthosis, to talk through his fears, anxieties and problems linked to the wearing of this device. They should be encouraged to socialize as normal for teenagers of this age group.
- Parents as well as the patient often have the need to express their fears and anxieties. The nurse must provide time for this to happen.
- The patient may experience local problems caused by rest enforced by the orthosis. These will be prevented by:
  - (i) Exercise. Active exercise and, wherever possible, normal use of all of the joints not immobilized. Isometric exercises may be taught and should be encouraged for the joints which cannot be moved, e.g., quadriceps exercises for an immobilized knee joint. These will overcome such potential problems as stiff joints, muscle wastage and weakness, and increase the circulation. These exercises will also aid the feeling of well-being and decrease the risk of the patient feeling disabled.
  - (ii) Care of the orthosis or any other such device used to immobilize will prevent the onset of skin complications.
  - (iii) Care of the skin.
  - (iv) Prevention of oedema. Where possible elevation of the immobilized limb will aid this and help venous return. Limbs should be fully supported when elevated and care taken not to put joints of such limbs into abnormal positions, e.g., it is very easy when elevating an arm to put the shoulder joint into an over extended position.
  - (v) Observations to prevent the onset of neurological and circulatory problems. The onset of numbness, pins and needles, abnormal colour, pain and swelling should immediately lead the orthopaedic nurse to suspect some neurovascular complication. This should be reported immediately and expert help sought. Patients and their relatives should be taught the importance of these observations, how and when to take them and who to contact when problems arise. These instructions should not only be given verbally but be written down and handed to the patient or relative.

There are many types of orthoses used for a variety of deformities. Although it is not possible to include all types available, some of the more common ones used are described below with the specific nursing considerations. Some orthoses are discussed with the specific conditions for which they are used.

CALIPERS

A caliper is an orthosis used for the lower limb. Its main functions are:

1. To control deformity of a limb.
2. To restrict movement of joints.
3. To provide stability for paralysed, weakened and unstable joints and limbs.
4. To relieve weight bearing, thus providing rest for joints affected by disease.

Walking calipers

These may be weight relieving or nonweight relieving devices worn to support an unstable knee joint by keeping the knee in extension or to take weight off the bones of the lower limb.

A ring or moulded leather 'bucket top' fits against the ischial tuberosity. The body weight is transmitted from the tuberosity to the ring or bucket top through metal side bars to the shoe and then through the shoe to the ground. Older people are generally fitted with the bucket top as this provides greater comfort for them and because their caliper is normally to be worn indefinitely. It may be necessary to incorporate a knee locking device, particularly in adult calipers, to allow for flexion of the knee joint. The metal side bars must be strong but light. They are attached to the ring or bucket top and terminate in small spurs which slot into the shoe.

For children, the ends of calipers are adjustable so they can be lengthened to accommodate growth.

The shoes worn with calipers should be of a laced type with a firm leather upper and sole and a flat heel. A slight raise may be necessary on the heel of the shoe of the unaffected leg to compensate for the orthosis. This is important to prevent deformity of the patient's unaffected limb and the spine.

The patient should be taught to stand with his weight evenly distributed on his feet, which should be apart as far as the width of the shoulders, and he should be taught to walk without clutching at furniture or swinging the caliper outwards (see Figures 5.1 and 5.2).

Toe raising devices

When dorsiflexion is weak the patient has difficulty in walking, particularly over uneven ground.

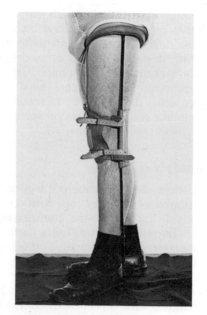

Fig. 5.1 Ring caliper applied to patient.

A method may be employed to provide the patient with an active measure to overcome this disability.

A below knee double iron is used, which is a short version of the long weight relieving caliper with a ring. A spring is attached to the double irons by a Y-shaped strap. The irons fit into the shoe with spurs, and an ankle strap is employed to stabilize the ankle joint.

When the disability is not great, a toe raising device may be fitted within the heel of the shoe.

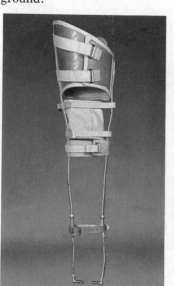

Fig. 5.2 Bucket topped caliper.

A below knee double iron is used and wire springs inserted into the heel. This is a more easily concealed device which may be cosmetically desirable (see Figure 5.3A).

T-straps

When an inversion or eversion deformity is present, a below knee iron with a T-strap may be used. A T-strap is made of leather and is attached to the side of the shoe between the sole and the upper. The straps are cut sufficiently long to go round the ankle and the side of the caliper bar with the buckle on the other side of the leg. The strap provides stability and compensates for weak invertor or evertor muscles.

When tibialis anterior and posterior muscles are weak, but the peroneal muscles are unaffected, the foot will be pulled into a valgus (away from the mid-line) position. This may be seen in such conditions as poliomyelitis or spasmodic flat foot. The deformity can be controlled by the use of an outside iron and inside T-strap.

When the opposite occurs and the peroneal muscles are weakened the foot may be pulled into a varus position. An inside iron and outside T-strap will help to control this deformity (see Figures 5.3 B & C and 5.4).

Cosmetic long leg caliper

Many of the previously mentioned long leg calipers are cosmetically unacceptable by today's standards. They have further disadvantages in that they are frequently cumbersome and uncomfortable. With the new, light weight, easily malleable materials, cosmetic calipers have a part to play in lower limb orthoses. These calipers are of value in controlling a flail lower

Fig. 5.4 Inside: iron and outside: T-strap to aid eversion; the reverse consequently helps inversion.

limb and provide the patient with a far more acceptable orthosis (see Figure 5.5).

ALTERATIONS TO SHOES

The orthopaedic nurse is often called upon to give advice regarding footwear and, in particular, those shoes which require some form of alteration as ordered by the surgeon.

Shoes should be well fitting, have a strong, leather upper, a rounded toe and a flat heel. The sole should be of leather in preference to one of the manmade materials, although cost may need to be taken into consideration. Most modern

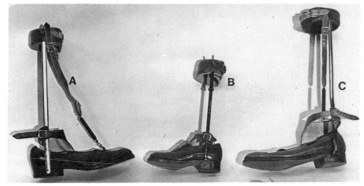

Fig. 5.3 (a) Inside: T-Strap; outside: iron with centre toe-raising spring; (b) inside: T-strap; outside: iron; (c) inside: T-strap; outside: iron with flat socket ankle joint and side spring to help the dropped everted foot.

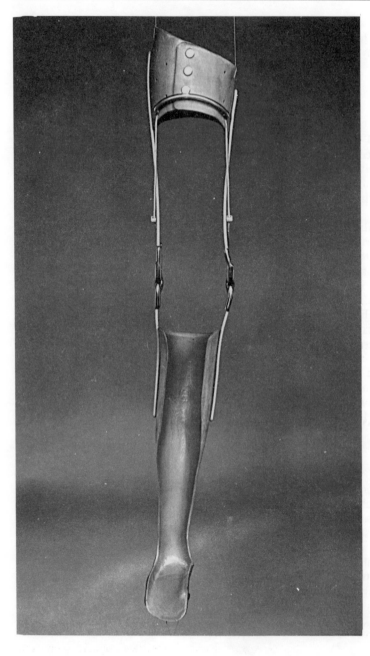

Fig. 5.5   A cosmetic caliper.

shoes have a hollow heel and this can lead to problems when shoes need to be altered to accommodate the spurs of calipers. The shoes must be of the lace-up type. In today's society the fashion-conscious woman may have difficulty in accepting this type of shoe, but the advantages in relation to her orthopaedic condition should be explained to her.

Raising of one side of the heel

Inside raising of the heel

This is used to alter the line of weight bearing in an abducted foot. It is occasionally used to correct a knock knee deformity in children. A wedge of leather, according to the surgeon's wishes, is placed between the upper and the sole on the inner side of the heel of the shoe. This enables the shoe to be repaired normally. This heel is known as a 'crooked' heel (see Figure 5.6).

Fig. 5.6   Inside raising of heel.

Floated heel

Occasionally the heel may be 'floated' out on the lateral side to increase the weight bearing surface. A combination of an inside wedge and floated heel may be used when the peroneal muscles are weak.

Outside raising of the heel

Alterations to the shoe may be carried out in exactly the same way as inside raising. This is used to prevent a varus deformity such as may be seen in talipes equinovarus, particularly in late treatment of this condition.

A Thomas heel

Where a greater degree of inversion of the foot is required, the inner margin of the heel is elongated for up to two-and-a-half centimetres to come to rest under the navicular bone of the foot. This gives support to the medial longitudinal arch and is the classic Thomas heel (see Figure 5.7).

Alterations to compensate for leg length discrepancy

Uneven gait can be physically tiring, look unsightly and cause secondary complications, in particular to the vertebral column.

The measurements taken to decide these discrepancies are discussed in Chapter 7.

When there is slight shortening, between one

Fig. 5.7   Thomas heel.

to two centimetres, the heel is raised and bars are placed on the sole, one behind the tread and one about five centimetres from the toe of the shoe.

For greater shortening, the heel and sole are removed from the upper and the shoe built-up with layers of cork to the required height. It is shaped to give a rocker like action. The shoe is then reassembled and the cork covered in the same type of leather as the shoe. This is known as 'universal raising' (see Figure 5.8).

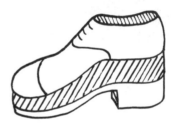

Fig. 5.8   Universal raising.

Metatarsal bar

This is used as a pain relieving device for metatarsalgia. It is also used for hallux valgus and claw foot. A bar of leather two-and-a-half centimetres wide is securely applied to the sole of the shoe obliquely behind the metatarsal heads (see Figure 5.9).

Insoles

Insoles are generally made of leather, although materials such as 'plastazote' may be used.

These are placed inside the patient's shoe. This is convenient for the patient as they can be transferred from one pair of shoes to another.

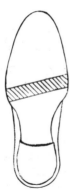

Fig. 5.9   Metatarsal bar.

A   B   C

Fig. 5.10   (a) Ski-front surgical shoe; (b) space shoe; (c) shoe with deep cork raise sometimes known as a bridge cork.

The insoles may be required to be used in conditions such as a permanent flat foot when one or both longitudinal arches may need to be supported.

SURGICAL FOOTWEAR

Commercially produced shoes and boots are available for purchase to accommodate deformed feet (see Figure 5.10). However, such products, while having a part to play, should be treated with caution as they are made in factories far from the patient and without the individual patient's foot being seen. Consideration should be given as to whether a shoe or boot is desirable: boots give a much better grip to the foot than shoes. The style and size of the opening of the shoe and the type of material it is made from should all be taken into consideration made when such shoes are ordered.

REFERENCES

1   Bunch W. & Keagy R. (1976) *Principles of Orthotic Treatment*. St. Louis: Mosby Co.

SUGGESTED FURTHER READING

Stewart J.D.M. & Hallett J.P. (1983) *Traction and Orthopaedic Appliances*, 2nd Edn. London: Churchill Livingstone.

6

MANAGEMENT AND CARE OF PATIENTS IN PLASTER CASTS

All orthopaedic nurses should have a basic understanding of the techniques used in the application of plaster casts. They should be able to apply simple casts effectively in uncomplicated cases. However, the best way to acquire this knowledge is by practical handling of plaster under the guidance of an expert. The technique of good plastering is not an easy one and it is not easily acquired. It takes practice and time to become proficient.

The care of the patient wearing a cast is an essential part of the orthopaedic nurse's work and, while some consideration will be given to the basic principles of casting, most of this chapter will concentrate on the care of patients in casts.

MATERIALS USED IN THE APPLICATION OF CASTS

Over a number of years, many new synthetic-type casting materials have been introduced. These new materials often have distinct advantages over the older and more widely known plaster of Paris. The advantages of these new materials are:

1. They set rapidly and form a light, tough cast. This means that the patient is able to be discharged more quickly from hospital and that the cast seldom requires a long period of time for drying before weight bearing in leg casts commences.
2. They do not absorb body fluids and thus stay clean.
3. They are water resistant and allow the patient to perform a variety of activities involving water.
4. If used to immobilize a fractured limb the synthetic materials allow x-ray penetration without distortion, leaving the healing process of bones undisturbed by frequent changes of the cast.

However, these materials also have disadvantages. They are far more costly than plaster of Paris and need a skilled technician to apply them, as they set rapidly leaving little time for accurate moulding. This, in turn, may lead to a rough exterior to the cast, added to which they are usually dull or yellow-brown coloured which leaves an unpleasing sight to the eye. It is often necessary to use rubber gloves to protect the technician from the temperature produced during the chemical changes which take place and to prevent skin reactions occurring to the handlers.

TYPES OF AVAILABLE CASTING MATERIALS

Plaster of Paris or gypsum

This material is obtained by mining. Its chemical composition is calcium sulphate plus two molecules of water ($CaSO_4.2H_2O$). The gypsum is ground to a fine powder, heated in an autoclave, then mixed with a solvent and various additives to improve handling. A special woven fabric is immersed in this liquid type plaster and the solvent is removed by heating in a dry oven. Bandages and slabs are produced from this plaster material. The bandages are wound around a cruciform central core to enable the full penetration of the water to take place when the bandage is immersed in water.

Water activated polymerizable materials

For example Baycast, Scotchcast, Crystona.
These contain chemicals which are coated onto fabric to form bandages. Contact with water activates the chemical and starts polymerization.

Nonwater activated materials

For example Glassona.
This group is prepared in a similar way to the

water activated group but, instead of using water, a chemical solvent or catalyst activates the polymerization.

Low temperature thermoplastics

For example Plastazote, Orthoplast.

These are prepared sheets of inert plastic which, when heated, become soft and pliable and which harden again when cooled.

Specific nursing points

Due to the fact that plaster of Paris is the most likely material the orthopaedic nurse will learn to handle, the necessary requisites for its application are set out below:

- Plaster bandages and slabs of the required length. These may be dry slabs prepared by folding the bandage to form slabs of not less than six layers.
- Two or more buckets of water at a temperature comfortable to the hand. If the temperature of the water is too cold the plaster setting time is lengthened, if too warm the setting time is much quicker leaving little time for accurate moulding. The water in the buckets should be changed frequently otherwise the bandages will not soak properly. Pouring away the water at the end of the procedure should take place through a special drain, or the bucket should be allowed to stand until the plaster settles at the bottom of the bucket. The water is then carefully poured off and the plaster which has settled at the bottom of the bucket is disposed of in the rubbish bin.
- Padding materials are also prepared. These may include stockinette, to cover limbs and to line plasters where swelling is anticipated, and splint-wool, heavy felt or wool bandages to protect bony prominences. It may be necessary to stitch the felt and a needle and cotton should be readily available in this case.
- Plaster knives, bandage scissors and plaster shears should be available to trim plasters. Plaster knives should be kept sharp and have a non-slip handle.
- Indelible pencil for marking the cast.
- Protective gowns, gloves, boots and plastic sheets to protect the handler, the bed and the patient.

- Pillows covered in waterproof material and towelling on which to place and support the plastered limb during the drying process.
- Materials for cleaning the area of skin around the cast to remove any excess plaster material.

APPLICATION OF A PLASTER OF PARIS CAST

Care and preparation of the equipment

- All equipment is prepared and laid out before commencing the procedure.
- Before application of the cast the following points must be clear:
  - (i) Why the cast is being applied and the extent of the patient's disability.
  - (ii) Where the plaster is to extend from and at which point it will end.
  - (iii) Whether the cast is to be padded or unpadded.
- The surgeon will position the part to which the cast is to be applied and will maintain the position during application of the plaster.
- Each bandage is immersed in water at an angle. This ensures the centre of the bandage is soaked. It is held in the water until air bubbles cease to rise from it. The bandage is then lifted out and very gently squeezed towards the middle. The free end is loosened and handed to the operator. Alternatively the free end of the bandage may be held between the operator's thumb and first finger to secure it prior to soaking.
- The next bandage is then placed in the bucket ready to soak. This practice may vary. Individual bandages may be soaked only as they are required.
- The wet bandage is rolled round the limb, contact between the limb and the bandage being maintained the whole time.
- Special attention must be paid to moulding over bony prominences to prevent uneven pressure which may cause the formation of sores. This is achieved using the palm of the hand, never the fingers, during the moulding process.
- Two-thirds of the previous turn of the bandage is covered by the next turn and the cast is constantly smoothed by the free hand. This ensures no air is trapped between the layers of the cast which would weaken it and

also prevent pressure, particularly over bony prominences.

- When the cast is complete the edges are trimmed. It can be finished by turning the stockinette back and fixing it with a small-piece of plaster bandage. All plaster should be carefully washed off the skin areas to provide comfort for the patient and clean extremities to facilitate easy observations to take place. The aim of the cast is to supply the patient with a well supporting, solid mass, and not a series of layers of plaster. The cast must be smooth inside, and perform the function for which it is applied (see Figure 6.1).

General care of the patient in a plaster of Paris

Nursing care of the patient while plaster casts dry

Plaster of Paris does not gain its full strength until completely dry and this will take from 24 hours for a small arm cast to 96 hours for a total body cast. To enable drying to take place the following points should be observed:

- A fracture board should be placed under the mattress to provide a firm, supporting surface for the cast.
- Rest the limb, or part, on a soft structure with preferably one or more pillows covered with a waterproof cover which, in turn, is covered by towelling material to absorb moisture. This must be changed frequently and the cast should never be left to lie on wet material as this will hinder drying.
- Under no circumstances should the cast be rested on a hard surface as this will cause uneven pressure to a wet cast. Particular attention must be paid to bony prominences such as the heels or sacrum which should never receive direct pressure.
- Wet plasters must never be covered. They should be exposed to free circulating warm air to aid drying. When dry a plaster cast is white and shiny unlike the grey, musty smelling cast when wet. Areas of the limb not enclosed in plaster should be kept warm by covering them with a blanket or sock.
- Artificial heat is not used to dry plasters as

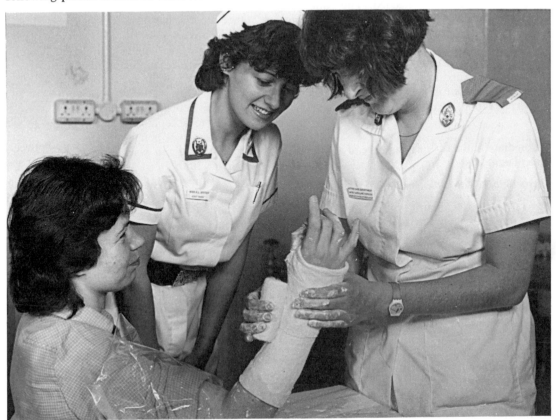

Fig. 6.1 Application of plaster of Paris.

this will result in a brittle cast. If rapid drying is necessary, a heat cradle may be applied in exceptional circumstances but, the time it is switched on and the amount of bulbs used inside the cradle is carefully controlled. Any areas not covered by plaster must be protected against burning by covering them completely and the patient should not be left unattended while the heat cradle is on. The heat cradle may be switched off for regular periods during each hour it is in use to ensure that no excessive heat or condensation occurs within the area inside the cradle or within the cast itself.

- To aid the even drying of large casts the patient should be turned every three to six hours. When handling a wet cast the flat of the hand is used with the fingers extended to prevent fingertips digging into the plaster which may result in pressure to the underlying skin.
- At least two nurses are required to turn a patient in a spica and frequently, for the safety of the patient and the nurse, more than two nurses are needed. The patient is always turned onto the side which does not have the leg in plaster to prevent cracking of the cast occurring. Where a double spica is used the patient must be lifted clear of the bed and turned in the air.
- Limbs encased in plaster should be elevated to aid venous return and to prevent oedema.

Immediate and daily nursing care of a patient in a plaster cast

Maintaining a safe environment

- Two- to four-hourly observations of the extremities should be undertaken during the initial drying period of the cast to check the neurovascular status. This may be reduced to daily checks once the plaster has dried.
- Each individual digit should be checked for temperature, colour, sensation and mobility to ensure that circulation and nerve conduction is unimpaired. It is not sufficient to test one or two digits. All individual digits should be tested each time.
- Circulatory impairment will be seen in a cold, oedematous, blanched or blue, painful digit. Capillary return should be tested for by the blanching test when the nail of the thumb or great toe is compressed and

immediately released. The colour should go from white to normal with great rapidity.

- If return to normal colour is slow, then frequency of observation is increased.
- Wherever possible, comparative peripheral pulses for rate, rhythm and volume should be taken although this is often difficult with the position of the plaster.
- Patients should be able to move and feel each toe or finger and the doctor's opinion sought if any suspicion of numbness or inability to move them is found.
- No observations can be carried out successfully unless the extremities are clean. Each day the patient's toes or fingers should be carefully washed and dried. Not only will this allow accurate observations, but will add to the comfort of the patient.
- If the observations show there is any neurovascular impairment, the cast must be split immediately throughout its entire length. Care must be taken to cut through any padding or bandage lying beneath the cast. Both an upper limb and lower limb cast may be split along the front edge.
- Once the cast has been split and bare skin is visible, a length of orthopaedic felt is placed along the whole length of the split. A crepe bandage is then applied around the cast.
- The affected limb of the patient is then elevated. Observations are continued to ensure the neurovascular status of the limb returns to acceptable levels. Failure to relieve excessive, potentially damaging pressure may result in permanent damage to the patient's limb.
- If the impairment is due to compression within a muscle compartment, surgical intervention will be necessary.
- It is necessary to monitor the pain levels of the patient carefully and to try to ascertain whether the pain is from the site of the surgery or fracture, or from pressure of the cast, particularly over a bony prominence. The nurse should discover from the patient the exact location and description of the pain before administering analgesia and then take appropriate action.
- If the pain is over a bony prominence it may indicate the onset of a plaster pressure sore. These sores may be caused by:

(i) *Pressure* from careless handling when the cast is wet or, when being moulded, insufficient padding over bony prominences or the rough edges of a cast. Inspection of the skin at the edges of a plaster should be part of the daily routine observations carried out by the nurse. The patient is taught to gently ease the skin under the edges of the cast, not to pad under the edge, but to report any discomfort. Pressure may also be caused by foreign objects such as plaster and food crumbs, ends of knitting needles or beads pushed down to relieve an irritation and then left inside the plaster.

(ii) *Friction* from a plaster which is too loose. If there has been a considerable amount of swelling due to the original incident, as this subsides the plaster may become too loose and cause rubbing particularly over bony prominences.

- Delay in repairing cracks which appear in the cast may also cause friction and chafing of the skin, between the rough edges.
- The indications that a plaster sore is forming are:
  - (i) Irritation under the plaster and/or a burning type pain. As the pressure increases the patient loses sensation of the area and the pain ceases. Any complaint of pain from a patient should be investigated and never ignored.
  - (ii) There may be a rise in temperature and an area of local heat may be felt through the cast.
  - (iii) Disturbed sleep, fretfulness and restlessness in children.
  - (iv) A reappearance of swelling of the digits.
  - (v) An offensive smell from under the plaster.
  - (vi) Finally a discharge will appear.
- At the first sign of any complaint from a patient a window is cut over the area. If there is no sore the window is replaced and plastered back into position. If there is a sore this is treated as an open wound and cared for aseptically. When the dressing is complete the window is replaced and taped back into position to prevent swelling.
- Pain experienced by a patient in a cast must never be ignored. It may be caused by the onset of a plaster sore or it may be from the application of too tight a plaster. Swelling at the site of surgery or injury may cause a cast to fit too snugly. If the pain persists, investigations will have to be undertaken. A plaster which is too tight may cause, eventually, ischaemia of muscle compartments which may lead to irreversible damage.

Communicating

Patients must be allowed to express their fears of being encased in a plaster. This is particularly important with those patients in a body cast. They experience fear of not being able to breathe, eat, drink or move. With gentle explanation and reassurance these worries can be alleviated. Teaching the patient the correct way to handle the cast and the procedures for caring for it and the skin around should be part of the routine care given. This may go some way towards the patient accepting the cast.

Breathing

- Breathing may present difficulties for those patients in body casts. Reassurance and repositioning of pillows may ease this problem. Encouragement to deep breathe will help to reduce the risk of chest infections.

Eating and drinking

- Nutrition may cause anxiety to patients in casts. Those in body casts or hip spicas should be advised to avoid large, heavy meals and to take a 'little and often' and easily digestable food. An overhead mirror attached to the bed may aid a bedfast patient to see what he is eating and where it is on the plate. Patients with arm plasters should be provided with mats to hold plates firmly in place and will require their food to be cut up for them. Feeding patients is often degrading for the patient and, therefore, it is necessary to enable the patient to maintain their own independence and dignity.

Eliminating

- The use of bedpans and urinals will be difficult for those patients in body casts. Waterproof tape should be applied to the plaster around the toilet area and the use of nonabsorbent cotton wool placed between the bedpan and the patient may prevent soiling of the cast. Privacy is vital for the patients and may assist in successful use of bedpans and urinals. Patients with leg plasters must have room to sit down on a lavatory with the leg extended and supported, and those with arm casts will need help to adjust their clothing and wash their hands following use.

Mobilizing

- Mobilizing should only be undertaken when leg and body plasters are fully dry and have been trimmed as necessary. Unless otherwise ordered, exercises of the patient's joints above and below the immobilized part will maintain joint function and minimize stiffness in the joints. All unaffected limbs should be put through a full range of motion at least twice daily to maintain muscle strength and prevent complications of immobility. Specific exercise for the muscles of the affected limb should be taught to the nurse and to the patient by the physiotherapist. The nurse is then able to supervise these exercises in the absence of the physiotherapist and encourage the patient to maintain the exercise programme.

Sleeping

- Sleeping in a body or limb cast presents problems for the patient. The sheer weight of the plaster may prevent the patient turning easily in bed. Positioning themself sufficiently comfortably to enable sleep may take time and patience. A patient's leg in a plaster should be securely held on pillows. If it slides off a pillow in the middle of the night this will lead to a poor night's sleep. A patient's arm in plaster may suddenly bump the patient's head and wake them. A wakeful night will lead to problems the following day when the patient will be tired and irritated by lack of sleep.

A daily routine of checking plaster casts must be carried out by the nurse. All plasters should be checked to ensure they are not too loose or too tight, that they are not becoming soft and that no cracks are appearing in them. If they are softening, or there is evidence of cracks, the plaster must be renewed or repaired without delay to prevent a sore forming under the crack.

Personal cleansing and dressing

- The majority of patients are able to maintain their own personal hygiene while in a cast, although it is necessary to help the patient with those areas of their body that they are unable to reach. A plastic bag placed over the patient's arm or hand cast will enable the patient to continue their own hygiene. Brushing and combing the hair presents difficulties which may be overcome by the use of long handled combs. Plaster casts should be left uncovered as this aids evaporation of body moisture and, therefore, clothing should be kept from casts if possible. Dressing can be aided by replacing seams temporarily with velcro fastenings or tapes. Vests under body casts are changed daily. Bed linen is changed daily and is kept wrinkle- and crumb-free. Crumbs from the plaster can cause pressure on exposed areas of the patient's skin, which may result in the formation of sores. Pressure areas other than those associated with the cast are at risk as patients in casts are frequently less mobile in bed than those patients without casts. The nurse must maintain observation twice daily of these potential pressure areas to prevent the formation of sores occurring and encourage the patient to change position in bed frequently, if this is possible. Irritation under the cast is a problem experienced by some patients. At all costs they must be discouraged from sticking anything down the plaster to relieve the 'itch'. It should be explained to patients that if anything is pushed down the plaster it may cause extra pressure, crease up the lining of the cast or damage their skin. If the irritation persists, medical advice should be sought as there may be a skin reaction to a material used in the application of the cast.

INSTRUCTIONS GIVEN TO A PATIENT LEAVING HOSPITAL IN A PLASTER CAST

Patients in newly applied plaster casts should never be allowed to leave the plaster room until the nurse is certain that the neurovascular status of the extremities of the limb are satisfactory and have no signs of interference, that the patient has received both verbal and written instructions (see Table 6.1) on the care of their plaster and that their domestic arrangements are such that they are able to cope with their disability at home.

The verbal instructions are reinforced by giving them to the patient in a written form as in Table 6.1.

Table 6.1 Verbal instructions given to the patient.

1. Keep the plaster dry. Do not allow it to become wet as this will soften the cast and decrease its efficiency. Use a plastic bag or rubber gloves as protection if necessary.

2. Do not apply any external heat to the plaster to aid drying.

3. Keep the affected limb elevated when sitting down. Legs in plaster should be rested on a stool and arms in plaster rested on cushions or pillows. A sling is an effective measure in which to rest an arm, particularly while the cast is still wet, but it must be remembered to remove the sling to enable exercise to take place.

4. Wash the skin around the plaster daily. Make sure the skin under the edge of the cast is not becoming sore by inspecting it for redness.

5. Twice daily check the fingers or the toes of the affected limb. There are four major points to observe:
    (i) Colour. Ask yourself if the skin is the normal colour of each finger or toe.
    (ii) Sensation. Is the feeling normal in each finger or toe? Are there any areas of numbness or feeling of pins and needles?
    (iii) Movement. Can I move each finger or toe? Not just wriggle them but fully bend and stretch each one.
    (iv) Has any swelling recurred or increased of the fingers or toes or the surrounding area?

6. Check the plaster each day to make sure there are no unpleasant smells coming from it.

7. Carry out the exercises taught to you at the hospital at the times requested.

8. If an irritation occurs under the plaster, never stick anything down it to scratch.

9. The telephone number to ring if you have any worries about your plaster, or if you experience any pain, is . . .

REMOVAL OF A PLASTER CAST

The removal of a plaster cast is the job of a skilled person but the orthopaedic nurse should have knowledge of how it is performed in case she is called on to remove a plaster in an emergency.

Under normal circumstances, plasters are only removed once the instruction to do so has been given by the consultant. The tools required to remove a cast include an electric saw, shears, scissors, knives, plaster openers and protective covering for the patient and clothes (see Figure 6.2)

The patient is shown the equipment to be used and the operator must be confident in all the moves he makes. The saw makes a noise and the patient should be introduced to this and shown that the blade oscillates not rotates and will, therefore, not cut the skin. This can be demonstrated by the operator on their own skin.

Lines are drawn on the plaster and the plaster is bivalved, that is, cut in half, along the predetermined lines. If shears are used, the cutters are held at right angles to the plaster and a little of the cast is cut each time. The plaster is removed without haste. It may be necessary to retain the posterior half of the plaster to use as a resting splint and the limb should not be removed from this until inspection by a doctor has taken place. Special attention is paid to areas where there is a bony prominence. Care is taken to cut the plaster behind bony prominences.

Constant reassurance of the patient by the nurse is essential during this operation.

Care of the skin and the limb following removal of a plaster cast

- The patient should be warned prior to removal of the cast that the skin underneath will be covered with areas of dead skin tissue and on no account should this be removed with force.

- The limb should be handled gently and supported at all times. The patient will feel the limb is weak and it may ache in various areas following the removal of the plaster.

- The skin should be soaked in warmed oil and then carefully washed in warm water and soap. Do not scrub the skin area. The soap is rinsed off and the limb patted dry on a soft towel, never rubbed dry. This procedure may need to be repeated several times before all the dead tissue is removed.

- The limb is supported on a pillow or by the use of bandages, elastic stockings or, in some cases, an orthosis. If the knee joint has been immobilized the patient should be warned not to allow the knee to be moved quickly as atrophy of the quadriceps, however slight, will lead to instability of the knee joint.

- Exercise should be encouraged within the

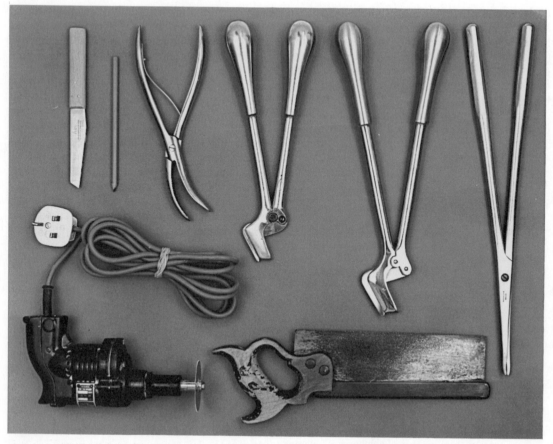

Fig. 6.2 A selection of plaster instruments: 1. spreaders; 2. large shears; 3. small shears; 4. benders; 5. indelible pencil; 6. cobbler's knife; 7. saw with wooden handle; 8. electric saw.

limits of pain and stiffness. Soaking the limb and attempting to move stiff joints in warm water may help.

- Rehabilitation of the affected limb should be undertaken with care and no undue force or pressure applied.

NURSING CARE OF PATIENTS IN SPECIFIC CASTS

Care of the patient in a full leg plaster cast

- The patient should be told the plaster will feel cold during the drying process after the initial feeling of warmth when the plaster is first applied. The reasons for exposing the limb and the frequency and reasons for turning the patient should be explained and reinforced.
- A semi-recumbent position, well supported

by pillows, is the optimum position in which to nurse the patient. Elevation of the affected limb is essential and this must be accomplished with an awareness of the necessary safety factors. The limb may be elevated using a Braun's frame, two pillows or more, or by elevating the foot end of the bed.

- The relevant exercises should be demonstrated to the patient and the time that these are to be carried out explained. The nurse must reinforce these instructions.
- With lower limb casts the activities of daily living are seldom interrupted once the plaster is dry. The use of bedpans may present a problem as the limb encased in plaster may be awkward to manoeuvre into a comfortable position and this may lead to complications of elimination. Encouragement and privacy for the patient will help to alleviate this problem.

- Cleansing of the toes of the affected limb may be the other activity which is hindered by a lower limb cast and the nurse may need to intervene to assist the patient with this task.
- Mobilizing is one activity where active help from the nurse is very necessary. If the exercises have been performed by the patient consistently, then the muscle tone and the joints of the unaffected leg and other limbs will have been maintained. The patient must have a firm, well fitting shoe for the un-affected leg: a lace-up type with a flat heel is advisable.

Care of a patient with a lower leg cast

- Routine care is carried out as for a patient with a full leg cast.
- If a walking heel is to be fitted to the plaster to enable partial weight-bearing to take place, the heel of the opposite shoe should be raised to ensure that there is no discrepancy in leg length and that the patient will then not have an uneven gait.

General activities for patients with full or lower leg casts

The following general activities should be performed by the patient with either a full or lower leg cast:

1. Transferring from bed to wheelchair is the first activity to be undertaken. The bed and the wheelchair at all times should be locked into position and the patient taught how to transfer from bed to wheelchair with the use of crutches, observing the boundaries of safety. The patient should be instructed how to elevate the affected limb when sitting down in order to avoid the extremities from swelling and turning blue in colour. He must be advised to take every action slowly and to avoid rushing any steps.
2. The physiotherapist should instruct the patient and the nurse in both transferring the patient from bed to wheelchair and in crutch walking.
3. Crutches need to be inspected frequently for wear and to ensure they are the correct size for the patient. The rubber tips of the crutches should be intact and not smooth or they will slip on the floor causing the patient to stumble and fall.
4. The surgeon will decide whether the affected limb is able to bear weight or not. The appropriate device will be fitted to the plaster and allowed to dry before any weight bearing on the plaster is allowed.
5. The patient who has been confined to bed for some time must be mobilized with care. Suddenly sitting up or standing for a patient who has been bed-bound may lead to the patient becoming lightheaded or dizzy.

PRECAUTIONS FOR A PATIENT ON CRUTCHES

The following precautions should be taken by the nurse when a patient walks with the aid of crutches:

- Initially there should always be two people to support the patient starting to walk on crutches. Weight is taken on the hands holding the hand grips of the crutches and not under the axillae. As confidence and competence increase, the number of people supervising the walking is lessened to one person until the patient is sufficiently safe to walk alone. However, in a ward setting, it is advisable for the nurse or other member of the clinical team to supervise the patient during any attempt to walk in order to maintain a safe environment at all times.
- Such manoeuvres as sitting, standing and going up and down stairs should all be attempted before the patient is discharged home. Relatives as well as the patient need to be confident before this event takes place. Instruction and careful explanations should be given to both. Questions and worries should be given due attention and help provided when necessary.

It is recommended that further reading in this subject is undertaken and this is included in suggested reading at the end of this chapter.

CARE OF PATIENTS IN HIP SPICA

Patients in hip spicas require special consideration. The hip spica is applied with the patient lying on a special table and, if conscious, the patient may experience a great deal of apprehension requiring careful reassurance and explanation from the nurse.

The majority of hip spicas are applied with the patient still under the effects of anaesthesia. This enables the patient to be totally relaxed and the hip manipulated into the correct position and maintained by the doctor while the plaster is applied.

A single hip spica will extend from the nipple line to below the knee of the affected limb and may or may not include the foot. It is trimmed at the groin of the sound leg to allow for unobstructed flexion of the good hip to a right angle.

One-and-a-half hip spicas extend from the nipple line to either above or below the knee of the affected limb (the foot may or may not be enclosed) and to above the knee of the unaffected limb.

A double hip spica encloses both legs and may have a bar fixed between the legs to maintain a degree of abduction decided by the surgeon. The hip is held in extension and neutral rotation, the knee is held in five to ten degrees of flexion to prevent genu recurvatum occurring.

The spica is trimmed around the buttocks at the level of the coccyx and at the front to allow for toileting and nursing purposes. The edges of the plaster at this area are protected by waterproof tape to prevent soiling occurring during elimination.

The bed the patient is received onto must be prepared with sufficient pillows to support the patient entirely.

This usually means a minimum of five pillows: one under the head and one under the shoulders, one under the small of the back and one placed lengthways under each leg. Each pillow is covered in a waterproof cover and then covered by some form of towelling material.

The rule is to support the patient in a spica in its entirety until it has dried. The pillows may need adjusting once the patient is placed on them.

A double hip spica may take up to 96 hours to dry. During this time the patient needs to be kept warm, comfortable, and informed of what is happening.

Turning the patient every three to four hours throughout this time is essential to ensure even drying of the cast. The patient is turned supine to prone and vice versa. A minimum of three nurses are required to support the patient and the cast. Careful assessment may necessitate the need for more than three nurses and no attempt should be made to turn the patient with less nurses than are thought necessary for the safety of both the patient and the nurses.

The rules for handling wet plaster should be observed (see page 49), the pillows under the patient removed and their pillow cases and towelling renewed if damp.

The patient in a single or one-and-a-half hip spica is always turned towards the unaffected side.

The patient in a double hip spica should be lifted and turned in the air. On no account should the supporting bar between the legs be used to turn the patient as this may crack the plaster.

Prior to turning the patient their toes should be observed for colour, sensation and mobility and, when turned, extreme care must be taken that the extremities are kept free of hindrance from the bed and re-observed to ensure no impairment has occurred to blood vessels or nerve conductivity during the turning process.

Nursing care for a patient in a hip spica

Maintaining a safe environment

- A warm room with free circulating air will help to dry the plaster and then maintain it in good condition. Bedside lockers should be kept within easy reach of the patient and a nurse call bell given to the patient should they need assistance.

Communicating

- It is important to tell the patient every move that is to be made, particularly during the turning operation.

Breathing

- Patients may feel claustrophobic in hip spicas and this may lead to respiratory embarrassment. The hip spica should be positioned so as to prevent this occurring. Careful trimming around the nipple line and positioning of pillows under the chest area will ensure breathing remains within normal limits.

Eating and drinking

Nutrition may present problems for these patients.

- The use of an overhead mirror and small meals which may need to be cut up will help. The use of 'bendy' straws and beakers may help the patient retain independence in drinking. Vague complaints of abdominal pain and discomfort, accompanied by nausea, should never be ignored as these may be signs of intestinal obstruction occurring and should be reported to the doctor.
- An increased fluid intake will help to reduce the possible complication of renal calculi caused by the immobilization of limbs. This may cause reabsorption of calcium from the bones resulting in deposits in the kidneys. An accurate fluid balance chart is maintained.

Eliminating

- Eliminating by the use of both a bedpan and urinal may be embarrassing and uncomfortable unless they are both carefully positioned and the patient left in privacy with a nurse call bell close at hand. Once the nurse has left the patient in a hip spica on a bedpan he is virtually a prisoner as the patient is unable to move by himself. There is also the danger that the patient may roll off the bedpan, and therefore, while ensuring privacy for the patient at all times, the nurse should be close at hand in case of accidents occurring.

Personal cleansing and dressing

- Personal cleansing for these patients is practically an impossible task for them to undertake, although independence must be encouraged.
- The patient's hands and arms are free and they are able to wash their own face, hands and arms and usually their chest areas. This takes careful planning on the part of the nurse for a bowl of water inaccurately placed may lead to a scald or a wet spica. Therefore, while encouraging independence, it is unwise to leave these patients alone with a bowl of water, particularly behind drawn curtains.
- All exposed skin areas must be washed and dried carefully and skin at the edges of the plaster inspected as described on page 53. Small amounts of talcum powder are used.

Controlling body temperature

- Once the spica is dry, handling the patient becomes less difficult. They are able to turn themselves with the aid of one nurse and controlling their body temperature becomes much easier. Patients in damp plasters are often cold. All exposed areas of skin should be covered and the atmosphere kept as warm as possible. This will not only help the patient but will aid the drying of the plaster. Normal dressing for the upper part of the body is possible. Trouser seams can be split and tapes or velcro applied to secure them. Modesty must be observed and the patient's genital area covered by some form of pants with ties.

Mobilizing

- When the spica is dry, and the surgeon gives permission, the patient may be gradually mobilized to walk with crutches.
- Prior to this procedure, all unaffected limbs should be put through a full range of motion at least twice a day and this exercise programme is encouraged and maintained by the nurse.

Sleeping

- Sleeping in a hip spica is another uncomfortable experience and sleep patterns are often disturbed. Ensuring the patient is pain free, as comfortable as possible, both physically and mentally, will help to improve the situation.

CARE OF THE PATIENT IN AN UPPER LIMB PLASTER

The majority of patients with a plaster cast on the arm will be treated as outpatients, although there will always be some admitted to hospital for observation with other injuries or for social reasons. The first three items below may, in some circumstances, equally apply to a patient in a lower limb cast.

There are several major areas for the concern of the nurse dealing with these patients:

1. All rings and jewellery must be removed from the affected limb prior to application of the plaster and until it is removed.

If the fingers swell, circulation may be impaired by a tight encircling band.

2. All nailpolish should be removed to facilitate accurate observations of the colour and capillary return of the fingers.

3. Careful observations for compartment syndrome occurring, particularly if the area of injury or surgery is in close proximity to the elbow joint. Ischaemia of the superficial and deep flexor muscles of the forearm may occur as the result of partial or full occlusion of the brachial artery by swelling under a tight plaster, the application of too tight a plaster cast, or when the artery is compressed or severed such as may occur in a supracondylar fracture of the humerus. If left untreated, secondary changes occur in the peripheral nerves. Irreversible damage to the muscles and nerves will begin after six hours and in 24 hours the limb will be useless due to paralysis and contractures. The classical example of this is Volkmann's ischaemic contracture of the hand. The condition my occur less severely in the lower limb when the popliteal artery is affected.

To avoid this complication occurring, vigilant observations by the nurse must be taken every 15 minutes at first. The observations are known as the five Ps.

(a) *Pain*. This is felt in the forearm and is increased when passive movement of the fingers is performed.

(b) *Pulselessness*. The radial pulse must be observed for rate and volume and compared with the radial pulse of the unaffected limb.

(c) *Pallor*. The fingers become white and cold.

(d) *Paralysis*. An inability to flex and extend the fingers.

(e) *Parasthesia*. A feeling of numbness and/or tingling in the fingers.

All symptoms are important, but all may not be present. The initial symptom is pain, the order of the others is variable but action must be taken quickly in order to relieve this distressing condition.

The action taken is to firstly elevate the limb; secondly to inform the doctor. If the symptoms persist after one hour, the plaster is removed and surgical exploration of the artery may be undertaken by the surgeon.

4. Breakdown of skin in skin creases. If the arm is to be totally immobilized in an above elbow plaster, the patient must be instructed in the care of the skin in the axilla. Likewise, patients in a below elbow plaster should be taught similarly about the elbow creases. Both types of patient should be taught to care for the skin between the fingers of the affected hand. These areas should be kept clean and dry at all times. A small pad of 'gamgee' or gauze inserted in the crease may aid this, but the pad must be changed regularly.

5. Swelling of the fingers may be prevented in the initial drying phase by elevation of the arm or by the use of a sling. The sling may be either a broad arm sling, a high arm sling or collar and cuff. All patients should be taught exercises of the unaffected joints and told when they should discard their sling. They and their family should be instructed how to reapply the sling following its removal for the purposes of caring for the skin.

6. Before being discharged the nurse must ensure the patient has been given both verbal and written instructions (see Table 6.1) on the drying and care of the plaster and that they have been understood.

SUGGESTED FURTHER READING

Bell R. (1987) *Plaster Cast Techniques*, 1st edn. London: Hodder and Stoughton.

Farrel J. (1983) *Illustrated Guide to Orthopaedic Nursing*. New York: Harper & Row.

7

NURSING CARE OF PATIENTS UNDERGOING COMMON TESTS USED TO AID MEDICAL DIAGNOSIS

The nurse is frequently required to assist the doctor while he is carrying out a variety of tests. Her main concern is with the welfare of her patient both before, during and after these tests. As each test is described the nursing needs will be identified. Many investigations take place in the outpatient department and the nurse has to quickly form a relationship with the patient to gain his trust.

SPECIAL NURSING NEEDS FOR OUTPATIENTS

Patients in the outpatient department have special nursing needs, which include the following:

Maintaining a safe environment

- Safety of their personal belongings. These should be kept with the patient at all times.
- Safety of the patient. This is ensured by a chaperon being present during all investigations and the patient being made aware of all of the steps of the tests which are being carried out.

Communicating

- Communicating all relevant data to the patient and answering any questions posed by the patient.
- Providing facilities in which the patient can maintain his own dignity.
- Reinforcing and repeating instructions given to the patient.
- Allow the patient time to talk to the nurse or his relatives.
- Providing reassurance for the patient and his relatives by a professional approach to the

patient and providing appropriate knowledge about the tests.

Controlling body temperature

- Controlling the temperature of the department to make sure it is comfortable for the patient to remove his clothing.

Expressing sexuality

- Maintaining the patient's modesty and preventing embarrassment will help provide reassurance.

GENERAL EXAMINATION OF THE PATIENT

This is not only a medical investigation, but will enable the nurse to make a physical examination of the patient as an aid to the nursing assessment and the planning of the patient's care.

The patient is asked to undress except for his/her underpants and is generally laid on a bed or couch and covered by a blanket for examination. The patient is looked at as a whole at first by carrying out a general physical examination of the general systems of the body. This will aid the nurse to assess her patient's general physical state and provide a basis for planning care. If an individual part of the body, such as a limb, is identified as being the problem when it is examined, the sound limb should be used for comparison.

Examination takes place by:
1. Observation.
2. Touch.
3. Measurement.
4. Stability.
5. Peripheral neurovascular status.
6. Psychological outlook.

Observation

- The general alignment and position of limbs and the body.
- Any unusual posture assumed by the patient.
- Any deformity or shortening of bones.
- Any visible evidence of soft tissue swelling or abnormal contours or muscle wastage.
- Any redness, cyanosis, pigmentation or discolouration of the skin.
- The presence of any scars and how they were caused.

Touch

- The temperature of the skin, whether it is normal and equal on all sides.
- Any abnormal thickening of bone or abnormal bony prominences.
- Any swelling to see if it will fluctuate or if it is tense.
- Any areas of tenderness are felt to see if they relate to a particular area.

Measurement

- Measurement of a limb is often necessary and the orthopaedic nurse should always have a tape measure in her pocket to facilitate this task.

- The length of a limb. This is particularly important in the lower limbs for leg length discrepancy.

- There are two particular measurements the orthopaedic nurse should be able to perform:

  1. *'Apparent' or false leg length discrepancy*
     The usual cause of this is a fixed adduction deformity at one hip, giving an appearance of shortening on the same side, or a fixed abduction deformity of the hip giving an appearance of lengthening. The patient is laid supine with their legs parallel and in line with the trunk. The tape measure is placed on a fixed point in the mid-line of the body, e.g., the xiphoid process or the umbilicus. Measurements are then taken by placing the other end of the tape measure on each medial malleolus in turn.
  2. *True length of the legs*
     The patient is laid supine and the limbs

placed in comparable positions to the pelvis. If one limb is adducted, the other limb must be adducted. If one limb is abducted the other must be abducted to the same degree. One end of the tape measure is then placed on the anterior superior iliac spine, the other end is placed on the medial malleolus of the leg on the same side. The procedure is repeated for the other leg.

- The circumference of the limb at its greatest width. Compare this measurement with the measurement of the other limb taken at the same place. This will give an indication of muscle wastage, soft tissue swelling and thickening of the bone. It may be necessary for the nurse to carry out this test frequently to monitor the progress of a condition. For example, whether a patient with haemophilia is continuing to bleed into the soft tissue of a limb.
- The circumference of the patient's calf at its greatest width compared with a measurement of the other calf will be of value in patients with suspected venous or saddle thrombosis.
- The range of movement of a joint. This will be of particular value to a nurse when planning the patient's care as she is able to assess how much a patient is able to help themselves. For example, is the joint painful to move, are the passive range of movements greater than the active range, what is the active range of movement and is there any crepitation on moving the joint?

Stability

- If a joint is unstable the nurse needs to be particularly careful when positioning the limb so that she does not cause pain or encourage fixed deformities of a joint in an abnormal position.

Peripheral neurovascular status

- Examination of the colour and temperature of the skin and nails should be carried out. Arterial pulses are assessed for rate, rhythm and volume and compared with the sound limb. This provides a baseline from which the nurse is able to work particularly following surgery. Sensation and movement of the extremities is noted as this will also provide a baseline for postoperative nursing care.

Psychological outlook

- The patient's psychological approach to his condition is important and this will enable the nurse to identify many of his nursing needs during any admission to hospital. A positive approach from the nurse will encourage a positive attitude from the patients and their relatives.

RADIOGRAPHIC EXAMINATION

X-ray examination of musculo-skeletal system is a vital aid to medical diagnosis. It has become complex and it is important for nurses to have an understanding of the procedures to enable the nurse to reinforce explanations given by the medical team.

Standard x-rays

These provide information about the degree of the disease or injury, aid confirmation of the diagnosis, the progress of the disease or its response to treatment. In general, there is no special preparation necessary except to ensure that the patient is aware of the impending procedure.

Computerized axial tomography (CT scan/CAT scan)

This is a noninvasive procedure which allows images of tissues taken in the form of slices (tomograms) through a horizontal plane to be examined. It is particularly useful for outlining the contents of the skull and the spinal column.

Contrast medium x-rays

This is where a radio-opaque dye is injected into the patient to allow examination of soft tissue structures. Careful explanations to the patient of the positions they may be placed in upon the x-ray table are essential and the nurse will often be called upon by the patient to interpret the doctor's instructions. An informal consent is generally obtained by the doctor from the patient. The patient must be asked if there are any known allergies he may have experienced

during similar procedures carried out previously.

All of the following procedures are invasive procedures and, as such, are carried out under aseptic conditions. Most x-ray departments will issue written instructions for the care of the patient following these procedures. Some of the major nursing points are included following the individual procedure. These examinations include:

1. Arthrography.
2. Myelography.
3. Arthroscopy.
4. Tests for instability of joints.
5. Tests relating to the neurological system.

Arthrography

This is used to outline the soft tissues within a joint.

This investigation may be done prior to proceeding to surgery such as a meniscectomy.

Nursing care following arthrography.
- The patient's limb is placed in a comfortable position, well supported.
- Pain levels are monitored and appropriate measures taken to relieve this. Pain may occasionally be caused by the onset of a haemarthrosis.
- Observation of the patient's temperature and pulse rate are continued four-hourly for at least 24 hours to monitor for the onset of infection within the joint.

Myelography

This is an examination of the theca and spinal cord and its nerve roots. The dye is introduced into the subarachnoid space by a lumbar puncture.

Nursing care of patients following myelography.
- The patient is nursed either with the head of the bed elevated or completely flat on a firm based bed according to which contrast media has been used. This knowledge must be obtained from the radiologist along with any special instructions regarding the patient.
- The patient is encouraged to remain quiet during the following 24 hours as excessive laughter or coughing will increase pressure in the spinal canal. This in turn may lead to a

shift of the dye causing headache and neuro-logical problems.

- Observation of the neurological status of the patient is maintained by recording the blood pressure and pulse rate hourly for the next six hours and ensuring the patient is orientated in person, time and space. There is a danger of reactions to some of the dyes used. These may take the form of meningism, photophobia, severe headache and vomiting. The nurse must be aware of these and observe for their onset.
- A fluid balance chart is maintained. The patient is encouraged to drink at least 200 mls of fluid hourly to aid removal of the dye from the tissues. This will also aid the formation of cerebro-spinal fluid.

Bone scan

An intravenous injection of a radio-isotope substance is given to the patient. This substance is then taken up into bone. The substance emits a form of radiation. The rays which are emitted are detected by a special camera. The amount of uptake reflects the bone turnover. This can then be interpreted to reflect the amount of bony destruction or repair which is taking place.

Arthroscopy

This investigation allows direct visual examination of the interior structures of a joint through a small instrument called an arthroscope. The most common joint examined in this way is the knee joint.

It is an aseptic procedure normally carried out in the operating theatre under local or general anaesthesia and may be performed prior to a decision to proceed to surgery.

TESTS FOR INSTABILITY OF JOINTS

Trendelenberg test

This is a test of stability of the hip joint. The patient is instructed to stand upon the sound limb and to raise the other leg from the ground. The patient then repeats the procedure by standing on the affected limb.

Normally, when one leg is raised from the ground, the pelvis tilts upwards on that side. The test is negative if this occurs. However, if the pelvis fails to rise on the side of the lifted leg, then the test is positive, indicating an affection of the limb being stood on. This may indicate weak abductor muscles of the hip or loss of the fulcrum of the hip joint (see Figure 7.1).

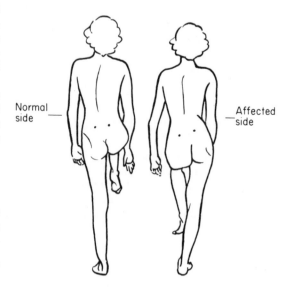

Normal side —   — Affected side

Fig. 7.1 Trendelenburg's sign. Positive for right hip, negative for left hip.

McMurray's test

This test is performed to elicit tears of the menisci.

The knee is flexed and then externally and internally rotated. At a certain point a click may be felt by the examiner as the cartilage slips over the centre of the joint. The patient may experience pain at this time.

The 'draw' sign or Lachman's test for ruptured anterior and posterior cruciate ligaments

This procedure is performed for ruptured anterior and posterior ligaments in order to provide evidence of cruciate ligament instability.

The patient lies down. The knee is flexed to 90 degrees and the foot placed flat on the couch and stabilized to prevent it from sliding. The lower leg is then gently pushed backward and forward to determine the amount of posterior and anterior movement.

TESTS RELATING TO THE NEUROLOGICAL SYSTEM

Lumbar puncture

A lumbar puncture is performed for the following reasons:

1. To obtain a sample of cerebrospinal fluid for diagnostic purposes.
2. To administer drugs and, in particular, antibiotics.
3. To introduce contrast media for x-ray purposes.
4. To estimate and possibly reduce cerebrospinal pressure.

Two nurses should be present whenever possible. One to assist the doctor and one to observe and reassure the patient.

The procedure is a frightening one for the patient and the nurse must reassure the patient by standing close to them and holding their hand, informing them of what is happening. The patient is laid on their side in the left lateral position, 'curled up' as far as possible.

The procedure is performed under aseptic conditions. A needle is introduced between the third and fourth lumbar vertebrae under local anaesthesia. This is known as an intrathecal injection.

Following a lumbar puncture the following nursing care is advisable.

- The patient lies flat on a firm-based bed. Headaches may develop as a result of low pressure of the cerebro-spinal fluid.
- Encourage the patient to take 200 millilitres of fluid hourly to help in the formation of cerebrospinal fluid.
- Neurological signs are monitored hourly for up to six hours.

Queckenstedt's test

During a lumbar puncture, Queckenstedt's test may be carried out to ascertain whether there is a free flow of cerebrospinal fluid in the canal.

The nurse is required, at a time given by the doctor, to compress the patient's jugular veins. If there is no blockage there is a sharp rise in the pressure of cerebrospinal fluid, as seen in the manometer attached to the spinal needle. This is followed by a rapid fall in the pressure when compression is released.

Lasègue test

This test is used for determining the degree of severity of irritation of the sciatic nerve in cases of low back pain.

The patient lies flat on the couch and the legs are raised by the examiner one at a time with the knee extended to the degree at which the patient feels pain.

Babinski's sign

This sign is present in disease or injury of the upper motor neurones. Babies who have not walked react in the same way, but obtain normal results when walking starts.

The patient is laid flat on the couch. The sole of the foot is stroked firmly from the heel towards the toes. The great toe bends upwards into dorsiflexion instead of downwards into plantar flexion.

SUGGESTED FURTHER READING

Thompson D. & Bowman G. (1985) *Medical Investigations*. London: Baillière Tindall.

8

CARE OF THE ADULT PATIENT WITH AN ORTHOPAEDIC PROBLEM

Orthopaedic problems in the adult have many implications for the patient and their family, and for the nurse caring for them. The family have a particularly important role where long-term disability is a feature, as they will become the principal care agents when the patient is discharged home. Whether long-term or short-term disabilities are concerned, it is important that the patient's family are involved from the beginning in the care and encouragement of the patient. They are included as part of the orthopaedic team with the patient from the start of treatment.

The patient's inability to move his joints through a normal range will have affected his lifestyle. He may well have experienced difficulties in the normal activities of daily life. Tasks such as dressing and being able to get in and out of the bath may have led to another member of the family having to perform these tasks for the patient. This in turn often leads to a loss of dignity and role within the family. A husband and father who finds himself having to rely on his wife to help dress him, help him into the bath or even drive him to work, may well feel guilty at adding to his wife's work. The wife and mother who finds herself unable to manage the housework or shopping will have to ask someone else to help with these. An active young man or girl who becomes unable to play sport or attend discos may become an introverted and unhappy person.

Sleep patterns are frequently disrupted by pain and this leads to tiredness during the day and often a lack of concentration.

Sexual relations with a partner are difficult because of pain from the affected joint. This may add stress to a marriage.

A patient's general health is often not affected by orthopaedic problems and this can lead to frustration at not being able to carry out tasks they feel capable of.

Disability, although better accepted by the general public in recent years, still presents a major problem to the patient. Simple tasks such as getting on and off a bus, going into and out of public places and walking round supermarkets become major ones when the patient has to manage a walking aid, cope with high steps or no lifts.

The patient with a long-term disability may have to face the possibility of alterations to their lifestyle and family life. Acceptance for a man that he may no longer be the major 'bread winner' of the family may be difficult.

Modifications to the home or to cars may help the patient to retain some independence and the avenues to enable these to take place must be explored.

NURSING CARE OF PATIENTS WITH HIP DISORDERS

The most common hip disorder seen in adult patients is osteoarthrosis (osteoarthritis).

Osteoarthrosis is a noninflammatory degenerative condition affecting the articular surfaces of synovial joints (see Figure 8.1).

The hip joint is particularly vulnerable as it is one of the major weightbearing joints of the body and the condition progresses to become one of the most disabling forms of arthritis. It may be of a primary or secondary nature (see Table 8.1).

The disease causes many problems for the patient including pain, which is a constant nagging pain relieved by rest but felt again when movement restarts.

Sleep patterns are interrupted as, during sleep, muscles relax and cause involuntary movement which, in turn, causes pain. Lack of sleep leads to irritability and tiredness during the day which leaves the patient and their family

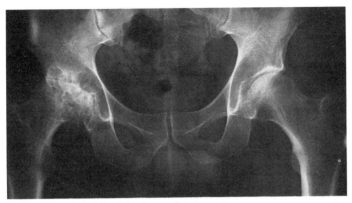

Fig. 8.1   Osteoarthritis of the hip joint showing joint destruction.

Table 8.1   The two categories of osteoarthritis

Primary/idiopathic osteoarthritis
- The articular cartilage fails and no definite cause is found.
- Most commonly found in women.
- Incidence increases with age therefore more common in the elderly.

Secondary osteoarthritis
- This is usually confined to one joint which is generally the site of previous disease or injury.

  Causes:
- Disease
    - septic/tuberculous arthritis
    - haemophiliac arthritis
    - rheumatoid arthritis
    - gout/pseudogout
    - Paget's disease
    - acromegaly.
- Injury
    - trauma causing articular surface fracture, e.g., from sports injury.
- Avascular necrosis due to
    - fractures
    - steroids
    - alcohol
    - sickle cell anaemia
    - decompression sickness.
- Congenital and childhood disorders
    - Perthes' disease
    - congenital dislocation of hip
    - slipped upper femoral epiphysis
    - scoliosis
    - inequality of leg length.

From Nursing Magazine (December, 1985, Vol. 2, No. 44) published by Baillière Tindall.

unable to enjoy the normal family and social pleasures.

Joint replacement or arthroplasty is becoming one of the most frequent procedures carried out in orthopaedic hospitals. It brings for the nurse, a very rewarding and satisfying nursing situa-tion. For the patient it brings dramatic relief of symptoms and, although it may not increase the amount of mobility, it does improve the quality of the patient's life.

Great curiosity is shown by the general public and the mass media about joint replacement. Many myths and much speculation about the operation abounds. The nurse needs to be able to answer her patient's questions truthfully to dispel any fears brought about by these myths and to prepare the patient and their family carefully for the postoperative regimes.

There are other measures which may be taken to relieve this condition: nonoperative and operative measures.

Nonoperative measures

- Physiotherapy in the form of heat and exercises to strengthen weakened muscles. These exercises may be in the form of:
    (i)   passive exercises to preserve the range of movement of the joint.
    (ii) active exercise to improve the muscle tone and strength. The use of hydro-therapy to aid active exercise may help. The buoyancy and warmth of the water will provide a relaxing medium in which exercise will be encouraged.

- Weight reduction to reduce the load bearing on the joint. This may be difficult to achieve if the patient has no desire to lose weight. Incentive to reduce pain and small targets set may help to achieve a satisfactory weight loss.
- The use of walking aids, such as a walking stick used in the opposite hand to the

affected hip may relieve mechanical stress. Ladies in particular need to be convinced of the value in using a walking stick as they often find this cosmetically unacceptable.

- The use of analgesic and anti-inflammatory drugs will help to control pain and reduce local inflammation caused by the destructive changes taking place in the joint.

Operative measures

Arthrodesis

This is fixation or fusion of the joint in a functional position. It is not an operation which is often attempted these days, but may be of value in young patients suffering secondary osteoarthrosis.

All movements of the joint are eliminated and the patient is therefore left with a stiff but pain-free joint. It is important that the patient has a good range of movement in the knee of the affected side, the opposite hip and the vertebral column, as these will now have to provide the means to enable the patient to move freely.

Osteotomy

Osteotomy is the division of the femur generally between the trochanters. The shaft is then displaced medially and internally fixed in its new position. By altering the line of weightbearing, pain is thereby decreased.

Patients are often nursed in Hamilton-Russell traction for up to three weeks postoperatively. Early mobilization on crutches, partial weight bearing is commenced at this stage.

Arthroplasty

Arthroplasty is the refashioning of a diseased joint, creating a new joint. The aim of surgery is to provide a stable joint with a good range of pain-free movements. It may be achieved in one of several ways such as pseudoarthrosis, interposition arthroplasty and replacement arthroplasty.

Pseudoarthrosis

This operation is often referred to as Girdlestone's operation as it was first performed by Mr G.R. Girdlestone. The surgery involves excision of the head and the neck of the femur. The resulting gap heals with fibrous tissue forming a fibrous joint which is pain free. There is a residual shortening which varies between 1.5–4 centimetres (see Figure 8.2).

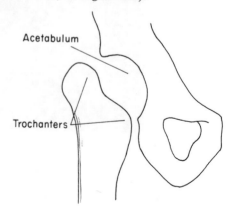

Fig. 8.2 Girdlestone's arthroplasty. Fibrous tissue forms in the gap between the acetabulum and the trochanters, thus allowing movement.

Interposition arthroplasty

In this type of operation a barrier of artificial material, usually Vitallium, is placed between the diseased surfaces of the joint.

Cap arthroplasty is the insertion of a cap over the head of the femur. The cap is not fixed into place but allows fibrocartilage to form under it while allowing pain-free articulation to take place.

This operation is often used in the treatment of young adults suffering from degenerative disease of the hip (see Figure 8.3).

Replacement arthroplasty

This is the complete replacement of the joint by artificial material.

Types of hip replacement prostheses

There are many types of hip replacement available to the surgeons. The most commonly used one is a Charnley prosthesis which consists of an acetabular cup made of high density polyethylene and a femoral component made of Vitallium or other inert metal. Each component is secured in place by a cement-like material, methyl methacrylate. Recent years have seen the development of prostheses which do not require cementing into place. One such prosthesis is the Lord's. This requires a carefully prepared femur

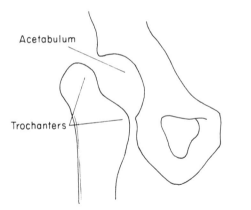

Fig. 8.3   Smith-Petersen cup arthroplasty in a young person.

and acetabulum. The prosthesis is then hammered into position, fitting very tightly into the prepared bone.

There are other designs of total hip replacement prostheses, each surgeon having their own preference as to which one to use (see Figure 8.4 and 8.5).

The nursing care both pre-operatively and postoperatively is similar whichever prosthesis is chosen.

Pre-operative nursing care: psychological preparation

Maintaining a safe environment

- A thorough explanation of what is meant by a 'total hip' replacement is made by the surgeon and this frequently needs reinforcing and re-explaining by the nurse. Many patients are keen to know the details of the prosthesis to be used and, if appropriate, photographs or an actual prosthesis may be shown to the patient and the family.

Communicating

- Explanations over the equipment which will be used following surgery should be given to the patient. Intravenous sets, abduction pillows, foam troughs and vacuum drains as used by the surgeon, may be shown to the patient if they wish to see them.
- The type of wound dressing which may be employed should be shown to the patient. The patient should be told of the risk of infection being introduced into the wound if the dressing is disturbed by any means other than an aseptic technique.
- It is often difficult for the patient to imagine that the pain experienced in the postoperative phase is frequently less than that which they are having pre-operatively. This may be overcome by introducing them to a patient of similar age who has recently recovered from similar surgery.
- The patient will be told about the precautions that will be taken postoperatively to avoid dislocation of the new hip joint by avoiding excessive flexion and adduction of the legs.

Physical preparation

Maintaining a safe environment

- Particular attention is paid to the skin of the

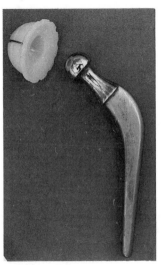
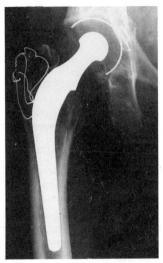

Fig. 8.4   Charnley total hip replacement: Charnley prosthesis (left); Charnley prosthesis in situ (right).

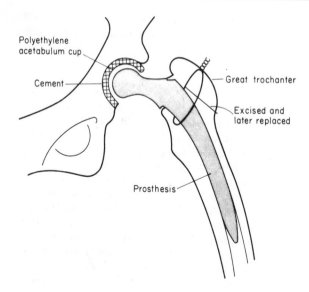

Polyethylene acetabulum cup

Cement

Great trochanter

Excised and later replaced

Prosthesis

Fig. 8.5 Charnley tool hip replacement. The great trochanter is removed at operation then replaced and held in position by wires when the prosthesis is in situ.

affected limb. It should be free from abrasions and clean. Skin preparation depends on the individual surgeon's preference. Some require a full pubic and limb shave, some prefer no shaving at all. Nursing research (1) (2) into shaving patients or the use of a depilatory cream have been inconclusive. Cost factors are an important factor. The medical team preferred the use of a cream.

- Oral antibiotics may be commenced the day before surgery as infection in joint replacement surgery is a serious postoperative complication.

- Careful assessment by the nurse of how the patient is to be lifted postoperatively is important. For the first 24 hours the patient may require total body lifting. The use of a hoist to achieve this may be used and the patient should practice this procedure with the nurse at this stage so they are confident in the postoperative phase.

- The physiotherapist, with the nurse, assesses the patient's present range of movement and gait. Exercises to be carried out in the postoperative phase are taught to the patient. These include deep breathing exercises, dorsi and plantar flexion exercises for the ankles and exercises to meet the patient's individual needs and to prevent complications such as deep venous thrombosis and chest infections.

- A home assessment may be carried out by the occupational therapist to see if the patient's home conditions are suitable for a planned early discharge. Such things as raised toilet seats, bath seats, access to the kitchen and to the bedroom are necessarily looked into. Patients following total hip replacement are discharged relatively quickly, often by the end of two weeks, and it is necessary that both the patient and the family are prepared for this.

- A mid-stream specimen of urine is sent to the laboratory for microscopy to ascertain urinary tract infection.

- If the prescribed pre-operative drug is to be given intramuscularly it is given into the opposite side to the one to be operated on. This will help to avoid the risk of introducing infection.

- Routine pre-operative preparation is carried out as for patients undergoing a general anaesthetic. Total hip replacement surgery may be performed under a spinal anaesthetic. If this is to be used the anaesthetist should issue special instructions to the nurse.

Postoperative nursing care

Maintaining a safe environment

- Patients following a total hip replacement often return from theatre pale, cold, with a rapid pulse rate and low blood pressure due to the anaesthetic drugs which have been administered. Observations of temperature, pulse, respirations and blood pressure are monitored every 15–30 minutes until they are stable. The recordings are then reduced to every hour, then to once every four hours for the first 24 hours. It may be necessary to use a 'space' blanket such as those used in the care of patients with hypothermia, to raise the patient's temperature to acceptable levels.

- The patient is nursed supine on a firm-based bed with one pillow under their head until they are able to maintain the patency of their own airway. They are then gradually raised to a semi-recumbent position, well supported by pillows. If the surgeon has used a posterior approach to replace the hip joint, the patient should never sit at more than a 45 degree angle until the wound has completely healed.
- Observation of vacuum drains to ensure that they are patent and freely draining is carried out hourly. The amount of drainage is recorded on a fluid balance chart. Drains are usually removed after 48 hours, or when drainage is complete.
- The wound dressing is observed for any soakage from the wound. A pressure dressing may be applied over the wound dressing and, if necessary, this may be replaced. The immediate dressing over the wound is left undisturbed, unless contraindicated by signs of infection, until the wound has healed. The sutures are removed at approximately 12–14 days.
- The patient's legs are held in abduction. This may be achieved by the use of a Charnley wedge abduction pillow, by foam troughs (see Figure 8.6), or other suitable devices (see Figure 8.7).
- Opiates may be ordered to relieve pain, but patients generally find that their pain levels are less than pre-operatively. It should be remembered that these patients frequently have other joints affected by arthritis and these may need care to help relieve pain. The effect of any analgesics given should be monitored by the nurse and the patient to assess their effectiveness.

Breathing

- As soon as the patient is able, deep breathing exercises should be performed for five minutes each hour to help improve the circulation. Similarly, ankle exercises to prevent stiff joints should be performed at the same time.

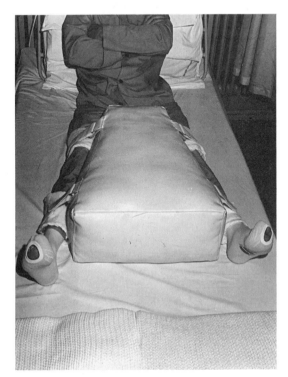

Fig. 8.6 Charnley wedge abduction pillow.

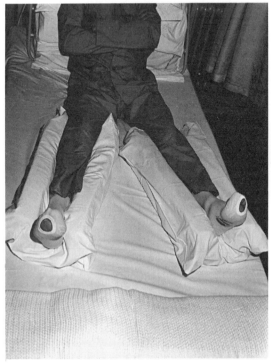

Fig. 8.7 Foam troughs.

Eating and drinking

- Any intravenous therapy requires monitoring and recording on a fluid balance chart. Providing the patient is not nauseous, sips of water may be given as soon as they are conscious. Once tolerated the patient can resume a normal diet and fluid intake. The intravenous infusion is discontinued on the doctor's instruction. This is usually when the patient is fully conscious and well hydrated.

Eliminating

- Elimination using a bed pan may be both painful and uncomfortable at first due to the position necessary to sit on the bed pan. A slipper bed pan may be used for the first 48 hours to aid the patient in successful voiding. After this, with care, a normal bed pan may be used with success. As early ambulation is encouraged in these patients, the use of bed pans should be for a limited period only. Constipation may be a problem for the patient during the postoperative period. Encouragement from the nurse to the patient to eat a well balanced diet, sometimes with added fibre, and to drink extra fluids may remove the need to use aperients.

Personal cleansing and dressing

- The patient will require an assisted bed bath during the first few days postoperatively. They are encouraged to retain as much independence as possible.
- Anti-embolic stockings are removed twice a day and the skin underneath them is checked for reddened areas which may indicate irritation. The skin is carefully washed and dried and the stocking replaced.
- Pressure areas are checked according to the nurse's initial assessment of the patient. Bed aids such as a sheepskin placed under the buttocks or under a heel may help. If a Charnley pillow is used to aid abduction, the skin of the legs resting against the pillow must be checked every four hours for signs of abnormal pressure.
- If a splint or other method is employed to maintain the affected limb in abduction, the nurse should check that the slings supporting the limb on the splint do not become soiled or wrinkled. These are easily replaced

if they do. Routine care of the pulleys and cords should be carried out.

Mobilizing

- Mobilization may begin with the patient standing at the side of the bed. The nurse should prepare the patient for this by explaining exactly what will happen and by ensuring she is present when the physiotherapist stands the patient up for the first time. The patient may, understandably, be apprehensive and may feel dizzy and weak.
- The patient is taught to always get out of bed from their affected side and get into bed from their unaffected side. Flexion of the affected hip in the first few days is kept to a minimum.
- Gradually the patient is introduced to walking between parallel bars and then onto walking with a stick, finally achieving walking, if at all possible, with no aids at all.

Expressing sexuality

- It is important during all stages of the patient's care to maintain their independence and to retain their sexuality. Hairdressers are frequently employed in orthopaedic hospitals to help patients with their hair, but if they are not available then the nurse should encourage patients to care for their hair and the female patients to apply their cosmetics.
- The patients and their family should be instructed in the 'dos' and 'don'ts' following a total hip replacement. Written instructions such as those shown in Table 8.2 will act as a reminder and should be given to the patient before discharge.

COMMON POSTOPERATIVE COMPLICATIONS

The following postoperative complications may occur following a total hip replacement.

Infection

The present incidence of infection is one in one hundred. New surgical techniques, effective pre-operative and postoperative preparation and care and the use of prophylactic antibiotics has helped to keep the incidence at this rate.

Table 8.2 Dos and don'ts for patients at home following a total hip replacement.

1. Dressing—don't attempt to put on your own shoes and stockings.
   —put on your pants/trousers by holding them in the opposite hand to your affected side.

2. Standing—don't stand with your toes turned inwards.
   —don't bend over to pick things up from the floor.
   —avoid lifting things up.

3. Sitting —never put your hip into a right angle when sitting. This may cause dislocation of your new hip.
   —always sit in a chair with arms and one which is not a low chair. You may use a cushion to increase the height of your favourite armchair.
   —you may need a raised toilet seat. The occupational therapist will advise you about this.
   —when you sit down put your affected leg slightly forward. When you get up, slide to the edge of the chair, put your affected leg in front of the other one and use the arms of the chair to help you rise.

4. Bathing —a bath seat may be supplied to help you in and out of the bath.

5. Sleeping—try to sleep on your back. If you are unable to do this then lie on your unaffected side with a pillow between your legs.
   —get into bed from your unaffected side.
   —get out of bed from your affected side.
   —sexual intercourse may be continued, but use a position where you lie underneath your partner on your back.

6. Driving —when you get into a car put your bottom in first and then swing your legs in. You will probably not be able to drive yourself for six weeks.

7. Never turn your hip inwards or outwards when standing, walking, sitting or lying in bed.

8. Never cross your legs when standing, lying, or sitting in a chair.

If you are at all concerned over your new hip, seek advice from your general practitioner.

Revision of an infected total hip replacement may be successful. If not possible, the infected prosthesis is removed and a Girdlestone's pseudarthrosis is carried out.

Dislocation of the prosthesis

This most commonly occurs in the immediate postoperative phase, but can occur at any time following surgery. The signs and symptoms of a dislocation are:

1. Severe, sudden pain in the affected hip.

2. The affected limb is shorter than the unaffected limb.

3. The affected limb usually lies in external rotation, occasionally internal rotation may be seen.

Preventative measures are taken pre-operatively to prepare the patient not to use extreme flexion and adduction of the new joint. If a posterior approach is used then medial rotation should be added to the above caution. These measures are reinforced by the nurse postoperatively and constant, gentle reminders given to the patient.

Fractures

Fracture of the femoral shaft, particularly in patients with rheumatoid arthritis as well as osteoarthrosis, may occur during surgery. If noticed at the time, wires may be used to hold the fracture and weight bearing is delayed.

A fracture of the shaft may occur sometime after surgery, just below the stem of the femoral component. Surgery is undertaken either to introduce a femoral prosthesis with a long stem or a Girdlestone's operation is performed.

NURSING CARE OF PATIENTS WITH KNEE DISORDERS

The knee joint is the major weight bearing joint of the body. Any condition which interferes with the smooth articulation of the joint leads to instability and rapid wasting of the quadriceps muscle. As with the hip joint degenerative disease is a major problem. It may be of a primary or secondary nature. Some of the predisposing factors to osteoarthrosis of the knee include:

1. Previous injury; fractures which affect the articular surface of the bones involved in the joint and torn menisci.
2. Chronic inflammation in such diseases as rheumatoid arthritis and tuberculosis.
3. Obesity.
4. Malalignment of articular surfaces as seen in genu valgum and genu varum.
5. Chondromalacia patellae.
6. Osteochondritis dissecans.

In all cases there is evidence of quadriceps

wasting to some degree, which inevitably leads to an unstable joint and pain.

Nonoperative treatments

These are similar to those used for osteoarthrosis of the hip joint.

* Treatment of underlying disease will halt the progress of the degenerative condition.
* Physiotherapy concentrates on building up the quadriceps muscle.

Operative treatments

Arthrodesis

Surgical fusion of the knee joint is only undertaken in a minority of cases, as the difficulties to be overcome by the patient with a permanently stiff knee are many. It may be done for an arthroplasty which for some reason has been unsuccessful, or if a successful arthroplasty has been performed on the opposite knee.

Following an arthrodesis the patient's leg is immobilized in a long leg plaster of Paris. The patient is mobilized nonweight bearing on crutches for 4–6 weeks. Gradual weight bearing is introduced following this until the plaster cast is removed at approximately 10–12 weeks.

Osteotomy

A tibial osteotomy may be performed to correct a valgus or varus deformity and to relieve pain.

The patient's limb is encased in a long leg plaster cast. Nonweight bearing starts at about the fifth day postoperatively and continues until the plaster is removed approximately 8–10 weeks after surgery.

Arthroplasty

This may take the form of either a partial or total replacement of the joint by the prosthesis. There are many prostheses available to the surgeon including the Insall Bernstein which is a cementless prosthesis for the knee joint (see Figures 8.8, 8.9 and 8.10).

Pre-operative nursing care for a patient having a total knee replacement

Much of the pre-operative care is similar to that

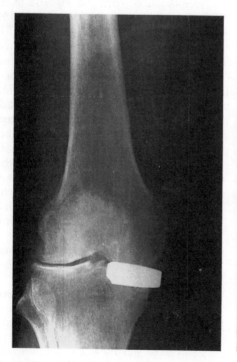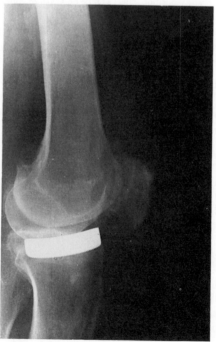

Fig. 8.8   Mackintosh's arthroplasty showing prostheses in place; anterior position (left); lateral view (right).

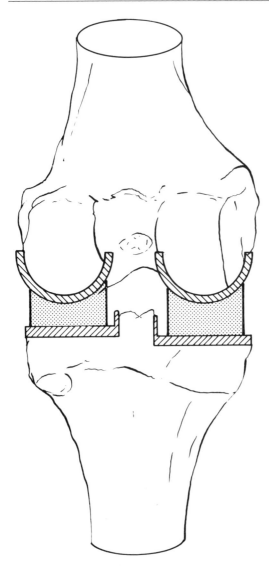

Fig. 8.9   Diagram of the Oxford Knee in situ.

Fig. 8.10   The Oxford total knee prosthesis.

for a patient having a total joint replacement of the hip. Therefore only the points specific to the knee joint will be elaborated.

- Preparation of the skin by shaving or use of a depilatory is performed according to the surgeon's wishes.
- Static quadriceps strengthening exercises are taught to the patient and practised by them.
- The patient should practise walking with crutches ready for postoperative mobilization.

Postoperative nursing care

Maintaining a safe environment

- The patient is nursed on a firm-based orthopaedic bed with the foot of the bed elevated to aid venous return and to prevent excessive swelling occurring at the knee. If a pillow is used under the patient's leg, this must be removed every two hours and the patient's calf gently massaged. There is a danger of deep venous thrombosis occurring from pressure under the calf.
- The knee is immobilized in either a firm Robert-Jones bandage or a pressure bandage over the knee with the leg held in a gutter splint. Occasionally a plaster cylinder may be applied, but this has the disadvantage of creating pressure on the joint and may increase the patient's pain.
- If a continual passive motion machine is used the patient may return from theatre with this in place. This machine provides gentle flexion and extension exercise to the knee joint continually over a 24 hour period. The degree of exercise to be performed will be set by the surgeon. The patient's leg must be removed from the machine every two hours and his calf gently massaged. There is a danger of deep venous thrombosis occurring from pressure under the calf (see Figure 8.11).
- Hourly observations of the wound dressing for seepage of blood-stained fluid are carried out for the first few hours.
- Monitoring of vital signs is continued until stable.
- Drainage into vacuum bottles is monitored and recorded on the appropriate charts. Drains are generally removed at 48 hours if drainage has ceased. There is a risk of

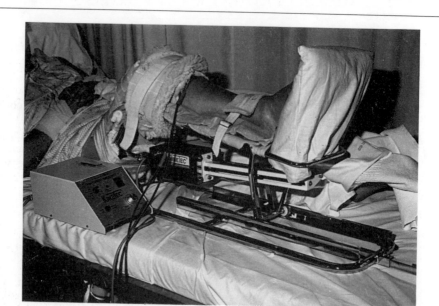

Fig. 8.11   Passive motion machine (kinetic knee machine).

haemarthrosis occurring and it is therefore important that free drainage is continued until it has stopped.

- Pain is a prominent feature and may need to be controlled by opiates. Before any attempt to exercise the affected limb starts, the patient should be given analgesia for the first few days, otherwise apprehension of pain will restrict progress.

- The neurovascular status of the toes should be monitored every 3–4 hours by examining each digit of the affected limb for colour, sensation and mobility. At the same time the pedal pulse should be taken and should be compared with the pulse on the unaffected foot. Checking the neurovascular status of the foot should continue routinely while any form of dressing remains on the knee.

- The pressure dressing and any back splint are removed 24 hours after surgery. The wound dressing should be left intact unless there are contraindications, until the sutures are removed at approximately 10–14 days, providing wound healing has taken place.

Mobilizing

- Exercises are started 24 hours after surgery. These are supervised at first by the physiotherapist and consist of passive quadriceps strengthening exercises and exercises for both ankles and feet. The joints of the unaffected leg should be put through as full a range of movement as possible, remembering that these patients may have some degree of osteoarthrosis in other joints.

- Active exercises of the affected leg in the form of straight leg raising is encouraged once a satisfactory degree of quadricep contraction is achieved. The regime of exercise then depends on the individual surgeon's preference.

- The patient may be mobilized using walking aids. It is important that the patient has a pair of well fitting laced shoes before starting to walk. The walking aid should be regarded as short-term and as soon as it is realistically practicable should be discarded. If, however, the patient feels unsafe walking without a stick, then it should be retained (see Figure 8.12).

- Once the patient is walking satisfactorily and the patient's home circumstances and family are ready, he is discharged home. It may be necessary for some form of outpatient physiotherapy to be continued until the full strength of the quadriceps is regained.

INTERNAL DERANGEMENTS OF THE KNEE JOINT

Osteochondritis dissecans

This condition is a common source of loose

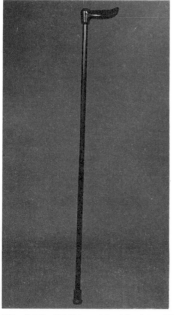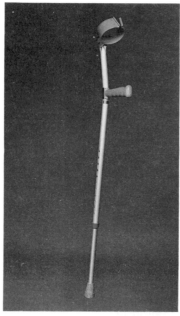

Fig. 8.12 Walking aids: (a) stick with moulded hand grip;   (b) forearm trough crutch; (c) elbow crutch.

bodies in the knee joint. It is a condition in which a small flake of bone with its cartilage becomes detached from the articular surface of the bone, most commonly the medial femoral condyle.

The patient complains of recurrent episodes of pain, a feeling of instability, locking of the knee joint and recurrent effusions.

The treatment is to remove the loose body or, if it is a large segment, to reattach it to the bone by means of a small nail or pin.

The nursing care is the same as for the care of a patient having an arthroplasty.

NURSING CARE FOR PATIENTS WITH FOOT DISORDERS

The human foot bears the weight of the body on its delicate bony structure. Overweight throws an increased burden on the feet which may be unable to stand the extra strain without causing some ill effect. Fashionable footwear often interferes with the normal mechanics of the foot and squashes toes into a small space. High heels throw the weight onto an area ill designed for such a purpose. As age increases so the feet begin to deteriorate.

Foot hygiene is important. Daily care of the feet by washing and careful drying between each toe is important. Corns and callosities should be dealt with by a trained chiropodist. Toenails, when cut, should be cut straight across.

Advice about footwear and foot hygiene are part of the orthopaedic nurse's role and should be given to any patient regardless of whether they have a foot disorder.

Pre-operative nursing care for a patient having foot surgery

- Careful foot hygiene is essential. Any abrasions, cuts or lesions on the feet should be reported to the surgeon as these may delay surgery.
- Pedal pulses should be taken and compared with each other to give a baseline for monitoring postoperatively.
- Any skin discolouration should be noted.
- Preparation of the patient for postoperative monitoring should be explained. The patient should be taught to be aware of the sensations received through his toes and how to move them.
- Footwear which will be worn in the postoperative phase should be explained to the patient and his family so they are ready to bring it to the hospital when it is required.
- Routine pre-operative nursing care is carried out.

Postoperative nursing care after foot surgery

Maintaining a safe environment

- The patient is received from the theatre onto a firm-based orthopaedic bed with the foot of the bed elevated to aid venous return and to prevent swelling of the foot.
- The patient's foot will either be dressed by a firm pressure bandage or a below knee plaster cast. Both of these should be observed for blood stained oozing from the wound and this should be monitored to ensure it does not become excessive.
- The immediate wound dressing remains intact unless contraindicated until the wound has healed. Sutures are removed at approximately 10–14 days.
- A metal pin or wire may be inserted through a toe following surgery to maintain its shape or position. The wire end extends through the dressing and must be protected by a cork. The patient must be made aware of the pin so that he does no harm to himself, and all members of staff should be aware of the pin so that they neither harm the patient nor themselves. A bed cradle will be used to ensure the bedclothes are kept away from this, or the patient may be nursed in a divided bed with the feet exposed.
- The neurovascular status of the toes must be monitored, although this may not be able to be fully performed due to the measures taken at surgery.
- Colour may be masked by solutions used in theatre. The blanching test may be difficult to perform if there is a pin through the great toe. This may also prevent the patient from moving his toes to ascertain movement.
- Postoperative pain is a major problem for patients following foot surgery and this may mask symptoms of sensation.
- Temperature therefore often remains the major way of assessing the neurovascular status of the foot following surgery.
- Pain levels are monitored frequently and opiates given as prescribed, noting their effectiveness. Analgesia is required frequently during the first few days.

Mobilizing

- When the patient first stands out of bed a throbbing pain is frequently felt in the foot. To avoid this the patient should be allowed to hang his legs over the side of the bed the day before walking starts.
- If the patient does not have a plaster cast on his leg, then some form of protective sandal should be worn. The patient is taught to walk on his heels with a walking aid.
- Foot exercises to mobilize the foot and to gain full strength of the intrinsic muscles are encouraged.

COMMON FOOT PROBLEMS AND THEIR TREATMENTS

Hallux valgus

In hallux valgus the big toe deviates laterally away from the mid-line at the metatarsophalangeal joint. The first metatarsal often deviates medially and an exostosis forms over the prominent metatarsal head. An enlarged bursa, called a bunion, forms over the exostosis and a painful corn may develop on the overlying skin.

Pressure and friction on the bunion may cause it to become inflamed and infected. Secondary osteoarthritic changes occur in the joint, leading to the condition of hallux rigidus (see Figure 8.13).

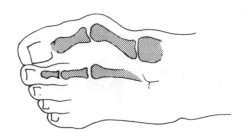

Fig. 8.13 Hallux valgus showing marked lateral deviation of the great toe.

Nonoperative treatments

This is undertaken in mild, early cases:

1. Felt padding is applied to relieve pressure on the bunion. Regular chiropody.
2. The patient is advised to wear wide shoes with a flat inner border.
3. Foot mobilizing exercises are taught to the patient.

Operative treatments

The aim of surgery is to relieve pain and to

enable the patient to buy shoes which are comfortable to wear:

1. Trimming of the exostosis and a bunionectomy to remove the bunion.
2. Arthrodesis of the metatarsophalangeal joint of the hallux.
3. A displacement osteotomy of the neck of the first metatarsal.
4. Arthroplasty:
    (i) Excision arthroplasty (Keller's method) of the proximal half of the first phalanx of the great toe. This creates a flail, freely movable false joint.
    (ii) Excision of the head of the first metatarsal (Mayo's method).
5. Transfer of the adductor hallucis tendon from the proximal phalanx to the metatarsal (McBride's method).

Specific nursing care points

- As patients receiving surgical treatment for this condition are frequently elderly, their susceptibility to pressure sores should be carefully assessed pre-operatively. Appropriate measures are planned and implemented to prevent this potential problem occurring.

Hallux rigidus

Hallux rigidus is osteoarthrosis of the metatarsophalangeal joint of the hallux. It is a very painful condition whenever the foot is used and walking becomes difficult.

Nonoperative treatments

A metatarsal bar may be fitted under the sole of the shoe at the level of the metatarsophalangeal joints.

Operative measures

These are advised when the condition is severe and either arthrodesis of the metatarsophalangeal joint in a position of slight extension, or a Keller's arthroplasty is undertaken.

Hammer toe

A hammer toe occurs when the metatarsophalangeal joint is extended and the proximal interphalangeal joint is flexed to a right angle. The distal interphalangeal joint may be extended or flat. The condition generally only occurs in the second toe but may occur in others.

Pain is due to a corn forming over the prominent proximal interphalangeal joint and it may interfere with the appearance and buying of normal footwear (see Figure 8.14).

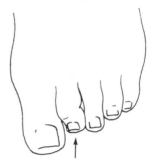

Fig. 8.14   Hammer toe.

Nonoperative treatment

This takes the form of strapping the toe with gentle stretching which may help in very mild cases.

Operative treatment

This is by arthrodesis of the affected toe or by filletting the toe.

NURSING CARE FOR PATIENTS HAVING UPPER LIMB DISORDERS

Many patients are surprised at how dependent they are on one particular arm. Surgery may leave them dependent on others to carry out quite simple tasks and this in turn may make them embarrassed and irritated.

It is therefore important that the patient should practice carrying out simple tasks with his nonaffected arm before having surgery, and his family are involved from the outset.

However if both arms are to be operated on, as will occur in a bilateral carpal tunnel release, then the patient becomes totally dependent on others for all activities of daily living. Even such simple things as blowing his nose may become a major hurdle for the patient with both hands encased in bandages.

The nurse has to develop a tactful approach of

watchfulness and to know when to help the patient and when to leave well alone.

The four major nerves of the brachial plexus—the musculo-cutaneous nerve, the ulnar nerve, the radial nerve and the median nerve—present major neurovascular complications for the patient having upper limb surgery. A skillful orthopaedic nurse will be aware of these potential problems and take care to position the patient's affected arm in such a way that no undue pressure is placed on nerves or blood vessels.

Irritation of the skin where two skin surfaces touch in the position the patient's arm is placed in during the postoperative phase may lead to discomfort for the patient. This happens particularly during hot weather. Cotton pads placed in the axilla, bend of the elbow or where the arm is held against the trunk will help to reduce discomfort for the patient. Careful changing of the pads, while the arm is held by a third person, may be accomplished. At the same time the skin is washed and dried thoroughly. A commercially prepared deodorant or alcohol applied on a cotton wool ball to the areas will help to dispel unpleasant odours and make the patient feel more comfortable.

Pre-operative nursing care for patients having upper limb surgery

Maintaining a safe environment

- The patient's axilla is shaved or a commercially prepared depilatory used if required by the surgeon. Many female patients will have done this before coming into hospital. The patient's axilla should be inspected for signs of abrasions.
- To ensure the fingernails can be observed postoperatively for normal colour, all nail polish is removed. The nails are cleaned and, if necessary, cut.
- All rings must be removed to prevent postoperative swelling of the fingers. Some ladies will find removing their wedding ring a distressing process and the nurse must be tactful when asking the patient to do this and give a logical explanation as to why this is important.
- Identification labels should be put around the patient's ankle. If they are put around the wrist they may be removed during surgery or if an intravenous infusion is inserted into one of the patient's arms.

- Whenever blood specimens are being taken they should be taken from the unaffected side. If bilateral surgery is to be performed then another area is used.
- Using the nonaffected arm for washing and other tasks is practised by the patient. Equipment such as nonslip mats to go under plates and 'bendy' straws to help with drinking can be obtained and their use practised.

Breathing

- If the patient's arm is held against his trunk in a body bandage (such as a Velpeau bandage) postoperatively, then the patient may experience breathing difficulties. In the pre-operative period the patient is warned about this and deep breathing exercises practised.

Controlling body temperature

- Body temperature may be difficult to control as the patient's arms are often covered in bulky dressings. A loose fitting jacket or back-opening nightdress, without sleeves, will help the patient to retain their dignity and feel warm.

Sleeping

- Sleeping with his arms elevated in slings at the side of the bed may be difficult for the patient and therefore should be explained during the pre-operative phase.
- Routine pre-operative preparation is carried out.

Specific postoperative nursing care

Maintaining a safe environment

- The patient is received from the theatre onto a firm-based orthopaedic bed and nursed flat until fully conscious. He is then gradually sat up into a semi-recumbent position, well supported by pillows.
- Vital signs are monitored every hour until stable and then daily as required.
- Any drains are checked hourly for patency and are removed after 24 hours, providing drainage has finished.
- The patient's arm may be held close to the

chest wall or it may be required to be elevated. This can be achieved by holding the arm in a roller towel or sling which is then attached to a stand at the side of the bed (see Figure 8.15). There are several points to remember when doing this. Make sure that:

(i)   the stand is stable;
(ii) the patient's shoulder is in the optimum and a comfortable position;
(iii) the patient's elbow is free from undue pressure, particularly on the ulnar nerve. Careful evaluation of the patient's fingers for altered sensation in the ulnar nerve distribution is essential. Ideally the elbow should be free from any pressure;
(iv) the stands are adjusted as the patient is sat up to prevent hyperextension of the shoulder joint.

- Observations of the patient's fingers for colour, sensation and mobility are monitored every half hour to begin with, then 4 hourly for 24 hours. These observations are continued twice daily during the patient's time in hospital. Each finger is examined separately.
- At the same time, the radial pulse is taken and recorded and compared with the radial pulse on the unaffected side.
- Analgesia is given to the patient to reduce postoperative pain and its effectiveness noted.
- The patient's locker is placed on the unaffected side of the patient within easy reach for the patient.
- Maintaining a sitting position for the patient may be difficult. Sliding down the bed may leave the patient prone to sores from friction, so constant adjustment of the patient's position by the nurse is necessary. The patient may be able to help the nurse by bending his knees and pushing on his feet to help lift himself.

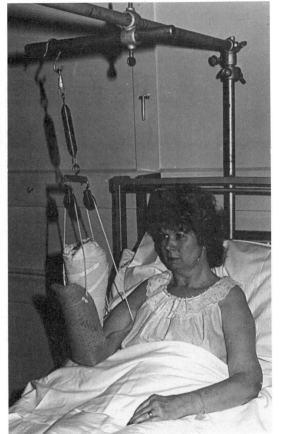

Fig. 8.15 A method of elevating the hand to prevent swelling.

COMMON UPPER LIMB PROBLEMS, THEIR TREATMENTS AND NURSING CARE

Recurrent dislocation of shoulder

This condition may be a congenital one or the result of an initial traumatic dislocation. The soft tissue structures are torn and an unstable joint remains. Repeated dislocation may then occur following minor movements involving abduction, lateral rotation or extension of the joint. The dislocation is nearly always in an anterior position. The head of the humerus comes to lie under the coracoid process in a subcoracol position.

Operative measures

Those undertaken are:

1. Reattachment of the capsule and glenoid labrum by the Bankart operation.
2. Shortening the subscapularis tendon by overlappng or reefing it by the Putti-Platt operation.

Specific nursing care points

- A collar and cuff are applied and the arm is

held across the trunk by means of a body bandage.

- Care is taken to insert a cotton pad in the axilla, bend of elbow and between the skin surfaces of the arm and trunk.
- The dressing and pads are left in place for seven to ten days when the dressing is removed, the wound inspected and, if healed, the sutures are removed.
- The axilla, arm and trunk are gently washed with minimal movement of the shoulder.
- A light dressing, pads and immobilization may be replaced depending on the individual surgeon. Alternatively just a collar and cuff may be applied to the patient's arm.
- Mobilization is at the surgeon's discretion. Gentle assisted exercises are started and gradually increased until active exercises are achieved. It may be some months before full use of the shoulder is restored.

Carpal tunnel syndrome

This is a condition where the median nerve becomes compressed in the carpal tunnel as it passes under the flexor retinaculum. It is characterized by numbness and a tingling sensation in the distribution of the median nerve distal to the carpal tunnel. The symptoms occur frequently at night and disturb the patient's sleep. It is a condition which particularly affects women during the post-menopausal era or during pregnancy. It may be a bilateral or unilateral affection. If left untreated a median nerve palsy may result.

Nonoperative treatments

1. Local injections of steroid preparations may help to relieve symptoms.
2. Use of a night splint with the wrist held in a neutral position may help to reduce the compression within the tunnel.
3. The use of nonsteroidal anti-inflammatory and diuretic drugs may relieve inflammation and reduce the swelling within the tendon sheaths in the tunnel.

Operative measures

There is only one surgical treatment and that is total division of the flexor retinaculum (transverse carpal ligament) and decompression of the median nerve.

Specific nursing care points

- If the patient has had bilateral decompressions, he returns from the theatre totally reliant on the nurse for the first 24 hours. Encouragement to retain some independence, if at all possible, is important for the patient's morale.
- The patient's arm/arms are elevated in bedside slings, but should be removed from these every four hours. The shoulder and elbow joints are put through a full range of movement at first, passively, by the nurse and later, actively, by the patient at these times.
- Observation of the colour, the sensation and the mobility of each digit is monitored half hourly during the initial postoperative phase. The fingers should remain pink and mobile with full sensation. If there has been considerable loss of sensation pre-operatively, then the pre-operative assessment of the movement and sensation possible at this time is important.
- If the surgery has been performed using local anaesthesia, then the nurse will need to be aware of this and reassure the patient that the sensation will return in due course.
- Patients following this surgery are often discharged two days after surgery. Home conditions must be investigated pre-operatively, particularly in the case of a patient with a bilateral problem. There must be some form of help available to them at home. Even the simplest tasks such as pulling up tights or holding a knife and fork are difficult.
- The dressings are reduced 24 hours after surgery and a light strip dressing retained over the wound. The sutures are removed once the wound has healed at 7–10 days, usually as an outpatient or by the patient's general practitioner.
- Advice is given to the patient to keep her arms elevated when sitting down and how to achieve this. A broad arm sling is applied with the wrist and hand well supported.
- The patient is advised not to get her hands wet and is shown how to cover them with plastic bags tied at the arm to prevent this happening.
- Encouragement to move her wrist and fingers as well as elbow and shoulder joints, which are put through a full range of movement every four hours.

- The patient is advised to avoid lifting heavy weights such as full shopping baskets for at least two months to allow time for the total healing of soft tissue structures to take place.

NURSING CARE FOR PATIENTS HAVING SPINAL DISORDERS

Low back pain is a familiar term to everyone and a 'slipped disc' conjures up all kinds of pictures to an imaginative mind. The fears associated with both of these terms and the fact that the patient's spine is involved with his problem will lead the nurse to involve themselves in long discussions with the patient in an effort to reassure him. The patient will often want his immediate family to be included in these discussions.

Times such as these present the nurse with the opportunity of providing health education for the patient and family alike.

Patients with back pain will often already have been subjected to a variety of investigations and nonoperative treatments. Relief of symptoms using alternative medicine such as provided by osteopaths and chyropracters has often been sought by those suffering from chronic back pain. When a decision is finally taken to undertake surgery, the patient is apprehensive and careful pre-operative preparation is necessary to ensure a smooth postoperative recovery.

Preoperative nursing care for patients having spinal surgery

Maintaining a safe environment

- As with all orthopaedic patients the patient is nursed on a firm-based bed but with only one pillow under the head. The patient is discouraged from sitting up for any procedure to enable him to become used to lying flat in bed for all activities of daily living.
- Some form of pelvic or leg skin traction may be applied to the patient to aid relief of pain and muscle spasm. This also acts as a reminder to the patient not to sit up. Routine care of patients in traction is observed.
- An overhead mirror is attached to the head of the bed and the patient is taught and encouraged to practise manoeuvring the mirror to enable him to see what is going on in the ward, and to aid him to eat and drink effectively without causing himself problems.

- Safety is of prime importance. The patient's bedside locker is placed within easy reach and the bed height adjusted to enable the patient to reach the locker without effort or sitting up.
- 'Log-rolling' is taught to the patient. This is a method of turning the patient from side to side, maintaining the vertebral column and legs in a straight line. It is not an easy movement to achieve and the patient is encouraged to practise this. Log-rolling is performed every four hours.
- From the position achieved during log-rolling, the patient is taught how he will get out of bed following surgery without causing damage to the wound and maintaining the spine in a straight line.

Communicating

- Talking to the patient and, if requested, to the patient's family about the various procedures is an important part of the nurse's role. Reinforcement of explanations given by the doctor are often needed by the patient.
- The patient is made aware of how he should bend, sit and stand in the future and this may be reinforced by giving him written guidelines as outlined in Table 8.3.
- Obesity puts extra strain on the vertebral column. If the patient is overweight then a gentle introduction to weight reduction is important. Cooperation from the rest of the patient's family will help to support the patient during this task. Advice from the dietician, if the patient wishes it, may be given.

Table 8.3 Sample of written guidelines for patient after spinal surgery.

1. Do not bend from your waist. At all times bend from your knees and hips.
2. Do stand with your head up, chin in and your back and pelvis straight.
3. Do carry heavy objects close to your body, never at arm's length.
4. Do not slump in your chair.
5. Do keep your back and neck in a straight line when sitting.
6. Do drive your car with the seat close to the pedals.
7. Do sleep or lie with your knees bent and on your side. If you have to sleep on your back, sleep with a pillow under your knees. Never sleep on your front.
8. Do rest your back when you are tired by lying down and placing either pillows or a stool under your legs which should be bent at the hips and knees.
9. Do not sit or stand in one position for long periods.

Breathing

- The patient may experience some difficulties in breathing whilst lying flat. He may be encouraged to take slow deep breaths to overcome this.

Eating and drinking

- Practice with eating while lying flat is essential. The patient may practise cutting up his food with it balanced or he may prefer the nurse to help him. Meals should be small and easily digestible. Not only will this be more comfortable for the patient but may aid weight reduction.
- Fluid intake is important to avoid urinary stasis and complications of immobility such as renal calculi. Practice with using 'bendy' straws is useful. Very hot drinks must be avoided to prevent the patient from accidental scalds.

Eliminating

- Elimination may be difficult postoperatively due to position and pain. Therefore, pre-operatively, the patient should familiarize himself with using bedpans or urinals. Some surgeons do allow their patients to use a bedside commode quite soon after surgery and the patient should practise getting out of bed and using this.

Personal cleansing and dressing

- The patient should be encouraged to maintain as much independence as possible over personal cleansing. An assisted bed bath will be necessary and pre-operative cleansing of the patient's skin according to the individual surgeon's wishes carried out.
- The patient's hair is washed. This is achieved using a bedfast rinser so that no undue strain is put on the patient's back.
- Pressure areas such as the bony prominences of the spine, the sacrum and the heels are vulnerable to breakdown. They are inspected every four hours for signs of pressure each time the patient is moved.
- Clothing is difficult, but open-backed gowns or jackets may be used to ensure the patient is comfortable.

Working and playing

- The medical social worker may become involved with the patient and his family, particularly if the patient will be unable to return to his original work.

Mobilizing

- Plans for postoperative discharge are made so the patient knows approximately when he will be returning home.

Sleeping

- Sleeping on his back may be difficult for the patient. If the patient's legs are placed in foam troughs, this will obliterate the lumbar lordosis and lead to less pain and discomfort. The troughs must be removed every four hours and the patient's calves gently massaged and inspected for signs of undue pressure.

Postoperative nursing care for patients having spinal surgery

Maintaining a safe environment

- The patient is returned from theatre lying flat on his back with no pillow under the head until he is able to maintain his own airway. At this time one pillow is placed beneath the patient's head. Two pillows are placed longitudinally down each side of the patient with his arms resting lightly on the top of each pillow. The patient's legs are placed in foam troughs to obliterate the lumbar lordosis, which has the added advantage of applying pressure to the wound in the lumbar region, reducing the risk of haematoma formation.
- The patient's vital signs are monitored half-hourly at first. The frequency of these observations is decreased as the patient's condition stabilizes. Spinal surgery is frequently lengthy in time and the patient may be cold and pale postoperatively.
- Sensation and movement of the patient's lower limbs is checked every four hours to ensure that there is no interference with nerve conductivity. It is important for the nurse to be aware of any numbness present prior to surgery. Ankle movement will aid circulation.

- The patient is generally nursed supine for the first three hours and then turned from side to back to side every four hours using the log-rolling technique. When the patient is lying on his side, the following must be observed:
  - (i) pressure areas, to ensure they are intact;
  - (ii) the wound dressing, for oozing. The outer pressure dressing is removed 24 hours after surgery. The wound dressing is left intact unless there are any adverse signs. Sutures are removed once the wound has healed between 10–14 days postoperatively;
  - (iii) any drains, to ensure they are patent and free draining. These are normally removed after 24 hours or when drainage has finished. The colour and amount of drainage is observed and recorded on the appropriate chart.
- Pain levels must be carefully monitored. These vary greatly in patients following spinal surgery. Some patients have experienced so much pain prior to surgery that they find they have little after surgery. Some patients are so used to pain that they wait until the last moment before asking for pain relief that analgesia given is not very effective. The skill of carefully assessing the patient's pain level is one which the nurse needs to acquire.

Breathing

- Deep breathing and chest expansion are encouraged to aid circulation. Gentle coughing may be assisted if the patient holds a pillow against his chest wall.

Eating and drinking

- Nutrition is withheld in any form until bowel sounds are heard as there is a danger of paralytic ileus following spinal surgery. The nurse should check these every hour. When there are signs of returning bowel activity, the patient starts drinking small quantities of fluid. If these are tolerated he progresses to a normal diet and fluid intake.
- Intravenous therapy is routinely observed.
- As oral intake is restricted at first, careful oral hygiene for the patient is essential to maintain the patient's mouth in a good

condition. This may be carried out hourly at first.

Eliminating

- Elimination may present problems for the patient, but if careful pre-operative preparation has taken place, these should be minimal. Urinary output is monitored. Shock to the sympathetic nervous system may cause a temporary loss of bladder tone. For this reason it may be necessary to introduce a urinary catheter. Careful recording of urinary output for the first three or four days is important.
- If a catheter is introduced, catheter toilet in the form of careful washing and drying of the genitalia is necessary at least twice a day.

Mobilizing

- The patient is encouraged to maintain the muscle tone of his arms. Gentle leg exercises under the supervision of the physiotherapist will take place twice a day.
- Some surgeons allow the patient to get out of bed two or three days after surgery. The patient is gradually sat up as he has been practising pre-operatively. There may be a tendency for the patient to feel dizzy and the nurse must be ready for this and not attempt to get a patient out of bed for the first few times on his own. The patient is discouraged from standing or sitting on the edge of the bed. He may sit in a high-backed chair for meals, but when the patient becomes tired he should lie down.
- Education in bending, sitting and standing is continually reinforced during this phase.
- Some surgeons prefer their patients to have support for their back in the form of a corset following spinal surgery. This should fit comfortably before the patient is discharged home. The care and maintenance of the appliance is carefully explained to the patient before he goes home.

COMMON SPINAL PROBLEMS, THEIR TREATMENTS AND NURSING CARE

Prolapsed intervertebral disc

Intervertebral discs are situated between adjacent vertebral bodies. They consist of a tough outer ring of fibrocartilage, called the annulus fibrosus, and a soft gelatinous inner portion, the nucleus pulposus.

In the condition of a prolapsed intervertebral disc the annulosus fibrosus may crack due to degenerative changes within its structure or tear due to sudden trauma. The nucleus then bulges through this rent and intrudes into the spinal canal. Depending on the position of the damage, the now bulging disc may compress one of the spinal nerves. This may happen at any level of the vertebral column, but the lumbar region is the most commonly affected. Compression of associated spinal nerve roots produces the symptoms which necessitate treatment (see Figure 8.16).

The patient may complain of a sudden onset of pain which rapidly becomes severe or they may experience a dull ache which gradually becomes worse, with pain in the limb. The pain is aggravated by such activities as stooping, sitting for long periods, coughing or sneezing.

Nonoperative treatments

1. Rest in bed on a firm-based bed and mattress for up to three weeks, usually with analgesics to relieve pain, and sometimes anti-inflammatory or muscle relaxing drugs to help. It is important to realize that a mother with a young family will have difficulty in succeeding in this treatment. Providing the family can be supported by relatives, these patients are better nursed in hospital.

2. Continuous pelvic traction or skin traction to both legs may help to reduce muscle spasm and maintain the patient in a relaxed recumbent position.

3. If it is essential to keep the patient ambulant, support for the vertebral column by means of a plaster jacket or corset may help.

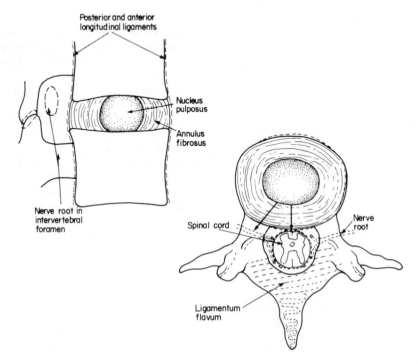

Fig. 8.16   Intervertebral disc as seen in longitudinal section of the spine (top); top view of intervertebral disc and its relations (bottom). The arrows indicate the usual sites of nuclear protrusion. Dotted lines and closely dotted areas represent sensitive structures which can cause lumbago or sciatica if pressed upon.

Operative measures

The criteria used to undertake surgical intervention are:

— when the sciatic pain is so great that it disturbs sleep and causes deterioration of general health;
— when there is evidence of severe neurological disturbance such as disruption of bladder and bowel function;
— when conservative treatment fails to control or relieve the sciatic pain.

1. *Laminectomy.* This involves removal of one or more of the laminae along with the protruding disc.
2. *Discectomy.* This involves removal of the prolapsing disc.
3. *Spinal fusion.* Both of the proceeding operations may be followed by a spinal fusion used to stabilize the vertebral column.
4. *Chemonucleolysis.* One of the newer techniques for dealing with a prolapsed intervertebral disc is chemonucleolysis. This procedure is performed under a general anaesthetic and is still very experimental. An enzyme, chymopapain, is injected into the affected disc. This then dissolves or digests the disc material. Precautions taken prior to this procedure include

ensuring that the patient is not allergic to meat tenderizers or the chymopapain itself. Severe anaphylactic shock may result if this technique is used on such patients.

Spondylolisthesis

In the normal vertebral column one vertebra articulates with the vertebra above and the vertebra below by means of its articular facets. If a defect occurs in the vertebral arch which carries the articular facets, then this articulation is impossible. Sometimes, as the result of a congenital deformity, the vertebral arch fails to ossify and fibrous tissue remains at the junction of each of the laminae and pedicles (the pars interarticularis). This is known as spondylosis.

In spondylolisthesis the affected vertebra slides forward together with the whole of the vertebral column above it, leaving the inferior articular process in situ. This condition most commonly occurs at the level of the fifth lumbar vertebra where it slips forward on the sacrum (see Figure 8.17).

Nonoperative treatments

1. Application of a plaster jacket is often beneficial in the early stages of the condition. This may be followed by some

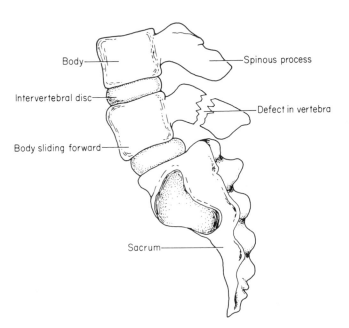

Body
Intervertebral disc
Body sliding forward
Sacrum
Spinous process
Defect in vertebra

Fig. 8.17 Sagittal section of the spine showing spondylolisthesis.

form of spinal support such as a Gold-thwaite brace.

2. Rest in bed with or without the application of leg skin traction may allow acute symptoms of low back pain to resolve.

Operative treatment

This is only undertaken when the acute symptoms fail to respond to non-operative treatment or there is neurological involvement. Spinal fusion is the operation usually performed.

REFERENCES

1   Winfield U. (1986) Too close a shave? *Nursing Times*, March.
2   Editorial (1983) Preoperative depilation. *The Lancet*, **8337**: 1311.

SUGGESTED FURTHER READING

Dickson R.A. & Wright V. (1985) *Musculo-Skeletal Disease*. London: Heinemann.
Farrell J. (1982) *Illustrated Guide to Orthopaedic Nursing*. New York: Harper & Row.
Powell M. (1986) *Orthopaedic Nursing and Rehabilitation*, 9th edn. Edinburgh: Churchill Livingstone.

9

CARE OF THE CHILD WITH AN ORTHOPAEDIC PROBLEM

To dare to be different
In a world of peers,

To be faced with constraints
During formative years,

To fear the unknown
Devoid of time frames,

To care about health
While others play games,

To become one's self
With an image of being,

That belies the distortion
Others are seeing.
Beverley Anderson, R.N., MSN. (1)

(Beverley Anderson is Director of Nursing Service, Encino Hospital, Encino, California).

When Dame Agnes Hunt returned to England in the early 1900s from pioneering in Australia with her mother, she was appalled by the sight of so many undernourished and crippled children whose parents were unable to manage or even afford their treatment and care. Dame Agnes founded the Surgical Huts for the Care of Crippled Children at Baschurch in Shropshire. She took these children herself to Liverpool for treatment by Robert Jones. Thus began an association between two of the great personalities in orthopaedics.

Robert Jones and G.R. Girdlestone recognized the need to establish a properly funded educational service for children with orthopaedic problems. Many years later through the Platt Report (2), the Tavistock Report (3), the Court Report (4) and the Warnock Report (5), the organization of a caring and carefully controlled environment within a multidisciplinary team for children in hospital has continued to reinforce the principles laid down by these people.

Today the orthopaedic nurse will seldom see children admitted to hospital for long periods. With the changing pattern of disease, children are admitted to hospital for a relatively short time; most of their care is carried out in the community by their family, the primary health care team and the community service team. The days of long hospitalization for osteomyelitis, tuberculosis and poliomyelitis are gone. New diseases have replaced the old ones and the orthopaedic nurse is more likely to have to deal with forms of birth defects, trauma from road and domestic accidents and nonaccidental injury to children.

Children with orthopaedic conditions are seldom acutely ill for long periods. The orthopaedic nurse learns many new skills to deal with children in her care such as how to turn routine exercise into play and how to teach parents to manage their child's care at home.

General nursing care

Maintaining a safe environment

Maintaining a safe environment within a children's ward is of prime importance. Children with orthopaedic conditions are not as mobile as their counterparts in a general hospital, but they still manage to get up to all types of tricks if care is not taken. The Hospital Building Act (6) for children's wards provides the statutory guide for the type, numbers and size of rooms required in a children's ward. Safety in placing handles on doors above a child's level, sliding doors on cupboards adjusted to prevent small fingers being caught and sharp corners on shelving rounded are some of the safety measures to be observed. Bright colours act as stimulation for children. The wards need to be decorated in primary colours to aid this. Appropriate sized beds are essential (see Figure 9.1). Children are not adults in miniature and therefore need appropriate equipment.

Children's wards should never be left un-

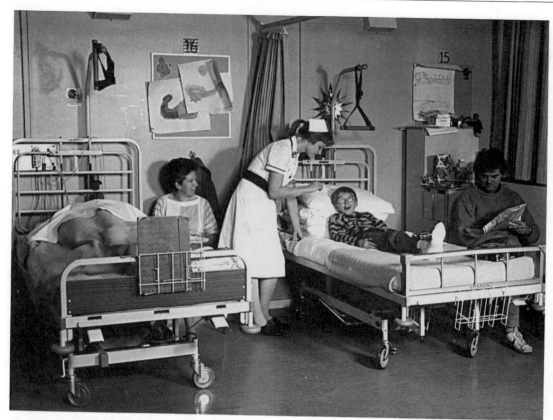

Fig. 9.1   Children's ward.

attended. This becomes an increasingly difficult problem where Nightingale wards are no longer used but the ward is divided into four or six bedded cubicles. Visitors should be reminded always to leave cot-sides securely in place when leaving the child. Toys brought from home should be checked for safety.

Special areas for play and education need to be set apart from the ward if this is practicable. The play leader works with all age groups of children, but she has an important role in the under school-age child's care (see Figure 9.2).

Mother and baby units should be available on the ward. These units are misnamed, as they may be used for children of any age whose parents need to stay at the hospital close to the child. Occasionally siblings may need to be accommodated as well, although staying overnight in a ward is undesirable for them.

Uniforms may frighten the child in hospital. The use of colourful tabards to cover uniforms is rapidly becoming the accepted practice in children's wards. The tabards need to be made of an easily washable material. Sufficient tabards must be available to allow for personnel to change them frequently when they become soiled.

Visiting should be unrestricted within acceptable limits. Obviously a child who is unwell will not welcome too many visitors. Family visiting and friends of the child are to be encouraged. This is particularly important for babies. Bonding between parents and the baby is essential. Time for cuddling both the baby and the child should be made. Parents should feel able to take an active part in the child's care under the guidance of a trained nurse.

Communicating

Communication at all levels is important for the transfer of information and care of the child. The child should be included in discussions with parents wherever appropriate. The nursing process provides the nurse with the opportunity to form a working relationship with both the family and the child. Assessment of both family and child should form the basis of care. Care is planned with the parents and with the help of

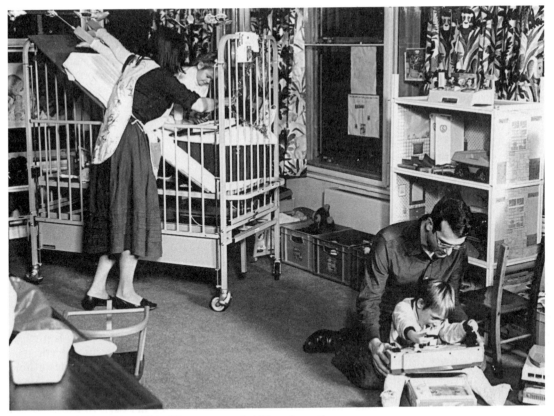

Fig. 9.2 Playleader with a child while a parent and child work together.

planned with the parents and with the help of the child. The care plan should be available to the parents and to all members of the team. This will mean that all carers involved with the child know what is expected of them.

It is important to know the child's own special language for everyday things. This can be written on the care plan. With individualized care this is not such a problem for the primary nurse, but should be available for supporting members of the team.

The majority of orthopaedic children are relatively fit. They often just require a period of rest for a particular part of the skeleton. Therefore most children will be up, out of bed and dressed in normal day clothes. Adherence to home routines such as bedtime is important and, within reason, should be continued for the child.

Eating and drinking

Nutrition for children in hospital needs to be carefully controlled by the ward sister in conjunction with the catering department of the hospital. Food should be appealing to the child as well as nutritious. Food brought in from home for the child should never be left in the bedside locker as this may pose a hazard both for the child and for other patients in the ward. Small portions of food should be supplied. Nutritious substitutes for meals, such as baked beans and eggs, can be available on the ward to tempt a child with a poor appetite.

Fluids need to be encouraged, particularly during a postoperative phase, to ensure adequate hydration. Flavoured milk drinks will provide an added source of calorie and vitamin intake.

Timing of meals should be regular and as peaceful as possible without interruption from other disciplines.

It is usually possible for breastfeeding of the baby by the mother to be continued and this is encouraged. A quiet area should be set aside to facilitate this.

Eliminating

Elimination may pose problems for the child.

Toddlers who have reached the potty training stage may regress. An understanding nurse and parent needs to deal with this without causing distress to the child. During immobilization periods the child may need a nappy to cover the genital area and this may lead to acute embarrassment. Privacy, even for the youngest child, is essential if elimination is to be successful. A bowl of water offered to the child afterwards is important in continuing his hygiene education.

Young girls who have just started menstruation may be particularly embarrassed during these times in hospital. A caring attitude and privacy will alleviate many of the problems which could arise.

Personal cleansing and dressing

Personal cleansing for some children is a task to be avoided. The nurse needs to ensure that all children maintain a good standard of hygiene during their hospital period. Parents are encouraged to help the child with this, but not to encourage them to become totally dependent on others for this activity. Education for the child about dental care and teeth cleaning can be incorporated into playtimes. Relevant posters displayed in bathrooms and play areas will reinforce teaching.

Dressing for children with orthopaedic problems is particularly important. Clothes need to be adaptable to accommodate awkward braces and splints. These should be of the correct length to prevent a child inadvertently falling over. Shoes need to be well-fitting and supporting. Children should be encouraged to dress themselves if they are able to do so. It may be quicker for the nurse to do it herself, but this can cause the child harm by encouraging him to become dependent. Fashionable clothes for a young girl are important. Advice from the nurse to a young patient wearing an unsightly brace may be welcomed. Whenever possible the child is encouraged to be dressed in their normal day clothes when out of bed. Operation clothes can be frightening for a young child. If a child is going to the theatre for surgery, he should be dressed in his own clean clothes.

Mobilizing

The normal developmental milestones for a child should be observed. By the age of 12–16 months the child should be walking. Whatever the orthopaedic condition the child has, these milestones are important. Attempts to allow a child with lower limb paralysis to stand at 12–16 months is vital. Supportive braces, tailored to the individual child's needs, assist this. Mobility provides independence for the child. This will help normal intellectual, social and psychological development.

Working and playing

Play, as already stated, is an important part of the child's day in hospital. Whenever possible, play can be used to help the child familiarize himself with hospital procedures and personnel, particularly prior to admission. Play can be used to introduce exercise routines for the child or as part of his normal education and intellectual development.

The Warnock Committee (5) suggested that education, by its normality, could help a child through his period of time in hospital. It further stated that education should begin at birth.

The hospital school's service provides a link between school and hospital. Many children leave hospital educationally ahead of their peers. The nurse and the teacher need to work closely with each other. Both need to appreciate each other's role within the team. Nursing duties should be minimal during school hours in order not to interrupt the educational programme.

Statutory examinations can be taken in hospital should the need arise and liaison between hospital school teachers and local educational establishments is important.

Hospitalization of a child may have adverse effects on the child's siblings. They may feel neglected by the parents and, where an orthopaedic condition is involved, may feel guilty at being normal themselves. It is important to include siblings in visits to the hospital and in helping with the care of the affected child. However, it is equally important that they are encouraged to live a normal life for themselves.

The affected child may feel himself to be the odd one amongst his peers, particularly if wearing a brace is part of the treatment. Friends should be encouraged to visit the child and to talk about the child's treatment to them. Normal everyday happenings at school and at home should be discussed with the child and not avoided as taboo subjects.

NURSING CARE FOR A CHILD UNDERGOING SURGERY

Pre-operative preparation

Operative procedures are frightening for adult patients and even more so for the child and his family. It is important that the nurse spends time with the patient and family in the pre-operative period to allow them to express their feelings and to clarify anything they have not understood. Emotional support for both the child and family is important at this time.

Maintaining a safe environment

- Safety precautions are observed in the pre-operative period in the same way as for an adult patient.
- One of the hazards the nurse has to be aware of is that the child may be fed by another child in the ward during the time when oral intake is stopped. If the child is too young to understand, and the parents are not available, then the nurse has to maintain a constant watch on the child to ensure nothing is taken orally.

Communicating

- Full understanding of the operative procedures should be given to the parents by the doctor. Postoperative nursing regimes are explained by the nurse and any equipment which will be used shown to the parents and child when appropriate.
- Talking to the parents of another child having had similar surgery should provide the parents with reassurance.
- It is often possible for the child to take a favourite toy to the theatre with them. The doll or teddy may be prepared in the same way as the child to provide reassurance for the patient.
- Once the child has had the premedication the parents should be encouraged to sit with him until he is ready to be taken to the anaesthetic room.
- The child may be pushed in his bed or cot to the theatre suite. Occasionally he is carried to the theatre by one of the parents. In either case the parents should be allowed to accompany the child and nurse to the theatre and to stay until the child has been anaesthetized, if they wish.

- The anaesthetic room may be a frightening place for a child. If it is possible, mobiles and murals on the ceiling may help to alleviate some of the fears experienced by the child.

Postoperative care

Maintaining a safe environment

- Safety for the child, like the adult, is important. Once the child is able to maintain his own airway, parents may be allowed to sit with the child if they wish. It is reassuring for the child if his parents are present when he first wakes up.
- The parents require reassurance that all is well with their child and will want to see the surgeon as soon as possible to find out the outcome of surgery.
- Pain levels in a child are difficult to determine. A fretful child, as a rule, is uncomfortable. This often means pain. Analgesia is given as prescribed and its effects carefully monitored.

Eating and drinking

- It is important that the parents realize that feeding the child too soon after anaesthesia may result in vomiting. They are then not tempted to overindulge the child with fluids too soon.

Personal cleansing and dressing

- The parents are encouraged to wash the child's face and hands and change him into his own nightwear as soon as is practicable. Handling of the child by a familiar, loving pair of hands may help to ease his fears.
- Observations of the child's extremities and vital signs are continued as necessary.

CARE OF THE CHILD WITH ORTHOPAEDIC PROBLEMS OF THE HIP JOINT

Diseases affecting the developing hip joint are of concern to the orthopaedic surgeon because, if not treated sufficiently early and with success, mobility and ambulation may be hindered at a later date. The nurse needs to understand the importance of maintaining the prescribed treatment and of providing support for both the child and the parents during this time.

Congenital dislocation of the hip

In congenital dislocation of the hip (see Figure 9.3) the femoral head is at first dislocatable. Once the soft tissues surrounding the hip joint have begun to accommodate the femoral head in its abnormal position, the hip becomes permanently dislocated.

The condition is more common in girls than in boys and more often unilateral than bilateral. There is some evidence to suggest there may be hereditary and hormonal factors which influence the condition. The true cause of the condition has not yet been established.

For correct anatomical growth to take place between the femur and the acetabulum, it is important that the two components of the hip joint form an early, correct relationship with each other. Therefore the earlier treatment for this condition is started the better the results.

The condition may be diagnosed in the newborn baby by the use of Ortolani or Barlow's test. These tests are performed by the doctor or midwife within hours of the birth of a baby. If the femoral head is found to be dislocatable then the orthopaedic surgeon will be notified and treatment started.

Different surgeons use different methods and each one needs to be treated on its own merits.

Nonoperative treatments

Splintage: To hold the head of the femur in the acetabulum. This will allow any lax ligaments to tighten and to then retain the head of the femur in correct anatomical alignment.

This may be achieved by one or other of the following splints:

1. *Von Rosen Splint*.   This is an 'H' shaped splint made of malleable metal covered in a waterproofed material. The splint is bent around the child's body and limbs. The child's hips are held in wide abduction and external rotation. The splint is worn for 24 out of 24 hours and never removed by anyone other than trained personnel (see Figure 9.4).

2. *Pavlik harness*:   This is a supple leather harness lined with a fleecy material which allows the baby a greater degree of freedom than the more rigid Von Rosen Splint. The child's hips are held in abduction. Normal movement of the hips is permitted and this encourages normal development of the hip joint (see Figure 9.5). Nursing care of a baby in this type of splint is similar to that for a Von Rosen Splint (see page 93), except that the baby cannot be bathed as normal. The harness must be kept dry so the parents are taught to wash the child all over each day instead of immersing the baby in water.

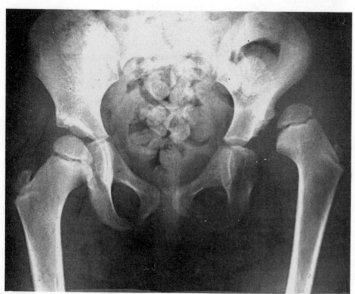

Fig. 9.3   Congenital dislocation of the hip.

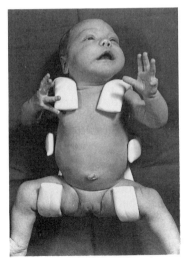 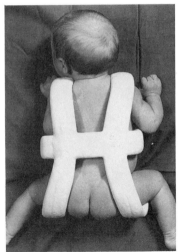

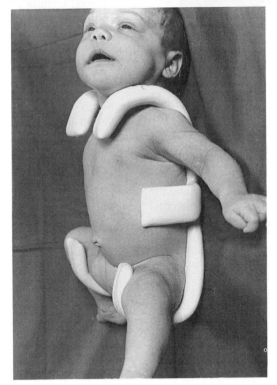

Fig. 9.4   A child in a Von Rosen splint.

3. *Frejka pillow and Putti's mattress*: Both these devices are similar to each other. They are both solid wedges, placed between the child's legs, held in place by straps. The baby's hips are again held in abduction and external rotation. The devices are removed each time the baby's nappy needs changing and then replaced by the parents.

Nursing care for the child in a Von Rosen Splint

The parents of the child need a very careful

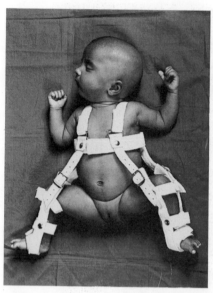

Fig. 9.5 Pavlik harness used for the treatment of congenital dislocation of the hip.

explanation by the doctor of how the splintage will help the baby. The nurse needs to be present during this explanation to reinforce the doctor's words and repeat explanations when necessary. Both parents require a great deal of reassurance to allay their fears and anxiety.

The baby is often only a few weeks old and the relatively new, proud parents suddenly find their child has a 'deformity'. Without care, handling the child may alternatively be rejected by them or the parents' own marriage may go through a serious stress period.

Maintaining a safe environment

- Handling the child in the splint as normal is vital for bonding to continue between mother and baby. Regular cuddling and playing with the baby are essential for normal intellectual development of the child to continue. The baby is often the firstborn child of a family so that handling young babies may be a new experience for both parents.

Personal cleansing and dressing

- Normal clothing is put onto the baby over the splint. It is important when changing the child's nappy to support the baby under his

buttocks instead of holding the baby's legs by the ankles.
- Normal washing and careful drying is encouraged after changing a soiled nappy, with particular attention paid to the creases found around the baby's buttocks and thighs.
- The baby may be bathed as normal in the splint. When the splint is applied there should be sufficient room between it and the baby for fingers to be carefully inserted. This allows the splint and the baby to be carefully dried following a bath. The nurse must make sure the parents are competent in achieving this before the baby leaves hospital.

Eating and drinking

- Normal feeding routines are established and continued.
- It is unusual for these babies to be treated in hospital. The parents need to be confident in the care of their child before they leave the hospital. They need to be given written details of who to contact in an emergency or if they are at all anxious over the baby. Good liaison and communication between the hospital and the community services are essential for the continued care of these children.

Closed manipulation of the hip joint

This is sometimes attempted within the first few months of life, but this method of treatment is not suitable for children over nine months of age as there is a danger of damaging the blood supply to the femoral head.

Following a reduction, the hips are held in the optimum position by the application of a frog plaster or batchelor plaster.

Frog plaster

A frog plaster extends from the nipple line to the ankles. The hips are held in full abduction and external rotation and the knees are flexed to the correct angle to maintain the hips in position.

Batchelor plaster

A batchelor plaster extends from groin to ankle on each leg. The hips are held in extension and internal rotation. A bar is then placed between the patient's legs and plastered into position (see Figure 9.6).

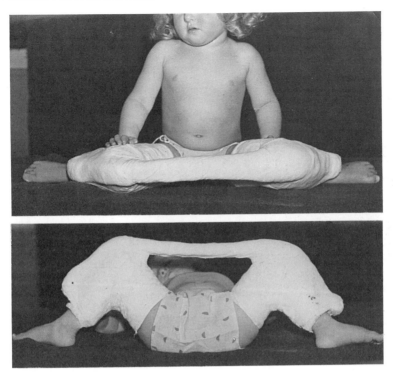

Fig. 9.6 Batchelor plaster showing wide abduction maintained by the broomstick incorporated in the plaster.

Nursing care of a child in plasters

- The child is placed on a firm-based cot on three waterproofed pillows covered with towelling. They are placed to support the plaster while it is drying. A kidney dish is placed between the pillows on the bed to catch urine and thus prevent soiling of the plasters while they are wet. A nappy can be placed over the genitalia and tucked under the plaster. This must be changed frequently.
- The child is turned every three hours until the plaster is fully dry. This may take up to 48 hours. When turned prone it is important to ensure the child's toes are not obstructed by any object.
- Normal observations of any patient in a wet plaster are maintained. The child's parents are encouraged to handle the child and to cuddle him, even while the plaster is wet. This is also encouraged even if an intravenous infusion is in situ.
- Once the plaster is dry, waterproof tape can be applied to the plaster around the genital area to prevent the plaster from soiling.
- Normal activities for the child, within the

limits of the splintage, are encouraged to allow for normal development to take place.
- It is essential to check the plaster frequently to ensure it is in good repair.
- Once the child's parents are confident in the care of the child in its plaster, they are discharged from hospital. All the equipment necessary to care for the child should be lent from the hospital. This should include a supply of nonabsorbant cotton wool which is placed around the child's toilet area to prevent urine tracking under the plaster. Specially adapted pushchairs or prams are available to allow the child to be wheeled out (see Figure 9.7).
- Contact with other children is important for normal development to be continued.

TRACTION

If early splintage is ineffective in reducing and maintaining the dislocated hip, then traction may be employed to achieve a satisfactory result.

The aim of using traction, if the hip is permanently dislocated, is to apply a gentle force

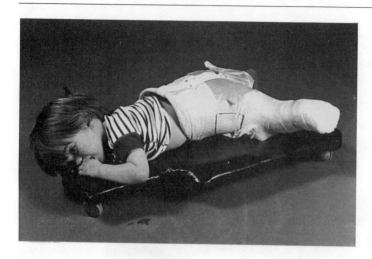

Fig. 9.7   Child on a platform with castors to allow mobility.

to the limb to stretch the soft tissues and to pull the head of the femur down opposite the acetabulum.

Children with congenital dislocation of the hip walk later than the normal stage of walking. They have a limp and the Trendelenberg's test is positive.

GALLOWS TRACTION

Adhesive or nonadhesive extension tapes are applied to the child's legs from the malleoli to above the knee joint. Even if only one hip is affected, traction is applied to both. This prevents an uneven pull on the good hip. A polythene back splint may be bandaged to the child's legs to prevent hyperextension of the knee joint. The extensions are generally applied 24 hours before the traction. This allows both the child and the parents to become accustomed to them and to observe for any allergic reactions the child may have to the materials used. A cord is attached to the extension tapes through a spreader.

The child's legs are suspended at right angles to the trunk to an overhead beam by means of weight and pulleys. The child's buttocks must be at least two fingers' width clear of the mattress. The child's body weight provides counter traction.

The child very rapidly adapts to its 'upside down' position.

Specific nursing care of a child in Gallows traction

Maintaining a safe environment

- Safety of the child is of prime importance. Children have a tendency to twist their trunks and tangle up the traction. Therefore regular observation of the traction every four hours is important to ensure the cords are running freely over the pulleys.
- If the extensions are nonadhesive they may be removed once a day for an hour. The child's legs are, at this time, washed, dried and gently massaged. If adhesive extensions are used the child's traction should be removed for the same length of time each day.
- The parents are encouraged to be present during this period. It provides an excellent opportunity for the child to be cuddled and played with.

Eating and drinking

- In spite of his position, eating and drinking are rarely a problem for the child. Normal diet and fluids for his age group are continued.

Eliminating

- Urine may back track during elimination. Nonabsorbant cotton wool placed around the child's buttocks may prevent this. Careful cleansing and drying of the genitalia will prevent soreness occurring.

- Particular attention needs to be paid to the occiput and scapulae while in traction as pressure is put on these areas and they are at risk from forming sores.

Working and playing

- Play is essential for a child in traction. While confined to bed, mobiles and story reading are helpful. The ceiling of a children's ward provides an area where interesting murals may be displayed. Toys and mobiles can be suspended from an overhead beam.

PUGH'S TRACTION

Skin extensions are applied to each leg and bandaged into position. The foot of the bed is elevated to an angle of 45 degrees by the use of a board under the mattress. Weights may be attached to the extensions by a cord through a spreader, or the cords may be tied to the end of the bed. This practice varies from centre to centre, according to the local surgeon's preference.

Children in Pugh's traction frequently find lying prone more acceptable than lying supine. The child's legs may be abducted slightly each day according to the doctor's wishes, until the desired degree of abduction is achieved.

Care of a child in a Pugh's traction

Nursing care is similar to that for Gallows traction. A harness is often put onto the child as a safety measure to prevent them falling over the side of the bed. Permission to use a harness must be sought from the child's parents and the paediatrician.

Traction provides slow reduction. There may be an infolding of the acetubular labrum which prevents successful reduction of the hip. This is seen if an arthrogram is carried out on the child's hip. The labrum, known as a limbus, is surgically removed by a limbusectomy.

Once reduction is complete, several courses are open to the doctor. If the hip joint is not stable, surgical intervention in the form of an osteotomy of either the femur or pelvis may be necessary to provide a stable joint. This is followed by immobilization in either a double or one-and-a half hip spica, with the hip held in a stable position. The cast is kept on for up to twelve weeks. The child's parents are taught how to handle the child in a wet plaster. The child is brought to the outpatient department every three weeks to check that the plaster is intact. At the same time it is ascertained that the parents are coping with the child at home.

Once the doctor is satisfied with the healing of any surgical measures and with the position of the limb, the child is mobilized very gradually. During the period of immobilization a reabsorption of calcium from the child's bones may have taken place. This leaves them osteoporotic and weak. Any sudden movement or spasm will result in a fracture, often in the supracondylar region of the femur. Very slow mobilization is therefore advisable. Each child's mobilization is individual to that child. He is gently weaned out of the plaster as children frequently feel insecure once the plaster is removed.

The plaster cast is bivalved and the child's leg carefully washed, patted dry and then bandaged into the posterior shell for 24 hours. When washing the child's legs a second person should place a hand gently over the child's knee to prevent sudden movement.

The physiotherapist will then start passive exercises.

During the next few days the child is turned prone and the posterior shell removed for short periods of time. The child is then returned to the posterior shell. Slowly, during the next few days, the child's legs are allowed to become more active. Warm baths and hydrotherapy are useful aids. It may be necessary to introduce hydrotherapy gradually in the form of water therapy. A 'lobster pot' walking device is helpful to encourage walking movements without full weight being taken on the legs.

PERTHES DISEASE

Perthes disease (Legg–Calve–Perthes disease, pseudo coxalgia) is one of a group of conditions called 'osteochondritis' (formally known as 'osteochondrosis'). It is characterized by avascular necrosis of the capital epiphysis of the femoral head (see Figure 9.8).

Many children are admitted to the orthopaedic children's ward with a diagnosis of irritable hip. Some of these children's problems will resolve following a few days rest in bed with gentle traction applied to both legs. For some

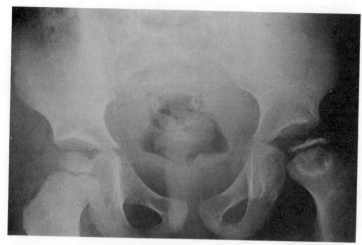

Fig. 9.8 Perthes' disease showing abnormality of right femoral head.

children the diagnosis will be Perthes disease and these require further measures.

Perthes disease affects boys more than girls. Commonly if affects one hip, although in some cases both may be involved. The affected age ranges from three to twelve years old. The course of the disease may take up to three years to complete.

The aim of treatment is to protect the femoral head from weight bearing stresses during the various stages of the disease. If the femoral head is subjected to weight bearing during the crucial 'soft' period of the disease, it will become abnormally shaped (usually mushroom shaped). This will affect normal use of the hip by the child.

The child's general health is good and this must be maintained during treatment.

Treatments vary according to the x-ray signs and the doctor's preference. Most children are treated as out-patients once treatment has been established.

Nonoperative treatments

- Rest in bed with bilateral skin traction. As the disease process takes up to three years to complete, this treatment is used only in the early stages while diagnosis is being confirmed to relieve pain and overcome muscle spasm. It was the chosen treatment in earlier years but it is now thought undesirable to confine children to bed for 2–3 years during their formative years.
- Orthoses, such as a Thomas patten-ended caliper (see Figure 9.9), Snyder sling or Harrison (Birmingham) splint (see Figure 9.10).
- Petrie plasters (see Figure 9.11).

NURSING CARE FOR A CHILD IN AN ORTHOSIS

The orthoses are all designed to relieve weight on the affected femoral head, prevent deformity and preserve the normal contours of the femoral head while recovery is taking place.

The child mobilizes on crutches whenever possible. Very young children will not be able to use crutches.

- Maintaining safety for a child in an orthosis on crutches is important. The child and his parents must be taught how to use the crutches safely before leaving the department.
- The child will need a well-fitting shoe for the unaffected leg.
- The child's parents will need to be made aware of the necessity of maintaining a safe environment for the child at all times.
- Care of the orthosis is taught to both the child and his carer. Vigilant observations of the state of the splint are essential, otherwise it will fail to achieve the desired result.
- The skin under the orthosis needs to be washed each day and inspected for signs of rubbing. The skin is carefully dried. The use of powder avoided as this may cause undue pressure on the skin if too much is applied.
- It is important that the child assumes a good

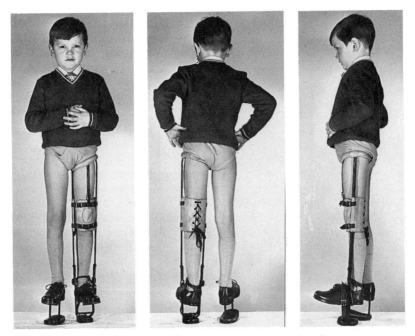

Fig. 9.9 Patten-ended weight-relieving caliper with compensatory patten to right foot.

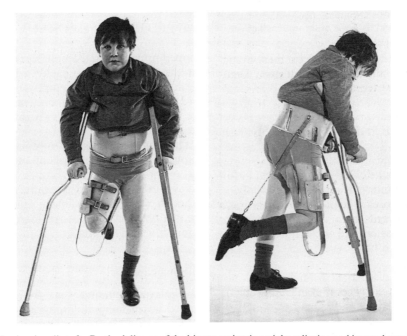

Fig. 9.10 Harrison's splints for Perthes' disease of the hips to maintain weight-relieving and internal rotation and movement of the hip. Note use of staggered crutch.

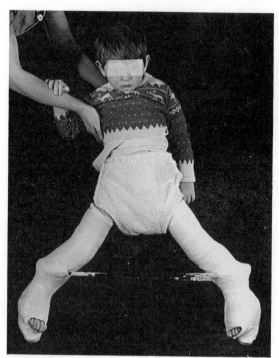

Fig. 9.11 Petrie plaster. Note the abduction and internal rotation of the hips and the angle of the walking heels.

posture when walking with crutches. Spinal exercises are taught to maintain good alignment of the vertebral column.

NURSING CARE FOR A CHILD IN PETRIE PLASTERS

In Petrie plasters the child's legs are fixed in full abduction and internal rotation by applying plaster of Paris to each leg and incorporating a broomstick between them. Walking heels are applied to the plasters and the children learn to move around with help.

- The child is discharged from hospital once the plasters are dry, comfortable and causing no problems to the child.
- The child's parents are instructed how to inspect the plasters each day for signs of rubbing or cracking.
- Written as well as verbal instructions on the care of the plasters should be available to parents.
- The child will be admitted to hospital at three-monthly intervals. The plasters at this time will be bivalved. Exercises to enable the

child's knee joint to be mobilized will be taught by the physiotherapist. The nurse supervises these exercises.
- As the disease affects children who are growing, new plasters need to be reapplied to accommodate growth.

OPERATIVE TREATMENTS

Pelvic or femoral osteotomies may be performed to contain the femoral head within the acetabulum.

Immobilization of the hip joints in either a double or one-and-a-half plaster hip spica follows surgery for 6–8 weeks. The child is then gradually mobilized to full weight bearing following removal of the spica.

Surgical intervention leads to minimal disturbance of the child's normal lifestyle.

The nursing care will cover the pre-operative and postoperative care for a child.

SLIPPED UPPER FEMORAL EPIPHYSIS

Slipped upper femoral epiphysis (adolescent cox vara) is a downward and backward displacement of the capital femoral epiphysis (see Figure 9.12). It occurs most commonly in boys between the ages of 12 and 15 years. It may be acute or chronic in nature.

The aim of treatment is to replace the slipped epiphysis, if possible, to maintain the reduction and restore joint function.

Treatment is most commonly surgical, although a period of skeletal traction may be used in chronic cases to try to reduce the slip before internally fixing.

Nursing care

The relevant nursing care for a child with slipped upper femoral epiphysis is as follows:

- Maintenance of the traction, if used.
- Following surgery the child is confined to bed until the pain has subsided. This may not be longer than 48 hours. Diversional therapy is important at this stage.
- The patient is nursed free in bed. All nursing care is carried out according to the nursing care plan to meet his needs.

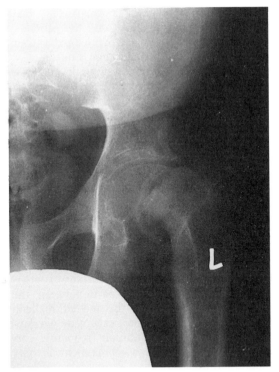

Fig. 9.12   Adolescent coxa vara: x-ray showing left slipped femoral epiphysis.

- Sutures are removed from the wound once it has healed, at about 10–14 days.
- The child is then mobilized on crutches, partial or nonweight bearing, until fusion of the epiphysis is complete. Once fusion is seen to be complete by x-ray examination, exercises are commenced and gradual weight bearing is started.

The condition is usually unilateral. Some surgeons will prophylactically pin the unaffected hip as there is an incidence of the unaffected femoral epiphysis slipping at a later date. Some surgeons prefer to adopt a 'wait and see' policy. Whichever method is used, the child is followed up in the outpatient clinic at regular intervals until skeletal growth is complete.

CARE OF THE CHILD WITH ORTHOPAEDIC PROBLEMS OF THE KNEE JOINT

There are very few occasions when a child with an orthopaedic condition of the knee joint will be admitted to hospital. The majority of these children are treated as outpatients. This ensures that parents and children are separated for as short a time as possible. A small number of children may be admitted for an arthroscopy to diagnose knee problems following sports injuries.

The outpatient department of a hospital is the 'shop window' of the organization. It is the place where many people have their first encounter with the hospital and its personnel.

The nurse assumes many roles in the department including one of teacher, counsellor, adviser and public relations officer. A warm, friendly reception helps the patient and his family to feel welcome to the hospital. Clear signs and indicators, and clear directions from personnel, will avoid confusion for the patient.

General nursing care

The following nursing care is relevant for a child with an orthopaedic condition in the knee joint in the outpatient department.

Maintaining a safe environment

- Safety within the department is the first consideration. As for any children's ward, the department must conform to all safety regulations.
- A play area with toys, books, blackboards and crayons will help amuse the patient while waiting.
- Waiting time should be kept to a minimum. This is only possible if a careful appointment system is in use.

Communicating

- The nurse should be allowed time to spend with the patient and his family. This will allow them to express their fears and anxieties. The nurse will then be able to provide reassurance and practical help by either asking another member of the team to help, e.g., the medical social worker, or by providing equipment or explanation herself.
- Time spent with the child prior to being seen by the doctor will enable a relationship to be started with the nurse who is then able to provide support for the child and the parents during subsequent examinations. It will also enable the nurse to make a rapid assessment of the child and the family to ensure that

nursing care plans can be accurately written.
- Teaching the child and the parents how to care for a variety of splints or plasters may be part of the nurse's role. This may vary if the department has an after-care service available. The teaching role may include teaching the child how to manage crutch-walking and exercises to be performed by him.
- Advice on the current footwear, particularly following a course of treatment, is important.
- Arranging transport to and from the hospital may be necessary.
- If a child is to be admitted to hospital, then the nurse needs to advise on the arrangements for admission. Pre-admission teaching and assessment may form part of her role in the department. Liaison with the children's ward staff is important. Whenever possible a pre-admission visit to the ward should be arranged with the child and his parents.

Specific nursing care

The following specific nursing care is relevant for a child having operative measures of the knee joint.

Pre-operative care

- General pre-operative preparation is given.
- The child's knee may need to be shaved if required by the surgeon. This is rarely necessary as a child's legs are generally hairless.
- Toe nails need to be cleaned and cut across. Children often experiment with nail varnish on their toes. This must be removed to facilitate postoperative observations of the feet.
- Quadriceps strengthening exercises are taught to the child. These may be in the form of a game. They must be practised under supervision.

Postoperative care

- General postoperative regimes are maintained.
- Wound dressings are observed for soakage and any excessive oozing reported to the doctor.
- Plasters require routine drying and support.
- The child's toes are observed to ensure the

neurovascular status is normal. This may also be turned into a game for the patient.
- Quadriceps exercises are maintained as soon as the child is sufficiently conscious.
- Pain levels are closely monitored. Analgesia is given as prescribed and its effectiveness noted.
- The child is generally mobilized with crutches if weight bearing is to be avoided within two or three days of surgery. Safety is of prime importance at this stage.

MANAGEMENT OF CHILDREN WITH COMMON ORTHOPAEDIC KNEE DISORDERS

Genu valgum

This condition (knock-knee deformity) is characterized by a decreased space between the child's knees and when the medial malleoli cannot be brought together, except by overlapping the knees. The condition frequently corrects itself spontaneously. Treatment is only undertaken in severe cases.

Nonoperative treatment

Application of a mermaid splint.

Specific nursing care for child with mermaid splint. Correct application of the splint by the parents is essential. The nurse should ensure that the parents are competent to do this before they leave the outpatient department.
The splint is applied as follows:

1. The splint is only applied at night.
2. The child lies on the bed with his legs parallel, his patellae and feet pointing forwards.
3. The splint is placed between the legs and the straps fastened. Wool is placed around the child's knees to protect them.
4. The splint is bandaged firmly into place from the base of the toes to the groin.

During the day the child wears shoes with an inside raise. Exercises are taught to increase the muscle strength of the legs.

Operative treatments

These are only undertaken in very severe cases

and are generally tibial or femoral osteotomies.

Genu varum

This condition (bow-leg) is where the tibia deviates away from the midline. The condition frequently corrects itself spontaneously.

The specific role of the nurse is to reassure the parents that the condition will correct itself and to reinforce the doctor's advice.

Chondromalacia patellae

Chondromalacia of the patella is softening of the articular cartilage of the patella. It is a condition which is more common in girls than boys. The condition is characterized by pain and instability of the knee joint.

Nonoperative treatments

1. Quadriceps strengthening exercises.
2. Drugs in the form of mild analgesics and anti-inflammatory drugs.
3. Supportive bandages and occasionally plaster casts in the form of a cylinder may be used.

Operative treatments

Surgery is only undertaken in extreme cases.

1. 'Shaving' of the roughened cartilage and sometimes the medial femoral condyle.
2. Very occasionally a patellectomy may be undertaken.

SPECIFIC NURSING CARE OF A CHILD WITH CHONDROMALACIA PATELLAE

- Reassurance by the nurse that the condition is a self-limiting one.
- Any prescribed drugs need to be explained to the parents. The correct dosage and time of the dose is repeated to them.
- The nurse needs to make sure the parents know how to apply the bandages to the child's leg.
- The exercises must be taught to the child and the parents; not only how they are done, but when to do them.

CARE OF THE CHILD WITH ORTHOPAEDIC PROBLEMS OF THE FEET

As with many children's orthopaedic conditions, if a condition affecting the foot is not detected early enough the long-term effects may be devastating. The inability to buy comfortable shoes, to take place in sporting activities at school or to walk any distance are among the most dramatic effects seen.

Treatment, to be effective, starts as soon after birth as possible. The prognosis will then be relatively good.

The nurse's role in dealing with children affected by foot conditions is, again, one of support and teaching. Most patients will be treated as outpatients, only being admitted to hospital when surgery is necessary.

Congenital talipes equino varus (club foot)

This is a condition characterized by plantar-flexion of the ankle and the forefoot is adducted and inverted (see Figure 9.13).

Fig. 9.13 Double congenital talipes equinovarus.

The condition is diagnosed if the child's foot cannot be passively put through a full range of movement. It is generally diagnosed soon after the birth of the baby. New parents are often shocked by the discovery of the condition and require much support during the first few days of treatment. Much of the success of the treatment will depend on the perseverance of the parents. Careful explanation of the treatments by the doctor is important.

Club foot is one of the oldest recorded deformities. There have been many attempts at correcting it. One of the earliest was forceful manipulation which had disastrous complications such as fractures and ischaemia of the developing tarsal bones.

Modern treatments are aimed at gentle correction over a period of time. It is sometimes necessary to use a soft tissue release or lengthening of the Achilles tendon. Once correction is obtained it is usually maintained by night splintage until the child starts to walk.

If the condition persists or regresses until the child is walking, more drastic surgical intervention may be given. This may take the form of bony procedures to realign the tarsal bones and operative measures to lengthen tendons to accommodate the new positions of the bones.

Nonoperative measures are aimed at gently stretching the soft tissues of the foot until the deformity is held in an over corrected position. This may be achieved by the application of strapping to the affected foot or the use of plaster of Paris casts. Serial strapping may be used. If it is it can be soaked off at home by the parent prior to the appointment at the hospital. This saves the child distress in the hospital when the strapping is removed. The strapping can then be reapplied with the child's foot held in its new position.

Nursing care for a child having had either of these methods used is the same as for any child following application of strapping or plasters. The nurse must satisfy herself that the circulation to the child's toes is normal before leaving the department. The parents, as with all of these procedures, must be adequately prepared and confident of looking after their child before they leave the department. Parents must be made aware that the length of the treatment may be up to one year. This should then prepare them to accept the time constraints.

CARE OF THE CHILD WITH ORTHOPAEDIC PROBLEMS OF THE VERTEBRAL COLUMN

Any condition relating to the vertebral column has an underlying fear that the spinal cord will somehow or other be involved. In the case of a child this is particularly relevant to the parents who see their child as being paralysed to a greater or lesser extent.

The nurse must listen to these fears and provide support for the parents whenever necessary. The emotional state of the child should always be considered when he is faced with plans of treatment. Parental support and cooperation is vital. This can be obtained by careful explanation of the condition by the doctor.

Scoliosis

Scoliosis is one of the more common conditions affecting the vertebral column which the orthopaedic nurse will see (see Figure 9.14). It is a lateral curvature of the spine accompanied by rotation of the vertebral bodies to one side. The resulting deformity is a 'C' or 'S'-shaped curve usually occurring in the thoraco-lumbar area. There is frequently a rib hump which occurs on the convex side of the major curve. In the early stages of the condition the deformity may be the main complaint.

Other signs and symptoms may be slight at first, but as the severity of the curve increases these may become more severe. There may be an aching pain in the back and eventually, due to the decrease in space of the thoracic cavity, respiratory and cardiac complications may follow.

The condition occurs at any age. If it is first noticed during the first few years of life the prognosis is poor.

The most common time for it to be noticed is during the pre-adolescent or adolescent period. The following management reflects that which may be used for this age group. It is commoner in girls than boys at this time. For girls the condition occurs at a particularly vulnerable age, when they are also facing physical and emotional changes. Suddenly to discover they have a curved spine may have severe psychological complications for them. It is difficult for them to accept a deformity they cannot see. Depression and withdrawal from their peer group are two such adverse effects which may be seen.

With the establishment of screening programmes many more children are diagnosed at an early stage of the condition.

The nurse needs to develop a sympathetic yet commonsense approach to these patients. She has to ensure that exercises are adhered to, orthoses are worn as necessary and normal routine development continues.

The child and the family faced with the diagnosis of scoliosis suffer all sorts of reactions from disbelief to panic.

Nonoperative treatments for patients with scoliosis

1. *Exercise* is aimed at strengthening spinal and abdominal muscles. The exercises help to retain mobility of the spine and to prevent the curve increasing.

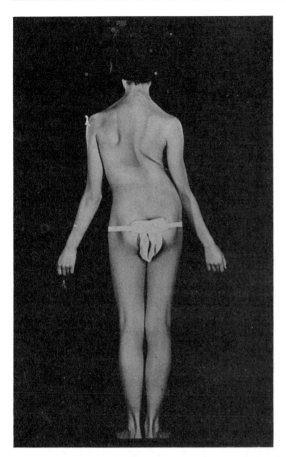

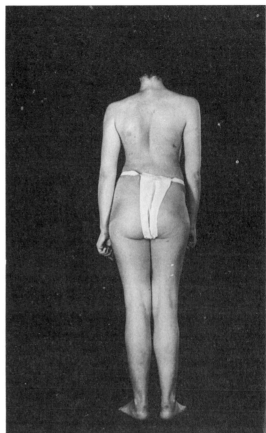

Fig. 9.14   Scoliosis showing curve to the left: (a) before and   (b) after surgery.

2. *Spinal orthoses* are many and varied. They are all used to hold the curve and to prevent it deteriorating. These devices are worn until skeletal maturity is achieved, unless operative measures are undertaken:

(a) *Milwaukee brace* is a formidable device which extends posteriorly from the occiput to the pelvis and anteriorly from the chin to the pelvis (see Figure 9.15). The child needs to be under the supervision of a dental surgeon to ensure that the growth of the lower jaw and teeth continues normally. The orthosis is worn for 23 out of every 24 hours.

(b) *Boston brace and Cotrell brace* are both made of synthetic materials and fit more closely to the trunk. They are largely hidden by clothing. Both are worn for 23 out of 24 hours.

(c) *Halo traction* is a metal skeletal traction device used usually prior to surgical intervention. Four pins are inserted into the skull under general anaesthesia. A halo is fitted around the four pins. Skeletal pins are then inserted into the pelvis or femur and held in place by a hoop, thus providing traction between two fixed points. These children are generally kept in hospital. Their nursing care is the same as for anyone in skeletal traction. Observations of their neurological status must be maintained due to the skull traction.

Nursing care for a child with scoliosis treated nonoperatively

Maintaining a safe environment

● It is important that the nurse has full

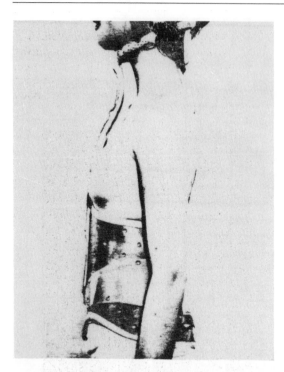

Fig. 9.15 The Milwaukee brace modified by Moe showing distraction obtained between the pelvis and the head.

knowledge of how the orthosis works and how it is applied. This will enable her to instruct the parents and the child on the reapplication of the device.

- Maintenance of each orthosis is important. The Milwaukee brace can be adjusted to allow for growth. Its pelvic girdle needs to be kept clean and dry. Both the Boston and Cotrell braces can be sponged to make sure they are clean. Buckles and straps on the Boston brace need to be checked to make sure they are safe. The Cotrell brace can be adjusted to allow for growth. The screwdriver necessary to release a child from the Cotrell brace should be kept safely and everyone have knowledge of where it is kept.

Communicating

- The nurse needs to allow the patient and the parents time to talk about the problems as they see them. The child in particular may find it difficult to adjust to wearing an orthosis.
- All possible information must be given to the patient before leaving hospital.

- If it is possible to introduce another child wearing a similar device to the patient, this may help. Parents also can gain confidence from talking to other parents.
- Local support groups and the national support group will help to allay fears. The nurse should have access to the addresses of these organizations to pass on to parents.

Breathing

- When the orthosis is first fitted the child may have some difficulty in breathing. Teaching him to take slow deep breaths and to remain calm will help to overcome this.

Eating and drinking

- Eating and drinking should not present any problems. If the child complains of feeling full he should be encouraged to take smaller meals. A nutritious healthy diet is important.

Eliminating

- Eliminating may be difficult at first until the patient becomes accustomed to the restrictions of the orthosis.

Personal cleansing and dressing

- The child is allowed out of the orthosis for one hour. During this time, showers or baths may be taken and the child's hair washed. Inspection of the child's skin for signs of pressure must be made at this time. Any reddened areas should be carefully dried and a light dusting of talcum powder applied. Some doctors advocate applying surgical spirit to the skin to prevent chafing from the orthosis; some allow a small light vest to be worn under the orthosis.
- The Boston and Cotrell braces do not allow for escape of sweat and this may encourage rashes to appear. If this happens the orthosis must be carefully sponged and dried before reapplication. Calomine lotion will help to cool the skin before the orthosis is reapplied.

  The Milwaukee brace may cause sores under the chin and on the occiput, so particular care should be taken of these areas.
- In spite of the fact that the Boston and Cotrell braces are hidden by clothes, these

children are very conscious of the fact that they are wearing them. Clothing should be chosen with care to help disguise this fact, but at the same time should attempt to be fashionable.

- High heeled shoes should be discouraged at all costs.
- Bed sheets may be damaged, in particular by buckles. It is important that the nurse warns the parents of this so that they are prepared should this happen.

Mobilizing

- Children wearing a Boston or Cotrell device should be encouraged to take part in swimming. Obviously if they are to do this there must be someone present who is able to reapply the orthosis following this activity.
- During the hour the orthosis is removed the exercise programme is continued.

Expressing sexuality

- Expressing sexuality is difficult for these children. They have a need to remain attractive to the opposite sex, but with their deformity and brace they soon have a wish to hide. It is important that the nurse and the parents encourage these children to retain an active social life and to mix normally with their peer group.

Sleeping

- Sleeping will present problems at first until the child adjusts to the brace. It may help if a board is placed under the child's mattress to help support him.

Operative measures for surgery

Criteria for surgery varies but frequently surgery is undertaken for those patients whose curve has increased to 45 degrees, even if skeletal maturity has been reached. This is because a curve of this degree may go on increasing even though growth has ceased.

Surgical intervention uses a spinal fusion usually with a metal rod to help achieve stability of the spine in a functional position. The other aim of surgery is to provide a cosmetically acceptable appearance of the patient's back.

The surgical methods currently used are:

1. *Harrington rod instrumentation*   Harrington rods are placed either on the convex side of the curve as a compressive force, or on the concave side as a distractive force. Bone is then used to provide a bony fusion (see Figure 9.16).

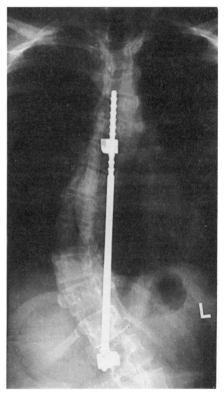

Fig. 9.16   The Harrington rod in situ.

2. *Dwyer cable instrumentation*   This type of surgery is performed through an anterior approach. Intervention is through the rib cage which may permit pulmonary complications.
3. *Luque wire instrumentation*   This is also known as segmental spinal instrumentation. It is performed through a posterior approach and involves wires around the laminae with supporting metal rods down the length of the affected area. Application of orthoses or plaster casts following surgery is not often necessary.

Specific nursing care for patients undergoing surgery for scoliosis

No spinal surgery is without risk. This should

be explained to the parents and the child by the doctor before the consent to operate is completed. The nurse assigned to the patient should be present to lend her support to the child during this time.

- Several investigations may be undertaken prior to surgery. The nurse must be aware of these and be prepared to support her patient through them.
  They include:
  (i)   Pulmonary function tests.
  (ii) Electrocardiogram.
  (iii) Myelogram.
  (iv) Moire fringe photography.
- It is important that all the factors relating to prevention of infection are taken into account.
- Careful psychological preparation of the child and the parents is important. A full explanation of the pre-operative and postoperative regimes by the nurse will help them to understand what is happening. The patient will already have gone through a period of having to adjust to his condition. The nurse needs an insight into the anxieties these children experience about being 'different' and feeling 'alone'.
- Routine deep breathing exercises and exercise for limbs are taught and practised. Deep breathing is particularly important if an anterior approach is to be used by the surgeon.
- An explanation that an indwelling catheter will be in place following surgery must be given. This is used to monitor accurately the urinary output of the child and to prevent the discomfort of using a bedpan in the early hours following surgery. It is far easier to introduce a catheter while the child is anaesthetized than to cause acute distress in either the pre-operative or postoperative period.
- Careful skin preparation is made. Some surgeons prefer the child to have several baths using an antiseptic solution. Research (7) on this is inconclusive as to whether bathing is effective. The child's hair is also washed at this time.

This type of surgery is usually a lengthy procedure and the child may be under anaesthesia for some time. During surgery a 'wake-up' test is sometimes performed where the anaesthetic is lightened to the degree where the child is asked to wriggle his toes. This determines the neurological state of the periphery. The anaesthetic is then resumed. Patients have no recollection of this test when recovered from the anaesthetic.

Specific postoperative nursing care

The following nursing care is for a patient who has had spinal surgery for scoliosis:

Maintaining a safe environment

- The child is nursed on a firm-based bed, flat, with one pillow to support the head. The legs are placed in foam troughs which help to reduce the lumbar lordosis.
- Blood loss is usually considerable. Replacement therapy is given through an intravenous line, usually into one of the patient's feet.
- Vital signs are recorded every fifteen minutes until they are within normal limits for the patient and stable.
- Paralysis is the fear of all spinal surgery. The neurovascular status of all extremities is observed and recorded every two hours for the first 24 hours and thereafter twice every day until the sutures are removed.
- The wound dressing is observed for signs of oozing. There is often some during the first few hours following surgery. Repacking over the existing dressing is carried out. If it becomes excessive the doctor is informed.
- To achieve inspection of the dressing the patient is turned onto his side by 'log rolling' so that the spine is kept in line and the patient does not twist.
- The sutures are frequently subcuticular and are removed at 10–14 days.
- The child's parents should be allowed to visit as soon as possible. This acts as a reassurance for all concerned.
- An overhead mirror is attached to the head of the bed to allow the child a view of the ward.

Breathing

- Gentle deep breathing exercises and encouragement to cough should be introduced as soon as possible for the child. If the nurse has formed a good relationship with the child, this will help to give the child confidence during this procedure.

- Pain from the operative site is not great, but pain from the bone donor site may be. Movement does, however, exacerbate any pain, and for the first 24 hours strong opiates are generally prescribed. These are given approximately 20 minutes before nursing care takes place to ensure the patient feels as little discomfort as possible. The effect of drugs given to any child should be closely monitored by the nurse.

Eating and drinking

- Paralytic ileus is another complication which may follow spinal surgery. Oral intake is withheld until the patient passes flatus or bowel sounds are present. Fluid intake is maintained by the intravenous route. Oral toilet is essential and should be carried out every two hours. Small pieces of ice to suck may help to relieve a dry mouth.

Eliminating

- Urinary output is observed and charted. Catheter toilet is performed every four hours.

Personal cleansing and dressing

- Care of the skin is necessary for the comfort of the patient and to prevent infection and breakdown. Pressure points are inspected for signs of pressure 3–4 hourly by 'log rolling' the patient.

The patient is encouraged to bath himself as much as possible. Movement of his arms to perform this task will help to exercise his muscles and joints. It is important that the parents and the nurse encourage the child as much as possible, within the limits of pain and discomfort, to be independent in daily activities. It is tempting, particularly for parents, to want to do everything for the child.

Mobilizing

- The patient starts mobilizing once the wound has healed and the sutures have been removed.
- Prior to mobilization a body cast may be applied to the child to support the vertebral column in its new position. An EDF* cast may be used. Application of the cast is a lengthy business and can be a frightening procedure for the patient.
- If individualized care has been planned, the patient and her nurse will have formed a bond of trust which will support the patient through the process of cast application. Once the cast has been applied it will take up to 96 hours to dry in a warm room. Once it is dry, pads are applied under the plaster to apply slight pressure in the rib hump to aid derotation of the vertebrae. The edges of the cast are trimmed to allow for free movement of the child's arms and to allow the child to sit down in comfort. The parents are taught how to change the vest under the cast.
- It is important to remember that the patient has been lying down for some time. Mobilization must therefore be gradual. When the patient sits upright for the first time they often feel giddy or nauseated. The child is often anxious to start walking, but short-term achievable goals should be set by the patient after talking to the nurse. It may take three or four days before the child is sufficiently safe in standing and walking before being discharged.

The cast is worn for up to six months. Regular hospital visits to the consultant are planned. Once the cast is removed it is sometimes followed by a plastic jacket which may be worn for up to a year following surgery.

CARE OF THE CHILD WITH SPINA BIFIDA

Spina bifida is a developmental failure of the neural arch of one or more vertebrae to fuse (see Figure 9.17). As a result, the meninges (meningocele) or the spinal cord and nerve roots (myelomeningocele) may bulge onto the patient's back. Hydrocephalus is often present and is treated with a ventricular shunt. The lesions are seen predominantly in the lumbosacral region of the spine (see Figure 9.18).

The orthopaedic deformities which may be present depend on the severity of the lesion. They include club foot (see Figure 9.19) and dislocation of the hip, both of which will present

*EDF = elongation, derotation and flexion.

NORMAL VERTEBRAE
Showing intact neural arch

SPINA BIFIDA
Least serious
defect

MENINGOCELE
Failure of fusion
allows protrusion
of the membranes

MYELOMINGOCELE
Sac containing spinal
cord

Fig. 9.17 Congenital abnormality in which the vertebral arch fails to fuse, thus allowing protrusion of the underlying membranes or even the spinal cord.

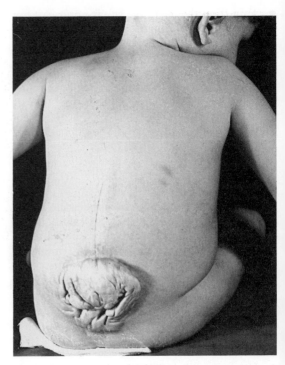

Fig. 9.18 A child with meningocele.

Nursing care of the child with spina bifida

Closure of the defect on the child's back is the first treatment which is undertaken. Following this the nursing considerations will be to promote healing of the area.

Maintaining a safe environment

- The baby is nursed prone to prevent undue pressure over the wound area which may cause breakdown of the skin.
- Particular attention is paid to elimination. Contamination of the wound by urine or faeces may lead to infection of the area. Therefore care is taken to ensure that urine does not 'back track'. Nappies are changed very frequently.

Medical treatments are sometimes delayed until after the child's first birthday and may continue for many years. Nursing considerations following surgical intervention are directed towards the prevention of complications in a paralysed patient.

- Because these children have insensitive skin over their paralysed limbs, a safe environ-

problems in any attempt to stand the child in an upright position. It is an aim of any treatment to attempt to make these children as independent as possible. Children with spina bifida are often not seen in orthopaedic centres until they are teenagers.

The degree of mental capacity of the child, and the willingness of the parents to support the child, need to be considered when the treatments are discussed.

The role of the nurse is aimed at maintaining communication between the child's parents and all members of the orthopaedic team. She helps to educate them about the likely associated problems and potential problems their child may encounter and encourages them to join support groups. The nurse is often a general 'sounding-board' for the parents and needs to spend time allowing them the opportunity and space to talk.

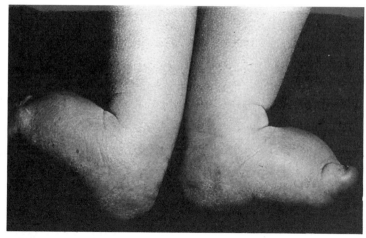

Fig. 9.19   Feet of a child with spina bifida showing calcaneovalgus.

ment is of prime importance. The skin is easily damaged by rough handling, by toys, or by sharp edges and corners. The child's pressure areas need to be relieved from pressure every two hours. Any sign of potential skin breakdown should be dealt with by increasing the length of time pressure is removed from the area.

- The skin is kept scrupulously clean over the buttocks and paralysed limbs.
- The ventricular shunt must be observed each day to ensure it is still in good working order. Twice weekly measurements of the circumference of the child's head will show if there is any increase in the hydrocephalus.

A nasal discharge, restlessness and fretfulness may indicate a block of the valve or the onset of meningitis. If the child complains of a headache it must not be ignored as this may be a sign of increased intercranial pressure.

Communicating

- Communications with the family will aid acceptance of the baby as an individual. Communication with all members of the health care team will enable continuity of care to be maintained.

Breathing

- It is important to keep the child free from chest infections. Vital signs should be recorded daily to monitor any rise in temperature. Visitors with colds should be discouraged from visiting.

Eating and drinking

- Normal bonding between the mother and baby should be allowed to take place. Support for the parents is important to allow them to accept the baby. This will enable the child to develop in a happy, loving atmosphere. Feeding times should be a time when both parents learn to handle the baby and to play with it.

Eliminating

- Care of the child's paralysed bladder is an important part of the nurse's role.

A high fluid intake in necessary. Gentle regular pressure over the suprapubic region may assist the bladder to empty. An ileal conduit loop may be surgically performed by the doctors. This is where the ureters are transplanted from the bladder into the ileum. The ileum is then brought through onto the abdominal wall. The urine drains into a specially adapted bag. This procedure is often used for females. The skin around the bag is carefully cleaned and suitably protected. Eventually the child will need to be taught to deal with this themselves. For males, a urinal is often attached directly to the penis.

- A child with a paralysed bowel needs to be trained to defaecate at a suitable, regular time. It is often necessary to administer an enema to the child every second day in order to achieve this. Older children may be taught to use manual evacuation.

Controlling body temperature

- Excessive heat may burn the insensitive skin of a child's paralysed limbs. Therefore hot water bottles or electric blankets should never be used to keep these children warm. Extra clothes or blankets are far safer.

Mobilizing

- Mobilizing is essential. The medical team's efforts are directed towards enabling the child to stand, even if walking is not possible. Encouragement from the nurse to the child to achieve this is important. Orthoses are often used to enable this activity to take place. It is important, because of the potential skin problems, that any orthosis used fits well and is kept in good repair and in good order.
- Finally, mental and physical stimulus is important to allow the child to develop as normally as possible. The nurse must encourage the child to take an active part in play therapy. Full exercise of all joints and limbs is important. Care must be taken when placing the paralysed limbs to ensure they are kept in a functional position.

CARE OF THE CHILD WITH SEPSIS OF BONES AND JOINTS

Acute osteomyelitis is an infection of bone occurring most commonly in boys under the age of 16 years. The condition occurs most frequently in the metaphyseal region of a long bone, often the tibia (see Figure 9.20). It is caused by a pyogenic organism, often *Staphylococcus aureus*. It is frequently taken to the bone from a primary focus of infection elsewhere in the body. The condition is then termed 'haematogeneous osteomyelitis'.

Chronic osteomyelitis may be the sequel to the acute form, or it may occur as a subacute or chronic disease itself.

Septic arthritis is an infection of the synovial membrane of a joint by a pyogenic organism.

In all cases the child is an ill child presenting a high fever, toxaemia, pain and occasionally a rigor.

Nursing care for a child with sepsis of bones and joints

Maintaining a safe environment

- The child should be nursed in a bed in either a quiet part of the ward or in a side room. It may be necessary to protect others from becoming infected, particularly if the primary focus is a sore throat.
- A cradle is used to take the weight of the bedclothes. Light nightclothes are worn by the child to encourage reduction of the child's temperature.
- Pain is a prominent feature. The affected limb may have traction applied to relieve muscle spasm and therefore reduce pain levels. A splint or a plaster back slab may be applied to the limb to provide support and rest for it. The limb is handled as little as possible, but when it is necessary, as gently as possible.
- Four hourly observations of the level of the child's temperature, pulse and respirations are recorded.
- Medical treatments will include intravenous therapy. Care and observations of the intravenous line are necessary. Intravenous antibiotics are given according to the prescription.

Eating and drinking

- The child is usually dehydrated. Fluid bal-

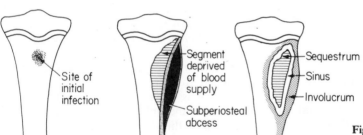

Fig. 9.20 The inflammatory process of osteomyelitis.

Site of initial infection

Segment deprived of blood supply

Subperiosteal abcess

Sequestrum

Sinus

Involucrum

ance is important. A careful check is made of all fluid intake and output and it is recorded on a fluid balance chart. Most fluid will be given intravenously as the child will, at first, not feel like taking fluids orally.

- A light, nourishing diet is offered to the child, although most children are anorexic in the early stages of this condition.

Eliminating

- Elimination may be limited. Due to the toxic condition of the child, urine is generally scant and constipation is also present. Both of these will resolve as the child's condition improves.

Controlling body temperature

- Tepid sponging may be attempted to reduce the child's fever. Iced drinks may also help this.
- Oral hygiene and mouth toilet should be very gently performed every two hours. Due to the fever and anorexia, the child's mouth may be furred and unpleasant. If the child is able to take them, citrus drinks may help to increase the flow of saliva and help to keep the mouth more pleasant for the patient.
- If antibiotic therapy is not successful within the first few days, surgery may be undertaken to release pus from the bone. Open drainage may be used or the wound covered with a dressing. The nurse will need to observe any dressing for soaking of pus or blood and redress accordingly.

Mobilizing

- Once the clinical signs have returned to within normal limits, mobilization of the child will start. Exercises for the unaffected limbs should start as soon as the child is well enough. Eventually the child may be allowed up, non-weight bearing on crutches without splintage, or weight bearing with a plaster cast on the affected limb.

REFERENCES

1. Anderson, B. (1979) *American Journal of Nursing.* Sept. 1979.
2. Platt Report (1959).
3. Tavistock Report (1982).
4. Court Report (1976).
5. Warnock Report (1978).
6. Hospital Building Act (1964).
7. Leigh D.A., Strong J.L., Marriner J. & Sedgewick J. (1983) Total body bathing with Hibiscrub in surgical patients: *Journal of Hospital Infection*, Vol. IV.

SUGGESTED FURTHER READING

Allum N., (1975) *Spina Bifida: The Treatment and Care of Spina Bifida Children.* London: Allen and Unwin.
Keim H.A. (1982) *The Adolescent Spine.* New York: Springer-Verlag.
Powell M. (1986) *Orthopaedic Nursing and Rehabilitation*, 9th edn. Edinburgh: Churchill Livingstone.
Weller B.F. & Barlow S. (1983) *Paediatric Nursing*, 6th edn. Nurses' Aids Series. London: Baillière Tindall.
Weller B.F. (1980) *Helping Sick Children Play.* London: Baillière Tindall.
Zorab P.A. (1970) *Scoliosis and Growth.* Edinburgh: Churchill Livingstone.

10

CARE OF THE PATIENT FOLLOWING TRAUMA

Nursing patients following trauma plays an increasingly large part in the orthopaedic nurses' role today. Many orthopaedic wards are filled with a majority of these patients, often at the expense of those patients waiting for elective surgery. They form the unpredictable numbers of patients which may need urgent admission to a hospital.

This chapter only gives a brief insight into the nursing care appropriate to some of the patients seen in the accident department and wards. Trauma nursing is a vast subject which can only be highlighted in this book. It is recommended that further reading in this subject is undertaken by any orthopaedic nurse specializing in this subject.

Statistics from road traffic accidents show a decline of approximately 10 000 over the period from 1978 to 1984 (see Table 10.1). Legal issues, such as the compulsory wearing of seat belts, crash helmets and drink and drive campaigns, have obviously had an effect. Total accidental deaths in 1984 (see Table 10.2) were 29 per cent lower than in 1961 (1).

The estimated cost of all road traffic accidents in Great Britain in 1984 was £2.7 billion. This included the cost for lost output, police and administration, medical and ambulance services, damage to property and an allowance for pain, grief and suffering.

FRACTURES

The following section deals with the local signs and symptoms which may be present in a patient with a fracture. This is followed by the patterns of fractures which may be seen, and the healing of bone following trauma. Nursing interventions which may be necessary for a patient admitted to hospital while this healing process takes place are then discussed. The section concludes by looking into the possible complications to which such patients may succumb.

Signs and symptoms of a fracture

If a fracture is suspected, the nurse should look for the following signs and symptoms:

1. Local features: Pain and tenderness due to the break in the continuity of bone, swelling caused by bleeding, bruising or blistering of the skin and deformity.
2. Abnormal mobility of the part.
3. Loss of function.
4. Soft tissue damage.

Patterns of fractures

The different patterns of fractures are illustrated in Figure 10.1. The cause of these fractures is set out in Table 10.3.

Table 10.2 Total number of *killed and seriously injured by age group for a ten year period.

Years	1974	1984
0–4	2 365	1 435
5–9	5 897	3 740
10–14	5 288	5 541
15–19	17 621	18 484
20–24	12 834	13 214
25–29	7 820	6 549
30–39	9 478	8 391
40–49	7 446	5 765
50–59	7 335	5 027
60 & over	12 780	10 512

Killed and seriously injured: Hospital patients, plus casualties with any fracture, internal injury, concussion, crushing, severe general shock, etc., plus death after 30 days.
All severities: 1974: 324 918
  1984: 339 673

Table 10.1 Total number of accidents in Great Britain on public roads, involving injury, which are reported to the police (2).

1974	1976	1978	1980	1982	1984
244 042	258 639	264 769	250 958	255 980	253 183

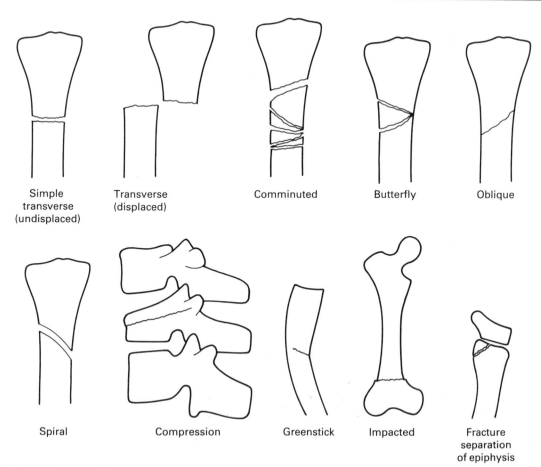

Fig. 10.1 Patterns of fractures.

Table 10.3   Type and causes of fracture.

Type of fracture	Cause/comments
Simple transverse (displaced) and transverse fractures	Often the result of direct violence
Comminuted fracture	More than three fragments
Butterfly fracture	Generally a stable fracture
Oblique and spiral fracture	May be as a result of rotational forces
Compression fracture	May be due to an indirect force, often from a fall from a height on to the heels
Greenstick fracture	Due to bending of immature bone, as seen in children
Impacted fracture	The direction of force causes two major fragments to be driven together
Fracture separation of epiphysis	Occurs in young people only prior to epiphyseal growth plates closing

A fracture is a break in the continuity of bone. It may be an open (compound) or closed fracture. It is caused by some form of violence, either directly at the point of injury or indirectly when a fracture occurs at a point distant to the impact (known as a nonpathological fracture). Pathological fractures occur in bones weakened by disease, e.g., Paget's disease, osteomyelitis, local tumour.

Open fractures provide a means for bacteria to gain entry into the body. The nurse needs to ensure that wounds are covered rapidly to reduce this risk. Patients with 'interesting' fractures need to be protected by the nurse from too many observers 'having a look'. Bone ends which may protrude through the skin need to be kept viable. The bone end is kept moist by applying a sterile pad over it which has been immersed in an antibiotic solution.

Fractured bones are dealt with by following the principles of reduction, realignment, restriction of movement, restoration of function and rehabilitation—the so-called 'five Rs'.

Reduction and realignment of a fracture take place only if it is necessary to enable function to be maintained and healing unimpaired. It may be by an open surgical method or by a closed manual method. The fracture may then be immobilized, if necessary, to maintain it in correct alignment. This may be by the use of plaster of Paris or some other form of external splintage. Open fractures are rarely internally fixed to maintain their alignment as this may increase the risk of infection. They may be held in place by the use of an external fixator, e.g., the Denham fixator or Oxford fixator.

The healing of fractures

Not all fractures require rigid immobilization. Some surgeons believe that movement between fracture ends encourages healing.

Different fractures heal at different rates. The age of the patient, the type of fracture and the general state of health of the patient are all factors which may influence the rate of healing of bone.

The bleeding which occurs at the bone ends, following a fracture in the bone, eventually forms a haematoma. This is the very beginning of healing and it is important to preserve this haematoma. This is the reason why nurses should handle limbs with suspected fractures very gently, and apply some form of temporary splintage as rapidly as possible.

Granulation tissue gradually replaces the haematoma as blood vessels from the surrounding soft tissues and periosteum invade the clot. Osteoblasts and osteoclasts are carried from the periosteum by these vessels.

Soft osteoid tissue, called callus, is eventually laid down between the fracture fragments. At this stage clinical union is said to have taken place. This may be seen by radiographs. However, the bone is not yet sufficiently solid enough for weight bearing to take place.

Gradually the callus becomes calcified as mineral salts are laid down. The bone is then remodelled and reshaped to as near normal as circumstances allow.

Nursing care

The following nursing care is relevant for patients in hospital during the immobilization period, waiting for fractures to heal.

Maintaining a safe environment

- To ensure the early stages of healing are allowed to develop, the means employed to immobilize the fracture must be maintained. Plasters are checked daily for signs of softening, or cracks. Walking heels are checked to make sure they are safe. Correct walking procedures with crutches or other aids are taught to the patient.
- Any traction or splints applied to the part are checked daily to make sure they are carrying out the function they have been applied for.

Communicating

- Knowledge of how the healing of bone takes place is explained to the patient to make sure he cooperates with his treatment and care.

Breathing

- The patient is encouraged to breathe deeply. Up to ten deep breaths every hour will ensure a good supply of oxygen to the tissues, and therefore promote healing of the fracture.

Eating and drinking

- The patient should be encouraged to eat a full nourishing diet. If at all possible a diet high in protein, calcium and roughage is beneficial. Milk drinks help to increase protein and calcium intake.

Personal cleansing and dressing

- The patient is encouraged to maintain his personal cleansing to a high degree to help prevent general infection occurring.

Mobilizing

- Passive and assisted exercise is performed for the patient if necessary to the joints close to the injured part. This will increase the blood supply to the area therefore promoting healing. It will further decrease the risk of such complications as a deep, venous thrombosis.
- Active exercises are taught to the patient as

Table 10.4   General complications of fractures.

General complications of long term immobilization of a patient with a fracture	Nursing actions to prevent onset of complications
Sores:	
Pressure	Relief of pressure from all points at regular intervals.
Splints or plasters	Accurate application of splints
(Due to immobilization)	and plasters. Observation of the principles of handling and care.
Renal problems:	
Urinary retention/ incontinence	Ensure the patient has an adequate fluid intake for his age and size. Maintain an accurate fluid balance chart.
Urinary tract infection due to immobilization and inadequate fluid intake and inability to maintain personal hygiene	Strict personal hygiene, assisting the patient whenever necessary. Weekly urinalysis.
Chest infection:	
Hypostatic pneumonia due to immobilization.	Teach the patient to take ten deep breaths each hour. Encourage venous return to the heart. Position patient so that breathing is unrestricted.
Confusion: usually in the elderly patient due to accident and removal from home routines.	Maintain normal home routine. Take time to talk to the patient. Encourage relatives and friends to visit the patient.
Thrombosis:	
Deep venous Coronary Cerebral (Due to immobilization)	Encourage the patient to take ten deep breaths per hour to maintain venous return. Active dorsi and plantar flexion of the patient's ankle joint for five minutes every hour.

Table 10.4   Continued.

General complications of long term immobilization of a patient with a fracture	Nursing actions to prevent onset of complications
Embolism:	
(Blood) pulmonary	As for thrombosis.
Fat, due to multiple fractures of long bones (A fat embolism is characterized by petechial haemorrhages within 72 hours of the initial injury. The patient may exhibit signs of mental confusion, tachycardia and restlessness.)	The doctor is notified and oxygen is administered at the first signs of onset. Regular checks of blood gases are monitored.
Myositis ossificans: (Bone deposits laid down in haematoma formation close to the fracture site), due to delayed reduction of the fracture, immobilization for an inadequate length of time and passive stretching of the patient's joint following healing of the fracture.	Ensure immobilization is maintained until the doctor decides to remove it. Encourage the patient to actively exercise the joints close to the injured part.
Tetanus: due to bacillus invading a deep, penetrating wound or an open fracture.	Ensure the patient is covered by antitetanus toxoid. Careful irrigation and cleansing of all penetrating wounds.
Gas gangrene: due to open fractures with extensive muscle damage.	Careful cleansing of all wounds.
Ischaemia: due to the interruption of the blood supply to an area (e.g., Volkmann's ischaemic contracture).	Check comparative pulses every 15–30 minutes. Observe the patient's extremities for colour, sensation and movement every 15–30 minutes. Make sure that bandages, splints and plasters are not constricting the flow of blood. Elevate the patient's limb to reduce swelling and therefore pressure.

soon as the doctor allows. The patient is then encouraged to carry these out.

Possible complications of fractures

Complications associated with fractures are di-
vided into general and local complications (see Tables 10.4 and 10.5). Specific complications will be discussed with individual fractures.

Table 10.5   Local complications.

Complication	
Delayed union	This is said to be present when the fracture does not unite within the expected time.
Nonunion	This is present when the fracture ends become rounded and sclerotic. The intervening space is filled with fibrous tissue and a painless, false joint occurs.
Malunion	The bone unites, but in a poor position.
Damage to nerves	This may happen at the time of the injury, or later.
Damage to blood vessels	This will result in haemorrhage and prompt life-saving techniques may need to be started. Damage may lead to avascular necrosis of surrounding structures and delay healing of the fracture.
Damage to skin and muscle	This may lead to delayed closure of wounds, loss of function and stability of neighbouring joints, and carries a risk of infection which may lead to osteomyelitis.
Osteoarthrosis	Particularly when the fracture extends into the joint surface.

ACCIDENT AND EMERGENCY DEPARTMENT

Not all patients seen in the accident department of a hospital will require admission. Many will be able to return to their homes for self care. They may, however, have sustained quite severe injuries which will necessitate them being off from their work for some months. Some of these patients may be left with a permanent disability as a result of their accidents, e.g., the machinist who sustains hand injuries may never return to his original job.

It must also be remembered by the orthopaedic nurse that injuries are not only sustained in road traffic accidents. Accidents in the home, at school, on the sports field, in a place of employment, and as a result of leisure activities, form a large part of the patients seen in an accident department.

The most recent statistics issued by the Department of Trade and Industry's Home Accident Surveillance System for accidents in the home are shown in Table 10.6.

Table 10.6   Department of Trade and Industry's Statistics on home accidents.

Type of case	Number in Great Britain
Fatal	5 500
Non Fatal	
Treated by hospital	2 200 000
Treated only by general practitioner	900 000*
Total	3 100 000

*Home Accident Surveillance System, 9th Annual Report, 1985 Data.

Age also has a part to play. With an increasingly elderly population, poor sight, decreasing inability to hear and an unsteady gait, many more elderly patients are being seen with a variety of traumatic problems.

The very young form a large proportion of the patients seen in an accident department. Between the ages of 1 and 19 years, accidental injury is the major cause of death. J.O. Forfar and G.C. Arneil (3) state that for every 1000 boys who leave school, 200 will be injured and three dead within ten years.

Drug and solvent abuse and the alcoholic patient pose particular problems for the nurse working in the accident department. There is an increased incidence of violence towards these nurses in the department from such patients. The stress levels of dealing with such accidents is obviously high and needs to be taken into consideration by any nurse working in an accident department.

Many complaints arise from the long waiting period patients have to undergo on admission to the accident department. Comfortable waiting areas, with provision for children to play, are important. If possible someone other than the nurse should be employed to supervise these children. Facilities to obtain a drink may also be of use, but it must be stressed that the patients who are waiting must never take any fluid until they have been seen by a doctor.

Because of the length of waiting time, it is important that there is always a nurse available, either close to, or at the admissions desk. The nurse will then be able to make a rapid assessment of the patient's condition and take a decision as to whether he requires immediate attention or can wait, and whether he can be placed on a stretcher or in a wheelchair or can walk to see the doctor. Any immediate observations of the patient's fingers or toes can be carried out. Whether the patient has a wound which needs covering or a sling which needs applying can also be assessed. The desk nurse (or triage nurse, as she is sometimes called) is also responsible for allocating the nursing team to the patients as they arrive in the department.

Most large hospitals have a written major incident policy. This relates to local conditions and the local fire, police and ambulance facilities. Rehearsals for a major incident are carried out to prepare the relevant services for action. All nurses working in the accident department must be aware of the part they have to play should such an incident occur.

NURSING MANAGEMENT OF PATIENTS IN THE ACCIDENT AND EMERGENCY DEPARTMENT

First aid takes place at the scene of the accident. It is important that nurses are familiar with the principles of first aid in case they are ever called upon to carry these out.

Many methods of forming a rapid assessment have been developed using a nursing model as a framework. Mike Walsh (4) states: 'After treatment, most accident and emergency patients return home, where self care becomes a reality.' He puts forward the case for using Orem's model in the accident department with conviction.

When the patient arrives at the accident department, the nurse receiving the patient needs to make a rapid assessment of the patient following the first aid principles. The patient needs to feel safe and comfortable. Reassurances are given to the patient. A sympathetic, but efficient, nurse will help to allay the patient's apprehension.

Ambulance personnel are experts in their job. If the patient has been brought to the hospital in an ambulance, the attendants will be able to provide a comprehensive history of the accident and the possible injuries the patient has sustained.

A clear airway is of paramount importance. It is the first thing to be checked by the nurse. Once this has been established, then signs of haemorrhage and injury are sought. Open wounds are covered with a clean, sterile dressing and left undisturbed until seen by the doctor. Any suspected fractures are splinted. Taking relevant data and ensuring relatives have been contacted are also carried out at this time.

The patient who has succumbed to injury has to make a rapid adjustment to his new situation. He has to learn to accept, without prior warning, discomfort and limitation of his normal activities of life. He suddenly finds himself unable to manage his own life. The patient will undergo emotional stress and will find himself, for some time, dependent on others.

The nurse working in the accident department of a hospital will not only have to deal with fractured bones. She will also see soft tissue injuries, sprained and dislocated joints, head, spine and chest injuries, to mention a few. To enable her to gain an insight into the possible complications of injury to a specific part of the body, she requires a reasonable knowledge of anatomy. For example, if the patient sustains a supracondylar fracture of femur, the nurse will be aware that the gastrocnemius muscle heads attach to the femoral condyles. This may cause a posterior displacement of the distal end of the femur. In turn, this may cause muscle spasm and intense pain for the patient. The nurse will have an understanding of why the patient is experiencing so much pain.

The pattern of the fracture will influence the way it is treated and immobilized. Knowledge of the patterns of fracture (see Figure 10.1) will assist the nurse with planning the care of her patient, e.g., an open or compound fracture may lead to osteomyelitis. Extensive soft tissue damage may lead to nonunion of a fracture if soft tissue is allowed to interpose between the fracture ends.

Observations of the patient's temperature, pulse rate, respirations and blood pressure are commenced. These will provide a baseline for future reference. They will also give information about the patient's present condition. Shock may be present and this is seen by a fall in the systemic blood pressure. The patient's pulse rate becomes rapid and feeble. His colour becomes pale and his skin feels cold and clammy. The patient's respirations become 'sighing'.

Shock is a physiological response of the body to injury, disease or emotion (see Table 10.7). It is a term which is used in many contexts. In injury, shock is most commonly caused by a haemorrhage. Often the haemorrhage is internal and not visible to the naked eye. Any patient with a fractured bone is liable to severe internal haemorrhage. This is a fact often ignored by nurses.

The body's blood volume is restored rapidly

Table 10.7   Cause and signs of various types of shock.

Types of shock	Causes	Comments
Anaphylactic (Allergic)	Injection of a protein to which the patient is sensitive.	May be seen following bee stings or injection of substances.
Cardiogenic	Coronary or pulmonary embolism. Heart failure. Cardiac tamponade following chest injury.	
Hypovolaemic (oligaemic)	A reduction in the volume of circulating blood.	May be seen in postoperative patients, or patients following severe burns or haemorrhage; patients with severe compound or closed fractures.
Neurogenic	Due to nervous or emotional factors. Often occurs immediately following an event.	Patient faints and the pulse rate is always slow and full.
Surgical (postoperative)	Follows operation or severe multiple injuries such as are suffered in major accidents.	As for hypovolaemic shock.

by the administration of intravenous infusion of a plasma substitute until crossmatched blood is available for the patient.

Nursing actions for a patient showing signs of shock

- The patient is kept warm and is handled gently. It is important not to overheat the patient thereby taking blood to the superficial tissues and away from the vital organs.
- Careful monitoring of the patient's blood pressure will provide a guide on the progress of the patient. Recordings are made every fifteen minutes. Central venous pressure will provide a more accurate guide. Some doctors may introduce a cardiac catheter to enable this to be done.
- Oxygen may be administered to the patient at the prescribed rate. This will help to reduce the 'air hunger' suffered by the patient. It will further ensure adequate oxygenation of the tissues.
- Pain will increase the patient's shock. Careful positioning of the patient's injured limbs and the use of prescribed analgesics will help to reduce this. Anxiety is known to increase

pain levels (5). Talking to the patient will help to relieve his anxieties.
- Nothing is given to the patient by mouth. A careful check is made and recorded of any urinary output.
- Care of the patient's relatives/friends is equally important. They frequently require a great deal of support and comfort during this time. Their distress may add to the patient's problems. The patient must always be dealt with before the relatives.

At the same time as general observations are recorded, observations of the patient's extremities, where a fracture is suspected, are performed. Observations of colour, sensation and mobility are noted. It is frequently necessary to compare the recordings of the pulse of the injured area with the pulse of a similar uninjured part, e.g., comparative radial pulses should be taken in injuries of the arm.

NURSING CARE OF PATIENTS FOLLOWING HEAD INJURIES

A head injury is any blow to the head which may

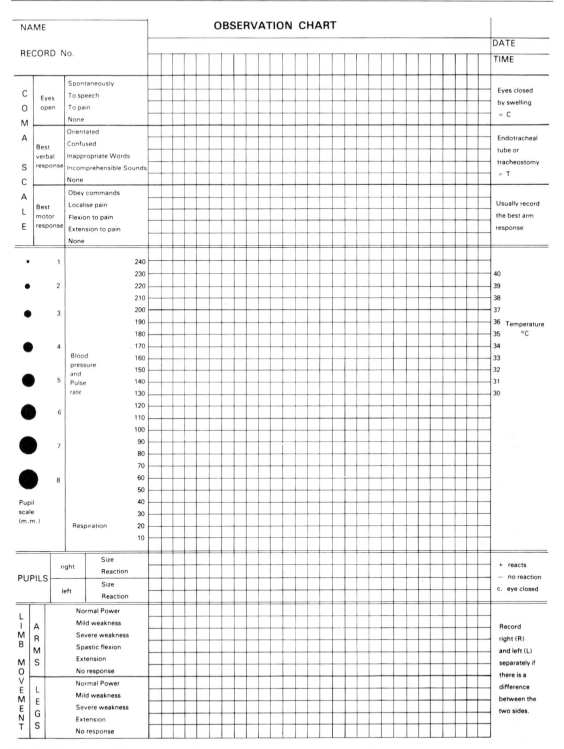

Fig. 10.2 An example of an observation chart.

or may not result in the patient losing consciousness.

In some centres, all patients who have had a head injury are admitted to hospital for observation for the first 24 hours following injury. This is a matter of local policy.

Careful observation of the patient's condition is vital. The nurse's role in maintaining these and accurately recording them may make the difference between life and death for the patient.

- A clear airway is essential for the patient. If the airway becomes obstructed then the patient will rapidly develop cerebral oedema. If the patient is unconscious when he is admitted to hospital, he should be nursed in a semi-prone position. It should be ascertained, prior to putting the patient into this position, that no neck injury has been sustained.
- Adequate ventilation of the patient's lungs will maintain adequate oxygenation of the patient's blood.
- Any haemorrhage will require to be stemmed by a clean pad and firm pressure applied to the area.
- Observations of the patient's temperature, pulse rate and volume, respiration rate and blood pressure are taken every fifteen minutes. These are recorded on a chart. Any change whatsoever in these recordings is reported to the doctor immediately. The frequency of the recordings will depend largely on the patient's condition. The more conscious the patient, the less frequently are observations recorded.
- With the recordings, observations are also made and recorded of the size and reaction to light of the patient's pupils. The size of each pupil is compared with the other to see if there is any inequality in size.
- The level of the patient's conscious awareness is also noted. This is the most important observation to be made. Statements about this should be accurate. The Glasgow Coma Scale is an excellent guide to this area of observations (see Figure 10.2).

The reason for noting these recordings is to identify very quickly any change in the patient's condition. Slowing of the pulse and respiratory rate with a steady increase in the patient's blood pressure recording, may indicate an increase in intercranial pressure. This is accompanied by constriction and later dilation of one pupil, rapidly followed by the other one. The level of consciousness is decreased. Despite popular opinion, surgical intervention of head injuries is seldom necessary. Careful monitoring of the patient's condition is often all that is required.

Nursing care of an unconscious patient

Maintaining a safe environment and breathing

- As previously stated, maintenance of a clear airway is of prime importance. To do this a tracheostomy may be performed by the doctor. Routine care of the tracheostomy is performed.

Communicating

- One of the last senses to go is hearing and it is one of the first to return. The nurse must talk to the patient as if he is fully conscious and inform him of all the procedures she is about to undertake on his behalf. Even though unconscious, the patient may be aware of his circumstances and talking to him may allay his fears.
- Careful assessment of the patient's general condition will lead the nurse to plan the management of the patient in relation to the prevention of the formation of pressure sores. Regular turning of the patient from side to supine to side will relieve pressure on particular areas. An alternating positive pressure mattress may be used as a mechanical method of relieving pressure.
- Turning the patient will also help to drain secretions from his air passages and allow full expansion of his lungs.

Eating and drinking

- A nasogastric tube is inserted to allow the patient to receive nutrition. This also allows for aspiration of the patient's stomach contents, which will avoid the patient vomiting.

Eliminating

- A urethral catheter is often inserted to prevent urinary incontinence. Routine catheter toilet is carried out.
- The patient will be incontinent of faeces. A

waterproof-backed sheet, left under the patient's buttocks, will help to collect the faeces. Careful washing and drying of the patient's anal area, following evacuation of faeces, is important.

- Accurate recording of the patient's daily fluid intake and output is recorded on a balance chart.

Personal cleansing and dressing

- The patient is fully dependent on the nurse to maintain his personal hygiene. The patient's skin must be kept clean, dry and lightly powdered. The patient's bed sheets must be wrinkle and crumb free.
- The patient's mouth is cleaned every 2–4 hours, or as often as required. He will have a lack of saliva which will lead to a sore, dry mouth.
- The patient's eyes are bathed every four hours, or more frequently if necessary, with a solution of warmed normal saline.

Mobilizing

- The patient's limbs are put through a full range of movement each time the patient is turned. This will prevent some of the complications of bed rest occurring.

MANAGEMENT OF THE PATIENT WITH A FRACTURED SPINE

Any patient admitted to the accident department with a suspected spinal fracture is treated with the utmost care to prevent complications. Spinal fractures can conveniently be divided into mild and serious fractures.

Mild fractures

Mild fractures are caused by twists, which result in avulsion of one or more of the processes of a vertebra, or by forced flexion which results in a crush fracture of the vertebral body. These are generally stable fractures (see Figure 10.3).

Patients with these types of fractures may be admitted to hospital for one or two day's bed rest. A support, in the form of a neck collar or plaster jacket, may then be applied to the appropriate area of the spine. The patient is then discharged home.

Serious fractures

Serious fractures are produced by severe violence and are generally unstable fractures. They often form part of a major incident which has happened to the patient. Because of the unstable nature of the fracture, the spinal cord is put at risk (see Figure 10.4).

Patients with unstable spinal fractures often have associated head injuries. If the patient is unconscious, information must be obtained

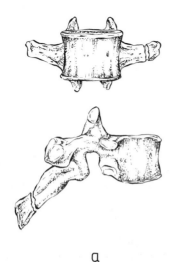

Nerve root in invertebral foramen

a   b

Fig. 10.3 Avulsion fractures of (a) vertebral processes, (b) simple crush fractures of vertebral body.

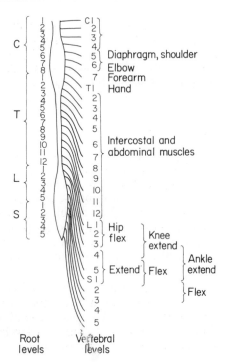

Fig. 10.4 Relationships between the levels of origin of spinal nerve roots and vertebral segments and the general localization of functions within the cord.

from the ambulancemen as to the nature of the accident.

If the patient is conscious, a careful history is taken and assessment of the patient is made before attempting to move or undress the patient.

All nursing staff involved with such a patient must be made aware of the precautions to be taken in dealing with the patient. The trolley must not be inadvertently knocked, or the patient moved with less than the required number of nurses.

Fractures or fracture dislocations above the first lumbar vertebra will result in the patient developing paralysis. Fractures below the first lumbar vertebra will result in damage to the nerve roots of the cauda equina. This may not lead to a permanent paralysis.

Medical management of fractures of the spine

Cervical region

Cervical traction, either by skull calipers or by the application of halopelvic or halofemoral traction (see Figure 10.5).

If skull calipers are used, the patient is

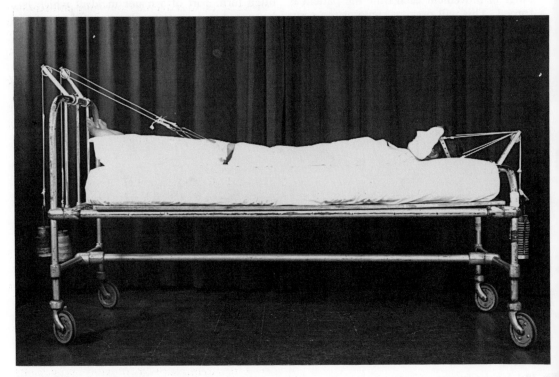

Fig. 10.5 Halo-femoral traction.

immobilized on bed rest for up to ten weeks.

Surgical fusion may be used to stablize the spine.

If paralysis is present, the patient may experience respiratory embarrassment.

Thoraco-lumbar region

Most fractures in this area are stable fractures. The force required to create an unstable fracture will result in a shearing effect on the spinal cord. This will cause paralysis below the level of the lesion.

Treatment consists of bed rest with the vertebral column extended, often on a bed or frame to facilitate easy turning of the patient. Spinal fusion may be undertaken if appropriate for the patient.

Specific nursing care of a paraplegic patient

Many of the nursing problems encountered when nursing an unconscious patient will be identified as those relating to a paraplegic patient.

Maintaining a safe environment

- The patient is nursed on a Stoke Mandeville or Egerton bed or a Stryker frame. These will facilitate easier turning of the patient.
- Because the patient will have lost sensation in his lower limbs, strict two-hourly turning of the patient must be carried out. Sheepskins, or other pressure relieving aids, must be used to protect the patient's skin from damage.

Communicating

- Allowing the patient time to talk and to express his feelings over his condition is important. The nurse needs to develop a listening ear.

Breathing

- Encourage the patient to take ten deep breaths every hour to reduce the risk of a chest infection developing.

Eating and drinking

- Because of the patient's emotional state he may not want to eat or drink. Small, light, tempting meals, using his favourite foods and drink, may help relieve this. The patient should be encouraged to drink 3–4 litres of fluid per day to prevent a urinary tract infection.

Eliminating

- The patient may develop a paralytic ileus. Patients should be carefully monitored to see if abdominal distension develops.
- Manual evacuation of faeces may be necessary. This will only be performed if a written prescription is obtained from the doctor and then only according to local policies. Laxatives and suppositories should be administered, as prescribed.
- An indwelling catheter may be used to drain urine or intermittent catheterization, using a strict aseptic technique, may be used as an alternative method. The aim is to develop an automatic bladder for the patient.

Once their condition is stable and during their time in an accident ward, these patients require a great deal of time to express their feelings. The nurse needs to remain encouraging and reassuring. She should never lie to her patient, but until accurate assessment by the experts in this field has been completed, she will not, herself, know the whole truth.

Patients with quadriplegia or paraplegia are transferred as soon as possible to a regional spinal injuries centre. Here they will receive expert care and assessment and be amongst others with similar problems.

NURSING CARE OF THE PATIENT WITH A FRACTURE OF THE UPPER LIMB

There are certain nursing points which are common to all fractures of the upper limb. These will be discussed before the specific measures for individual fractures are undertaken. Most patients with upper limb fractures will be dealt with in the accident department. Providing their home circumstances are satisfactory, they are then discharged home to be treated as out-patients.

- First aid measures are observed as necessary.
- If the patient is in a great deal of pain he

should lie down. This prevents him sustaining further injuries if he faints. If it is a child, he is better managed lying on a trolley.

- Pain must be carefully assessed and monitored by the nurse or the patient. If positioning the patient does not improve the pain then the doctor should be asked to prescribe analgesia, if possible, to help the patient through the waiting period.
- If possible the fractured limb is placed in a broad arm sling to provide temporary splintage.
- Rings and jewellery are removed from the affected hand and arm. It may be necessary to cut a ring off, but this should be the last resort when all other methods have failed.
- The patient's nails, if possible, should be free of nail colouring and dirt. This will enable accurate observations to be performed of the colour of the patient's fingers.
- Initial observations of the colour, sensation and mobility of the patient's fingers should be assessed and recorded. The fingers should be normal colour and, unless the damage is local, be able to move within normal limits as compared to the uninjured limb. Altered sensation should be reported to the doctor, as this may indicate the involvement of a nerve.
- Comparative radial pulses should be recorded. If the patient is a child, and the suspected fracture is in the supra condylar region of the humerus, all of the observations should be recorded at fifteen minute intervals. This is to exclude the onset of Volkmann's ischaemic contracture.
- The patient should be given nothing by mouth. This is a safety measure in case the patient needs a general anaesthetic to reduce and immobilize the fracture.
- The patient should be undressed sufficiently to enable the doctor to fully examine the appropriate area of the patient's body. If it is too painful for this to be successfully carried out, permission must be sought from the patient or his relatives to cut the patient's clothes off. If this is undertaken clothing should, wherever possible, be cut along seams to enable them to be stitched together again by the patient if desired.
- Once the patient is undressed he should be kept warm. He could develop emotional shock as a result of the injury. Exposure to the cold could exacerbate this.

- The patient's relatives should be allowed to sit with the patient while he is waiting to be seen by the doctor. This will provide reassurance for all.

Once the patient has been seen by the doctor and the necessary treatment has been carried out, if he is to be discharged home, the nurse must ensure the following points are observed:

1. Make sure the patient's plaster is comfortable and that all excess plaster has been washed from the patient's fingers.
2. Check that the colour, sensation and mobility of the patient's fingers remains within normal limits.
3. Redress the patient so that he is able to go home. Make sure the relatives are aware of the patient's limitations.
4. Give verbal and written instructions on the care of the patient's plaster and the exercises he is to perform.
5. Assess his home circumstances, making sure he is able to manage at home.
6. Give a follow-up appointment to attend the fracture clinic.
7. Give the patient and his relatives the opportunity to discuss any problems they forsee.

Normal use of the upper limb as a whole and of the hand in particular depends upon the absence of stiffness within the joints. It is important that those joints which are not immobilized are exercised from the beginning. To allow this to happen, immobilization of the affected area is kept to the minimal amount of external splintage.

Swelling hampers movement. Elevation and active movement are the most effective means of controlling swelling. Advice to the patient on how effectively to elevate an arm is necessary. When a broad arm sling is applied, the hand must be supported by the sling. It should never be allowed to hang over the edge of the sling from the wrist (see Figure 10.6). When either a broad arm sling or a collar and cuff are applied to the patient's arm, the patient should be instructed when he is able to remove them for active exercise to take place.

If the patient's arm is to be maintained against the patient's chest wall, the nurse must remember that wherever two skin surfaces touch there is a potential area for skin breakdown or intertrigo to occur. The area must be protected

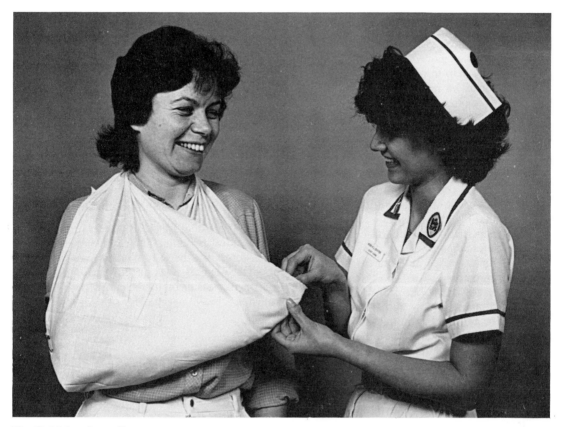

Fig. 10.6 A broad arm sling.

by a pad which is removed regularly. The patient's arm is supported by a second nurse whilst the pads are changed, the skin cleansed and carefully dried. The possible areas at risk are:

1. The axilla.
2. Where the arm lies next to the chest wall.
3. In the elbow crease.
4. Where the arm lies across the waist.

CARE AND MANAGEMENT OF COMMON INJURIES OF THE UPPER LIMB

Dislocated shoulder joint

A dislocation is a condition where the joint surfaces have been displaced by some form of violence. Anterior dislocation of the shoulder joint occurs usually as the result of a fall on to an outstretched hand, or a direct blow to the shoulder. It is a far more common injury than posterior dislocations.

Anterior dislocations occur quite commonly in young adult sportsmen or elderly ladies who fall on to their shoulders. The head of the humerus displaces forward into a subcoracol position. The normal contour of the shoulder becomes flattened.

Specific nursing care

● The patient should be admitted and placed in one of these positions:

1. Lay the patient prone with the affected arm lying over the edge of the trolley. Spontaneous reduction may occur once the patient relaxes and gravity traction occurs.
2. Sit the patient in a chair with the arm supported, either in a broad arm sling, or rested on a pillow placed across the patient's lap.
3. Lay the patient on a trolley in a semi-recumbent position with the affected arm supported on a pillow.

- During the dislocation the axillary nerve, or other branches of the brachial plexus, may have been damaged. Careful observation of sensation and movement of the patient's fingers will help to monitor this.
- Reduction is by manipulation under a general or regional anaesthetic, Entenox gas, analgesia and muscle relaxant drugs. Sometimes the patients require nothing. Whichever method is used, the nurse must be aware of the appropriate observations and precautions. If a general anaesthetic has been administered, the patient should:
  - (i)   always be attended until able to maintain his own airway;
  - (ii) never leave the department until fully conscious;
  - (iii) never leave the department without an escort;
  - (iv) never use public transport to return home;
  - (v)   be admitted as an in-patient if unable to fulfil any of these criteria.

  The methods used to reduce the shoulder are the Hippocratic or Kocher method. Once successful reduction has taken place, the arm is held in such a way as to prevent abduction and external rotation of the shoulder joint.
- The nurse will apply either a collar and cuff sling or a broad arm sling. The arm is then held against the patient's body by either a bandage or Netalast.

One of the major problems following a dislocation of the shoulder joint is recurrent dislocations. This is due to the damage of the structures within the joint during the initial dislocation, e.g., the glenoid labrum, and the joint capsule may be stripped from the anterior rim of the acetabulum. If this happens, the patient may be admitted for elective surgery to stabilize the joint. The operative measures taken may be a Putti-Platt procedure, or a Bankharts procedure.

Management of patients with fractures of the proximal end of the humerus

These fractures occur most commonly in the elderly and the young. They are often impacted fractures. Treatment is usually the application of a collar and cuff sling for a few days.

Specific nursing points

- The patient must be able to manage his own activities of daily living or have support at home before being discharged.
- Active exercises of the shoulder joint are shown to the patient before discharge. He is advised to remove the sling after three or four days and within his pain tolerance levels start assisted exercise of the affected shoulder joint. These then progress to active exercises.

Fractures of the mid shaft of the humerus

These particular fractures occur commonly in young adult patients. The radial nerve winds its way across the back of the humerus from the medial to lateral sides in the spiral groove. The nerve may easily be damaged in these fractures causing a radial nerve palsy or drop wrist.

Specific nursing points

- Initially the patient's arm should be supported in a collar and cuff sling. This is easier to apply than a broad arm sling. It also provides traction to the distal fragment of the humerus.
- Careful monitoring of the patient's wrist and finger movements is recorded every 30 minutes. The patient should be able to flex and extend the wrist joint.
- A 'J' or a Bohler 'U'-shaped plaster may be applied to the patient's arm to support the fracture (see Figure 10.7).

Fig. 10.7 J-slab for fracture of the humerus combined with a collar and cuff sling.

- If the radial nerve appears to have been affected, a radial nerve splint may be used, but spontaneous recovery of the nerve generally occurs.

Management of patients with supracondylar fractures of humerus

This type of fracture occurs most commonly in young children. The child arrives in the accident department, frightened, in pain and often pale. It is important that the child's parent stays with the child throughout all the procedures. A calm, confident, reassuring attitude by the nurse will help the parent to settle the child.

Specific nursing care

- Lay the child down on a trolley. Support the injured arm on a pillow.
- Gently remove the child's clothing.
- One of the conditions which may occur as a result of these fractures is Volkmann's ischaemic contracture. This is caused by damage or occlusion of the brachial artery (see Figure 10.8).

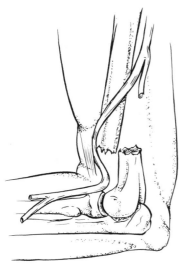

Fig. 10.8 Showing how adjacent structures can be injured by a supracondylar fracture of the humerus.

The nurse assigned to look after the child must observe both radial pulses every fifteen minutes, without fail. If the artery is affected the radial pulse is absent. There will be obvious further signs of:

(i)   pallor of the fingers;
(ii) pain in the forearm;
(iii) pain on extension of the fingers;
(iv) swelling of the fingers.

Unless prompt restoration of the circulation is taken, the flexor muscles of the forearm become hard and tender. Eventually they fibrose, pulling the hand and fingers into flexion.

If the fracture is undisplaced, the child's arm will be placed in a collar and cuff with the arm at more than right angles. The child is then discharged home with the parent.

If the fracture is displaced, then the child is admitted to the ward. The fracture is manipulated under a general anaesthetic. This is sometimes done as an open reduction when the brachial artery can be explored for signs of damage or occlusion. The child's arm is then rested in a right-angled back slab with a collar and cuff sling.

Specific postoperative nursing care

- Observations of the radial pulses are continued at fifteen minute intervals. Swelling under a constricting bandage or plaster may occlude the brachial artery. If any adverse signs appear, the doctor is contacted. The constricting bandage is removed.

Management of patients with fractures of the radius and ulna

These fractures occur quite commonly in children as greenstick fractures. They also occur in adults. The bones may fracture separately or together and be displaced or undisplaced fractures. The main aim in treatment is to maintain the length and relationship of the bones to each other. Pronation and supination are the two movements most likely to be involved.

The commonest areas where a fracture occurs are:

1.   Head of radius.
2.   The upper third of ulna, with dislocation of the radial head, known as a Monteggia fracture.
3.   Mid shaft of radius and ulna.
4.   The lower third of radius, with dislocation of the distal radio-ulnar joint, known as a Galleazzi fracture.
5.   The lower end of radius within 2.5

centimetres of the wrist joint, with or without avulsion of the ulnar styloid process. The distal fragment is tilted backwards. This is known as a Colles fracture.

6. The lower end of radius with anterior tilting of the distal fragment known as a Smith's fracture.

Treatment for all of these fractures, if undisplaced, is the application of a cast. This may be a long arm cast if there is a danger of rotation of the bones occurring.

If the fractures are displaced, they are manipulated under some form of analgesia or anaesthetic. The reduction may need to be open and the fracture internally fixed to provide stability.

Routine nursing measures, as previously described, are carried out.

Nursing care of a patient with a Colles fracture

The nursing care given to patients with a Colles fracture merits particular mention. The majority of patients seen in the accident department with this type of fracture are elderly. The fracture is seen very commonly during the winter months, due to the extra slippery ground.

The patients who are admitted with this fracture must be carefully observed for signs of hypothermia. They frequently fall and are not found for some time, particularly if they live alone. They may be anxious about an elderly partner left at home, or their pets while they are in the department. A friendly nurse will ensure that these anxieties are dealt with and are not ignored.

It is important that when they are discharged there is sufficient support for them on their return at home. Elderly patients are often fiercely independent and this must be respected. While giving due regard to this, the nurse must make sure her patient will be safe and not neglected when discharging him.

Management of patients with fractures of the wrist and hand

The specific regions where these fractures most commonly occur are:

1. *The scaphoid.* Fractures of the scaphoid are particularly common in young adults. They have a reputation for poor healing

as avascular necrosis of the distal fragment may occur. Displacement rarely occurs. The patient's arm is sometimes immobilized in a forearm cast with the thumb held in opposition to the other fingers. The thumb is immobilized up to the interphalangeal joint. Specific nursing care includes the necessity to ensure that the four fingers of the hand can move freely.

2. *Base of first metacarpal.* The base of the first metacarpal, including the carpo-metacarpal joint. This is known as a Bennett's fracture.

3. *Shafts.* Fractures of the shafts of the second to fifth metacarpals.

4. *Terminal phalanx.* A flake of bone may be avulsed when the end of the finger is forcibly flexed. The extensor tendon is torn from its insertion along with a flake of bone. This results in a mallet finger.

NURSING CARE OF THE PATIENT WITH INJURY TO THE LOWER LIMB

- Many of the problems related to swelling and stiffness of the upper limb apply equally to the lower limb. Elevation of the patient's leg should be on a chair, at least level with his hips, not on a low stool.

- Swelling will respond well to the pressure of a bandage. If a bandage is applied, the nurse must make sure it is sufficiently high to prevent swelling above and below its application, e.g., a bandage applied to a swollen ankle must extend to just below the knee from the base of the toes.

- If a long leg cylinder cast is applied, a bandage is applied to the patient's foot and ankle from the toes to prevent swelling of the patient's foot.

- If a Robert Jones pressure bandage is applied, it should consist of three layers of domette bandage, with a layer of wool encircling the limb between each bandage. The bandage extends from the malleoli to mid-thigh. Following its application, the bandage should be firm to touch and free from ridges and hollows. This will then provide firm immobilization for a limb with even pressure.

- The patient's perception of the injury to his lower limb needs to be carefully discussed with him. This may affect his attitude to his immobilization.

- Any traction which may be applied to the patient needs carefully explaining to him.
- Any wounds, particularly where there is an open fracture of the tibia, need to be dressed aseptically to prevent the onset of infection.
- Patients discharged from the accident department with a cast on their lower limb must be taught the correct use of crutches before leaving the department.

The length of the crutch is measured from 2–3 inches below the axilla to the side of the bottom of the foot 6–8 inches sideways from the heel. The amount of weight bearing the patient is allowed to do will be decided by the doctor.

The pattern of the gait should be as shown in Figure 10.9 for either partial or nonweight bearing. The patient is instructed to take his weight on his wrists and palms of the hands; never on his axillae.

- Never allow a patient to leave the accident department until you have seen them walk safely either on crutches, with a walking aid or unaided.

SPECIFIC NURSING CARE AND MANAGEMENT OF COMMON INJURIES OF THE LOWER LIMB

Management of patients with fractures of the neck of femur

Fractures of the neck of femur occur characteristically in women over 65 years of age. Because of the age group affected, these fractures carry a high risk to life. They take up to three months to unite. If the patient is confined to bed, all the complications of prolonged bed rest become life threatening. Therefore, the aim of the treatment is early ambulation to prevent these complications.

The fractures may be classified as intracapsular which includes subcapital and transcervical fractures, or extracapsular, which includes pertrochanteric, intertrochanteric and subtrochanteric fractures (see Figure 10.10).

As the patient is generally elderly, treatment will depend on the general state of health. Ideally, the fracture is internally fixed as soon as possible.

If the patient's general physical and mental

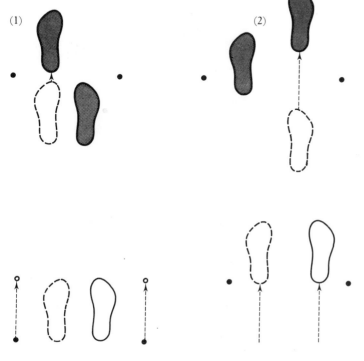

Fig 10.9 Partial weight bearing on crutches: (1) Both crutches and affected leg are brought forward. Weight and balance is transferred from the unaffected leg to the crutches. (2) The good leg is then taken forward.

Intracapsular fracture

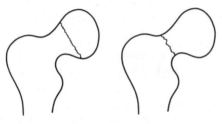

Subcapital fracture   Transcervical fracture

Extracapsular fracture

 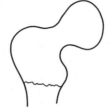

Pertrochanteric   Intertrochanteric   Subtrochanteric
fracture   fracture   fracture

Fig. 10.10 Intracapsular fractures: subcapital fracture, transcervical fracture; extracapsular fractures: pertrochanteric fracture, intertrochanteric fractures, subtrochanteric fracture.

condition is not good, then Hamilton-Russell traction or fixed traction on a Thomas splint may be the treatment used.

Specific nursing care will be routine care for patients on this type of traction.

If surgery is the treatment chosen, then routine pre-operative nursing measures are carried out.

With intracapsular structures the femoral head is generally replaced by prosthetic replacement, such as a Thompson or Austin Moore prosthesis.

If the fracture is extracapsular, dynamic hip screws, or a nail and plate, may be used to internally fix the fracture (see Figure 10.11).

Specific postoperative nursing care

Maintaining a safe environment

- The patient who is elderly will feel very weak post surgery. A gentle, reassuring, but encouraging attitude will help the patient feel secure and help him to retain some independence.

Communicating

- The patient may be confused due to removal from his home to hospital and as a result of

the anaesthetic. Talking to the patient and allowing him to have familiar things around him, e.g., family photographs, will help to alleviate this. Some elderly patients are very

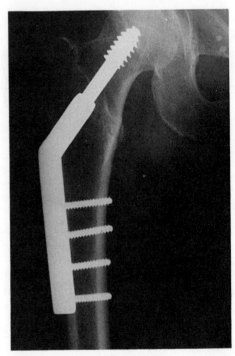

Fig. 10.11 A dynamic hip screw.

independent and determined to continue to follow their own routines. In spite of their pain they make attempts to get out of bed to go to the toilet. It is important not to misunderstand these actions and to label the patient as confused.

- If the patient is deaf, this can also lead to a misunderstanding on the nurse's part when the patient is labelled as confused. Clear speech, often rather than a raised voice, will allow the elderly patient to understand what is being said.

Breathing

- Careful observations of the patient's breathing are made. Hypostatic pneumonia may develop as a result of the patient's original fall. Encourage the patient to take ten deep breaths each hour and to expectorate, if necessary.

Eating and drinking

- Make sure the patient's dentures are replaced as soon as possible. Some patients will be undernourished and reluctant to drink. The nurse must encourage them to eat and to drink as much as possible.

Personal cleansing and dressing

- Careful assessment of the patient's potential to form pressure sores is made. Patients who lie on an operating table for any length of time are classified as 'at risk'. The elderly are even more at risk, therefore appropriate measures must be taken.
- Assessment as to whether the patient is to be lifted or rolled will be made. Any plan made should include how the patient is to be moved and how many nurses are required to do this.
- It is vital to encourage the patient to retain as much independence as possible. So many elderly patients believe the nurse has to do everything for them in the hospital.

Mobilizing

- Mobilization will begin, usually within 48 hours of surgery. The patient is sat out of bed with the affected leg elevated on a stool. This progresses to walking between the parallel bars or with a walking frame, then to walking sticks.
- Early assessment of the patient's home circumstances is necessary.
- It is important that the patient's relatives are aware of the patient's progress and are encouraged to take an active role in his care from the time of admission. This should mean they are prepared for his discharge.
- If the patient is unable to return home, then arrangements need to be made for long-stay accommodation. Unfortunately waiting lists are long with subsequent delay in discharging the patient from hospital.

FRACTURES OF THE SHAFT OF FEMUR

There are many causes of a fracture of the shaft of femur and any age group may be affected. Large numbers of the victims will be young men as a result of motor bike accidents.

Specific nursing care in the accident department

- Resuscitation is of prime importance. Up to 3 litres of blood may be lost by the patient into the soft tissue surrounding the fracture site. Observations of pulse rate, respirations and blood pressure are performed at 30 minute intervals.
- The colour, sensation and mobility of the patient's toes are observed at the same interval. The femoral artery and nerve and the sciatic nerve may become damaged or occluded as a result of the injury.
- Very severe pain is felt by the patient. This is caused not only by the fracture itself, but from spasms of the quadriceps and hamstring muscles. Temporary splintage of the fracture and analgesia will help to control this.
- Routine care regarding pain (see p. 15) should be planned.

Fixed traction using a Thomas splint may be applied with the patient using Entenox. This will take several nurses to apply successfully and rapidly. Other methods such as pillows or sand bags may be used. These may not be as successful as fixed traction, because every time the patient moves the muscles may go into spasm.

Nonoperative treatment of fracture of the femoral shaft

The fracture is manipulated. Traction is then applied. This may be balanced skeletal traction using a Denham or Steinmann pin. Hamilton-Russell traction may be used with balanced skeletal traction.

Fisk or Perkins traction may also be used.

Specific nursing care for a patient with a fractured shaft of femur in traction

Maintaining a safe environment

- Routine nursing care for a patient in traction is given to maintain a safe environment. Special checks are made for signs of developing drop-foot due to pressure on the lateral popliteal nerve by the splint.
- Observations of the patient's toes are continued, as started in the accident department, to look for changes in colour, sensation and mobility. These are recorded with general observations of the patient to look for change which may indicate the onset of infection or fat embolism.

Communicating

- Following careful assessment, the patient (once well enough) is taught how he may take part in preventing the complications which may arise as a result of confinement to bed. Careful planning of how and when this teaching takes place should be part of the nursing plan.
- The patient must be allowed time to adjust to his new situation and the sudden drastic change in his lifestyle. The medical social worker is asked to see him to discuss any problems which occur to him and to help him arrive at a variety of solutions.

Eating and drinking

- Patients with this type of fracture require a high intake of vitamins C and D, calcium and protein to aid bone and tissue healing. Milk is a good source of these and most young people will enjoy milk drinks. This not only provides a source of these, but also will improve the patient's fluid intake.

Personal cleansing and dressing

- Because the patient will be confined to bed for some length of time, it is important that his hair is washed when he requires it. The young patients learn many ways to enable themselves to do this, but an older patient may need the nurse to wash his hair for him.

Working and playing

- Boredom can become a problem for the patient who is confined to bed for a considerable length of time. Getting to know the patient and allowing time for him to talk will help to alleviate some of his anxieties, which in turn may relieve some of his frustrations.

The younger patient may create many difficulties through mischievousness brought about by boredom. The patient should be encouraged to use his time in hospital to develop some form of new skill, either educationally, or as an indoor hobby.

Operative measures for a patient with a fractured shaft of femur

An intramedullary nail or bone plate and screws may be used (see Figure 10.12). These are particularly used in unstable or irreducible

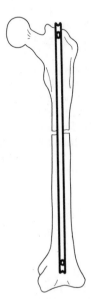

Fig. 10.12 Intramedullary (Kuntscher) nailing for internal fixation of femoral shaft fracture.

fractures. The patient's limb is then often placed in a cast-brace.

A cast-brace is a system of functional bracing when the fracture is held securely, but the joints above and below are allowed freedom of movement.

The limb has minimal padding applied. The plaster is moulded closely to the patient's thigh, allowing total contact between the skin and the plaster. It is shaped into a quadrilateral shape by applying an external plastic cuff, which is removed when the desired shape is achieved. The plaster extends from the groin to just above the knee joint. A pair of hinges are then applied and attached to a below knee cast. The patient's foot may or may not be included in the below knee cast. Normal routines for drying the plaster cast are observed.

MANAGEMENT OF PATIENTS WITH SOFT TISSUE INJURIES TO THE KNEE JOINT

Tears of the menisci (semilunar cartilage)

This is a common sports injury but may occur in those occupations which involve a squatting position, e.g., miners or painters and decorators. The medial meniscus is the one most commonly torn becuse of its position in being attached to the medial capsular ligament.

The tears occur in several ways (see Figure 10.13). The force required to acquire a tear is a rotational force on a flexed knee joint when the patient's foot is anchored to the ground.

In many accident departments on a Saturday, several patients will present with their knee 'locked' in position. Locking is the inability to fully extend the knee joint.

Initially, the patient's knee will be restored to an acceptable position by manipulation under a regional or local anaesthetic. The patient with a recurrent problem learns to reduce his knee himself, but will eventually find he has an unstable knee joint and will then be forced to seek medical advice. McMurray's sign will elicit a torn meniscus when the knee is manoeuvred to produce a 'clunk' as the tag of meniscus is moved back into place.

Once reduced, the patient's leg is encased in a Robert Jones pressure bandage or a long leg cylinder of plaster. The original Robert Jones bandage was a layer of cotton wool which encircled the limb and was then covered by a layer of fine Egyptian cotton bandage, later substituted by a domette bandage. This was repeated twice more. Most accident departments now modify this bandage by using a crepe bandage instead of a domette one.

The knee joint depends on the extensor mechanism for its stability. The extensor mechanism involves the large quadricep muscle of the thigh, the patella and its patellar ligament. Any injury or condition which affects the knee joint will result in rapid wasting of the quadriceps. It is an important part of the nursing care plan to ensure that the patient is taught quadriceps drill as soon as possible following a knee injury. This means that, before the patient leaves the department, the nurse must watch the patient practise contracting his quadriceps muscle. The patient is instructed to carry out these exercises for five minutes every hour he is awake. The consequences of failing to do this should be explained.

If the patient's meniscus is torn to the extent that recurrent locking of his knee joint and other associated problems continue, a decision may be taken to remove the meniscus, or the resulting tag, surgically.

Routine nursing as for patients with general orthopaedic conditions of the knee joint are planned according to the individual patient's needs.

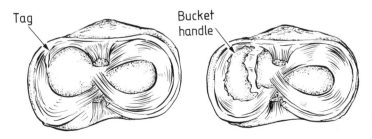

Fig. 10.13 Torn anterior horn (left); bucket handle tear of meniscus (right).

MANAGEMENT OF PATIENTS WITH FRACTURES OF TIBIA AND FIBULA

The fibula bone rarely fractures on its own. If it does, the fracture is usually a stable fracture which is well splinted by the tibia.

The typical injury which fractures the shaft of the tibia is one of direct violence, as commonly found in young motor cyclists. The force involved is considerable. There is frequently extensive soft tissue injury and loss of skin. These factors added together give rise to the risk of infection, delayed union and often nonunion of the fracture. The nurse must therefore take prompt emergency action to minimize these risks for her patient.

Immediate nursing care

- Routine resuscitation measures are carried out.
- Temporary immobilization of the patient's injured limb, by the use of a vacuum splint. Unnecessary movement of the limb will aggravate pain and increase the risk of shock. However, it is important to remove any clothing from over the wounds. The only way this may sometimes be achieved is by allowing the patient to use Entenox gas.
- Any wounds should then be covered by a clean, sterile pad.
- If possible the foot of the trolley or bed should be elevated to reduce the amount of oedema.
- The patient's pedal pulses are monitored and recorded every 15–30 minutes to check for vascular occlusion. These need to be compared to the uninjured leg. The colour of the affected limb is also checked. Sensation of the distal limb is checked in case of nerve injury.

Debridement of the wound and treatment of the fracture will depend on the type of fracture. The pattern of treatment may be as set out in Table 10.8 and shown in Figure 10.14.

MANAGEMENT OF PATIENTS WITH SPRAINS OF THE ANKLE JOINT

Sprains of any joint are characterized by pain, swelling, bruising and tenderness related to the attachments of ligaments to bone. The swelling is caused by an effusion of synovial fluid.

Table 10.8 Pattern of treatment for various types of fracture of the tibia.

Closed stable fracture, with or without a minimal wound	→ Long leg plaster applied for six weeks, followed by application of a Sarmiento plaster for a further six weeks. (A Sarmiento plaster is a patellar ligament-bearing functional cast, which allows use of the knee and ankle joints).
Comminuted fracture, with a moderate wound	→ Skeletal traction through the oscalcis for two weeks. This will help to allow time for the swelling to subside. A long leg plaster is then applied and the regime continued as for a closed fracture.
Closed comminuted fracture	→ A bone plate and screws are inserted, followed by the regime as for a closed fracture.
Severe compound fracture, with soft tissue injury & skin loss	→ An external fixator is applied for several weeks until the soft tissue injury has resolved and skin healing is beginning to progress. A Sarmiento plaster may then be applied to enable bony union to complete.

Sprains of the ankle are commonly seen in the accident department. They are generally as a result of a sudden inversion of the foot, which causes damage to the anterior talofibular ligament portion of the lateral ligament of the ankle. They are very painful and, unless treated correctly, may result in a permanently weak ankle.

Nurses often regard these injuries as trivial. The correct alignment and stability of the ankle is essential to normal walking.

Most patients will have their ankles x-rayed to eliminate the possibility of an avulsion fracture.

Most patients will require some form of support to their ankles before being discharged. This may be the application of a double layer of Tubigrip, a crêpe bandage or elastic adhesive strapping. In severe sprains the limb may be placed in a below knee nonweight bearing plaster of Paris.

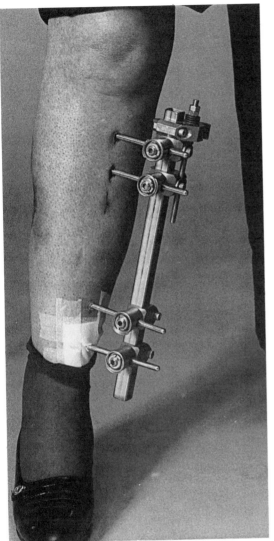

Fig. 10.14 The Oxford external fixator (courtesy of Oxford Orthopaedic Engineering Centre).

Nursing care for the patient with a sprained ankle

- Application of the support to the patient's limb.

Applying a crêpe bandage

- One, or two, four inch (ten centimetres) crêpe bandages are necessary for the average adult patient.
- The patient's foot is held at a right angle to the leg with slight eversion. This will help to relieve stretch on the lateral ligament and allow it to heal quickly.
- The bandage starts just below the toes and extends to just below the knee.
- The bandage must be applied firmly, evenly and mould to the contours of the leg. There must be no gaps in it to allow swelling to occur.

Applying elastic adhesive strapping

- Find out, before applying the strapping, if the patient has any allergy to it.
- A fine layer of stockinette will prevent the strapping sticking to the patient's hairs. Shaving the leg is unnecessary and uncomfortable for the patient. The stockinette must be applied smoothly and without wrinkles.
- A 7.5 centimetre (three inch) or ten centimetre (four inch) roll of strapping is usually satisfactory for the average adult patient.
- The strapping is applied from the toes to just below the knee without stretching it, as it is applied.
- It must be evenly applied, without excessive layers which could cause pain and swelling of the limb.

If the patient is unable to wear his shoe due to the support which has been fitted, then the shoe may be fixed with strapping to the patient's foot to enable him to walk on its upper part.

- Flat, wide shoes are important for the patient to walk for the 2–3 weeks while the support is in place.
- The patient should be encouraged to walk as normally as possible, without limping, before he leaves the department.
- Routine advice on the care of the support should be given to the patient. Advice about elevating the limb when sitting down and subsequent footwear is also given.

MANAGEMENT OF PATIENTS WITH PERIPHERAL NERVE INJURIES

A peripheral nerve arises from the anterior horn of the spinal cord. It conveys nerve impulses from the brain and cord to various structures in the body (see Figure 10.15). Table 10.9 and 10.10 outline causes of damage to a peripheral

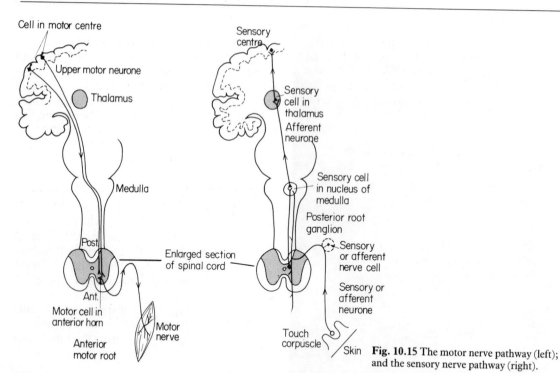

Fig. 10.15 The motor nerve pathway (left); and the sensory nerve pathway (right).

Table 10.9 Causes of damage to a peripheral nerve.

Type of injury	Cause
Laceration	This may be self-inflicted or accidental.
Compression	There are many causes of compression on a nerve 1. Tight, constricting, wrongly applied or ill-fitting bandages, plasters or splints, or the misuse of crutches (external forces). 2. Pressure from internal haemorrhage or haematoma formation. 3. Pressure from swelling, a fragment of bone or a foreign body.
Ischaemia	This will cause death of the axon, such as is seen in Volkmann's ischaemia.
Poison	Overdoses of arsenic or lead will cause damage.
Traction	Such as is seen in a birth injury (Erb's palsy) or as a result of traction between the head and shoulder in motor cycle accidents.

Table 10.10 Terms used to describe nerve damage.

Term	Description of condition
Neuropraxia	This is temporary damage to a nerve when there is interruption of the conduction of nerve impulses. Once the interruption is removed, the nerve usually recovers. Carpal tunnel compression is an example of this type of problem.
Axonotmesis	This is when there is damage to some or all of the fibres of the axon. Partial degeneration will occur distal to the damage.
Neurotmesis	The complete division of the nerve with destruction of the nerve cell body. There is loss of function distal to the injury.

nerve and the terms used to describe nerve damage.

Nonoperative treatments for patients with peripheral nerve injury

- An orthosis is applied to support the para-lysed limb in a functional position.
- Physiotherapy is prescribed to try to re-educate paralysed muscles and to reduce the risk of soft tissue contractures leading to a fixed deformity of a joint.

Operative treatments

- *Suturing of the nerve.* With the advent and progress of microsurgery, successful primary repair of the nerve may be undertaken.
- *Nerve grafts.* A graft taken from a non-essential nerve may be grafted between the

two ends of the nerve to bridge the gap.

- *Tendon transfers.* When there is no possibility of regeneration or repair for the nerve, the tendon of an active, less important, muscle may be transposed into the paralysed nerve.

Specific nursing care for patients with peripheral nerve lesions

- Wherever the patient has traction, orthoses, bandages or a plaster on, pressure on the affected nerve, it should be released as soon as possible.
- The affected limb must be kept at a normal temperature. The skin of the limb will be insensitive and applications of heat may cause burns. The patient must be warned not to put the limb near a radiator, hot water bottle or fire.

Cold can equally cause problems by making the limb go stiff.

- Any orthosis which is applied must receive routine checks as previously described. It must be removed at least twice a day to put the affected joints through a full range of passive exercise. This will prevent the formation of fixed deformities.

Paralysed muscles must never be splinted in an over-stretched position or they may retain that position, thus preventing normal use should any power return to the muscle.

- While the limb is removed from the splint it should be washed, thoroughly dried and inspected for signs of pressure.
- All of the unaffected joints, in close proximity to the paralysed muscles, must have their movements preserved. To facilitate this, all of the unaffected joints are actively exercised.

Common peripheral nerve injuries and their appropriate orthosis

Radial nerve

The radial nerve may be damaged in the axilla by pressure from crutches. This causes crutch palsy.

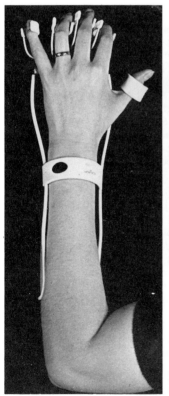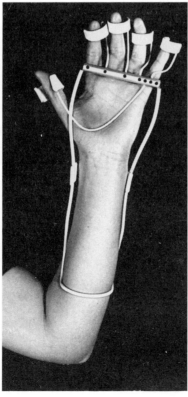

Fig. 10.16 A lively splint for radial nerve injury.

The radial nerve may also be damaged as a result of a mid-shaft fracture of humerus, particularly if the fracture is a comminuted one.

The patient will experience difficulty in extending his wrist and fingers, which results in the classical radial palsy of 'dropped wrist'.

Orthosis

The orthosis commonly used is a 'cock up' splint which holds the wrist in extension. This is a passive splint. Added to this sometimes are finger pieces to allow the fingers to be brought into extension. The splint is then called a 'lively' splint and it becomes an active splint providing movement for the fingers (see Figure 10.16).

Ulnar nerve

Damage to the ulnar nerve commonly occurs as a result of lacerations to the anterio–medial aspect of the wrist joint. Pressure on the inside of the elbow from a plaster of Paris, or fractures of the radius and ulnar together may also damage the nerve.

The typical deformity resulting in damage to the ulnar nerve is a claw deformity of the ring and little finger.

Orthosis

The orthosis commonly used is a knuckle-duster splint.

Median nerve

The median nerve is often damaged by bony fragments such as may be found in a supra-condylar fracture of humerus, or a Colles fracture. Carpal tunnel syndrome, when the median nerve is compressed as it passes through the carpal tunnel, will also give rise to symptoms.

The patient may have a claw-like deformity of the radial three-and-a-half digits. He will lose the ability to bring the thumb into opposition to the remaining fingers.

Orthosis

The orthosis used is to bring the thumb into a functional position to the remaining fingers, called an Opponens splint (see Figure 10.17).

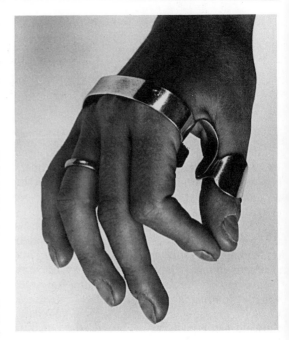

Fig. 10.17 Opponens splint.

REFERENCES

1. The Central Statistical Office (1986) *Social Trends*. London: CSO.
2. Road Accident Statistics From the Department of Transport, Scottish Development Dept and The Welsh Office (1986) *Annual Abstract of Statistics*. London: HMSO.
3. Forfar J.O. & Arneil A.C. (1985) *Paediatrics*, 3rd edn. Edinburgh: Churchill Livingstone.
4. Kershaw B. & Salvage J. (1986) *Models for Nursing*. Chichester: John Wiley and Sons.
5. Sofear B. (1984) *Pain: A Handbook for Nurses*. London: Harper & Row.

SUGGESTED FURTHER READING

Betts-Symonds G.W. (1985) *Fracture, Care and Management for Students*. London: Macmillan.

Bradley D. (1984) *Accident and Emergency Nursing*, 2nd edn. London: Baillière Tindall.

Cardona V.D. (1986) *Trauma Nursing*. London: John Wright and Sons.

McCrae R. (1983) *Practical Fracture Treatment*. Edinburgh: Churchill Livingstone.

Medical Research Council (1975) *Aids to the Examination of the Peripheral Nervous System*. London: HMSO.

Miller M. & Miller J.H. (1985) *Orthopaedics and Accidents*. London: Hodder and Stoughton.

11

NURSING CARE OF PATIENTS WITH RHEUMATOID ARTHRITIS

Rheumatoid arthritis is a chronic or subacute nonbacterial inflammation of synovial joints. It is usually polyarticular and of symmetrical distribution. The disease is a systemic one and it affects many parts of the body such as the skin, the lungs, the eyes and the arteries. It should be remembered by the nurse that this condition is a systemic disease involving connective tissue.

In 1969, 37 million days were lost from the work situation because of complaints arising from rheumatic disease. This number exceeds those lost from work which are attributed to heart disease and accidents.

There are approximately 1 000 500 people affected by rheumatoid arthritis in this country. Seventy per cent of these people will have complete remission from the disease if treatment is successfully started within the first year. If the disease is untreated forty per cent will recover with little or no deformity, the remainder will suffer deformity which will vary from mild to very severe. The disease may threaten the whole lifestyle of the sufferer and may disrupt family life and the family totally.

The patient requires long periods away from work with 'flare-ups' of the condition, and hospital admissions for treatment and reassessment. Due to this a man may lose his job. This in turn leads to a loss of earnings and consequently a lower standard of living. The wife may have to become the breadwinner for the family. Resentment at his loss of role, often accompanied by anger, leads to stress and tension within the family. Children of the marriage are affected by the lack of money, the alteration of the relationship between the parents and the loss of a father figure.

A woman affected by the disease may find herself unable to fulfil her role as wife and mother. She becomes unable to manage her housework, the cooking and generally looking after her children, particularly if they are young. Resulting deformities leave cosmetically unacceptable features and a woman may have difficulty in accepting these.

The management of this disease is one essentially of a team approach utilizing as many of the services available as possible. The patient and his family play a vital part within the team and are included at all steps of the treatment.

The cause of rheumatoid arthritis is still unknown, in spite of much research into the disease. Many suggestions have been offered as to why the condition occurs, and these include the following:

1. The environment.
2. Hereditary factors. These seem to have some influence.
3. Viral infections such as rubella and serum hepatitis.
4. Glandular; lack of steroid production.
5. Emotional crises.
6. Psychosocial factors.
7. Auto-immunity.

The last suggestion, auto-immunity, is the one which currently seems to be the most favourable. The rheumatoid factor, an antibody, is thought to be responsible for the disease. This factor may, however, be found in normal people, especially the elderly, and in diseases other than rheumatoid arthritis.

Although rheumatoid arthritis can affect many systems of the body, the majority of the cases nursed in hospital will have joint problems.

The disease starts with the appearance of swelling of the small peripheral joints. The overlying skin becomes warmer than the surrounding skin. It takes on a shiny appearance. The patient complains of pain in the joint and morning stiffness which may take up to and sometimes more than an hour to wear off. Sometimes the stiffness lasts all day. A fever is occasionally present.

Patients often complain of feeling generally unwell with anorexia, weight loss, tiredness and lethargy.

The pathology of the disease can be summarized as follows:

1. The synovium becomes thickened due to the chronic inflammatory process.
2. An effusion of synovial fluid produces a swollen joint.
3. The synovium encroaches upon the articular cartilage. This is called a pannus.
4. The cartilage and then the underlying bone are eroded by the pannus. This eventually leads to total destruction of the joint surface.
5. The joint capsule and ligaments are weakened which leads to instability of the joint.
6. Subluxations, or complete dislocations, occur.
7. Fibrous or bony fusions occur.
8. Secondary osteoarthrosis may impose itself on to the damaged joint surfaces if the joint remains mobile.

After many months or years the disease burns itself out leaving permanently damaged and deformed joints. Tendons soften and rupture and nodules may appear in the soft tissue close to pressure points such as the elbow.

Rheumatoid arthritis may be treated either medically or surgically.

Nonoperative management of rheumatoid arthritis

1. Improve general health.
2. Moderate exercise.
3. Rest of joints in splints.
4. Drug therapy.
5. Aids to daily living activities.

General health is improved by using controlled bed rest, achieving a balance between rest and activity. Any anaemia which is present is treated sometimes by blood transfusion. Depression, which is a feature of this condition, is dealt with by careful explanation to the patient and his family of the disease and the treatments being used.

Simple exercise routines, which are introduced gradually following rest periods, are started. Splints are applied to painful joints to achieve rest and relief of pain. These also aid the prevention and correction of deformities and help to fix a damaged joint in a functional position. Traction may be used to correct a fixed flexion deformity of a joint (see Figure 11.1). Reverse dynamic sling traction is applied to the affected joint. This gently stretches the contracted soft tissues. The traction is often used before surgical measures are undertaken.

Drug therapy in the form of nonsteroidal anti-inflammatory drugs and analgesics are started. It is often necessary to try several drugs before finding the combination which suits the individual patient. More advanced anti-rheumatoid drugs, such as gold salts and penicillamine, may be used. For patients with a severe unremitting disease or those who have very severe morning stiffness, corticosteroid drugs may be used. Table 11.1 shows some common drugs used in the treatment of rheumatoid arthritis.

Operative management of rheumatoid arthritis

1. Early phase:
   Synovectomy.
2. Intermediate phase:
   Tenosynovectomy.
   Tendon repairs.
   Tendon transplants.
3. Late phase:
   hands: Excision arthroplasty.
   Replacement arthroplasty.
   wrists: Arthrodesis of wrist.
   Excision of ulnar head.
   elbows: Excision of radial head.
   hips: Replacement arthroplasty.
   knees: Patellectomy.
   Arthrodesis.
   Osteotomy.
   Replacement arthroplasty
   feet: Arthrodesis.
   Excision arthroplasty.

Nursing care for patients with rheumatoid arthritis

Rheumatoid arthritis is a complicated condition. The nursing of such patients is physically and mentally demanding. The nurse needs detailed knowledge of the disease process and its treatment to be an effective agent in enabling the patient to achieve maximum independence with the individual's capabilities.

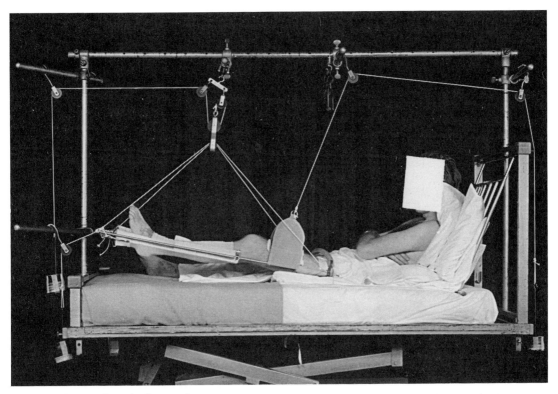

Fig. 11.1 Reverse dynamic sling traction.

Table 11.1 Some common drugs used in the treatment of rheumatoid arthritis.

Name of the drug	Possible side-effects	Comments	Information to be given to patients
Aspirin	Gastrointestinal discomfort, nausea, hearing disturbances, rashes	These are the first line nonsteroidal anti-inflammatory drugs used to relieve pain and stiffness. They may be supplemented by analgesic drugs as required. It is necessary to find out for the patient by trial and error which drug or combination of drugs gives the best relief with the fewest adverse side-effects	Aspirin should be taken after food. Report any indigestion, or change in bowel habits
Diclofenac sodium (Voltarol)	Gastrointestinal discomfort, headache, skin rashes		Drug should be taken after food or with milk
Fenbufen (Lederfen)	High risk of skin rashes. Less risk of gastrointestinal discomfort		As above
Fenoprofen (Fenopron)	Mostly gastrointestinal upsets		As above
Flurbiprofen (Froben)	As above		As above
Ibuprofen (Brufen)	As above		As above
Idomethacin (Indocid)	Headache, dizziness, light-headedness, as above. Ophthalmic and blood tests are advised		May impair the ability to drive. Report any urinary changes and as above
Naproxen (Naprosyn)	Dizziness, drowsiness and as above		Report any diarrhoea and as above.

Table 11.1 Continued

Name of the drug	Possible side-effects	Comments	Information to be given to patients
Chloroquine	Retinal damage leading to blindness. It is given for 9 months out of every twelve months	This is an anti-malarial drug. The patients eyes should be monitored by an ophthalmologist	Patients are advised to report any change in their eye-sight
Sodium aurothiomalate	Mouth ulcers, oedema		
Gold salts (Myocrisin)	Decreases platelet and white blood cell production by suppressing the bone marrow function. It may affect the renal tubules causing albuminuria. May cause skin rashes	Weekly blood test to include W.B.C. and platelet count. Weekly urinalysis to observe for albuminuria. The patient's skin is observed daily for the appearance of thrombocytopenia. Any irritation of the skin is investigated	Patients are advised to report if they start to bruise easily, develop a sore mouth or have any irritation of their skin
D-penicillamine	The same as for gold salts. Plus loss of taste and nausea	As above	Patients should be warned not to expect improvements for 6–12 weeks. Drug should be taken before food
		These three drugs are used as second-line drugs. They are far more toxic agents than the first line drugs. These are used for patients with severe unremitting disease.	
Corticosteroids (Prednisolone given orally. Hydrocortisone given by intramuscular or intra-articular injection)	Adrenal suppression, hypertension, oedema, muscle weakness, osteoporosis, peptic ulceration. May suppress growth in children	These drugs are used as a last resort in those patients with a rapidly progressive disease. They may also be used when a patient has an acute exacerbation of the disease. Corticosteroids are only used in short-term treatment. They are used with caution because of their side-effects. Their action is to suppress the disease process.	Patients should carry a card stating the drug and dosage they are taking

Maintaining a safe environment

• The patient is nursed on a firm-based bed, well supported by pillows. The patient's limbs are supported in a comfortable but optimal position. The bed needs to be in bright and cheerful surroundings to encourage the patient to feel better. Freedom from anxiety, stress and tension is important for the patient's well being. The nurse must take time to explain details of treatments to the patient and to take an interest in the patient's family. The nurse needs to provide a cheerful and optimistic approach to her patient without being over exuberant.

• Bedclothes are often too heavy for these patients and may be replaced by a duvet. It is important when selecting a duvet for use that fire precautions are observed by choosing a nonflammable material. Laundry facilities should also be taken into consideration.
• If a duvet is not the chosen method, bed cradles must be used to relieve pressure on painful joints.
• Patients with rheumatoid arthritis frequently have a frail skin due to both the condition and their drug therapy. Great care is taken to ensure the pedals of the bed are always turned to their safest position to avoid damaging the patient's legs.

- A careful assessment of the patient's potential risk of pressure sores is made and the appropriate measures included on the patient's care plan. The use of sheepskins for the patient to sit on, and sheepskin bootees to prevent heel problems will aid the prevention of the start of pressure problems.
- Pain control is of prime importance for the patient. Prescribed medication is given and its effectiveness observed by the nurse. The patient should be taught how to assess his own pain levels to enable effective relief of pain to be maintained.

Applications of heat and cold in the form of wax baths for the hands and ice packs carefully placed over hot, swollen joints will help to relieve pain.

Relaxation techniques may be of benefit. These may be taught to the patient by a well-informed person. There are commercially available relaxation tapes which may be employed.

- Drug therapy is important. The rheumatoid patient will be taking drugs sometimes for many years and self medication is an important part of the patient's education. In the acute stage of the disease the nurse will administer the drugs to the patient and will need a sound knowlege of their side-effects if she is to observe her patient accurately.

Self-medication can be taught slowly to the patient as his condition improves. If the patient is unable to undertake this task himself, then a relative or friend may be asked to take on this aspect of care.

- A balance between rest and activity is important for these patients. Rest periods on the ward must be jealously guarded by the nurse to ensure that the other disciplines do not interrupt them.
- Gentle exercises, taught by the physiotherapist, are carried out following rest periods. As the inflamed joints begin to improve so activity is increased.
- Splints may be used to rest acutely inflamed joints. The affected joint is splinted in the optimum position, often in a cuffed unlined splint (see Figures 11.2 and 11.3). This allows for observation of the joint without constantly removing the splint.
- Handling and lifting these patients may be difficult due to their fragile skin and painful joints. The patient will probably be able to advise the nurse on how he would like to be lifted. The nurse needs to assess which joints the patient will be able to use to help himself. This is one type of disease where the Australian/shoulder lift is often inappropriate as these patients frequently have their shoulders affected by the disease. Special attention to the patient's skin when handling them is important. Patients should be lifted well clear of the bed to avoid dragging on the

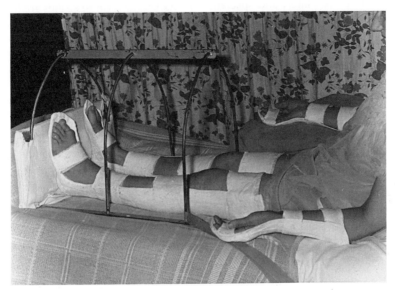

Fig. 11.2 Patient with resting splints applied.

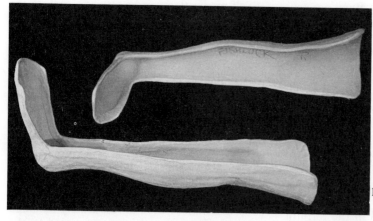

Fig. 11.3 Long leg plaster night splints, unpadded.

bed linen. The use of a hoist to lift the patient should always be considered.

Communicating

- Education of the patient about his disease, his treatments and his prognosis is important. The family will frequently need to be included in these teaching sessions.

Eating and drinking

- Meals need to be small, light, nourishing and tempting. Patients with rheumatoid arthritis are often anorexic and are unable to feed themselves due to their painful joints. Aids in the form of large handled cutlery, nonslip mats on which to place plates, and specially designed feeding cups are employed to enable these patients to retain their independence in this task.

Personal cleansing and dressing

- The patient will require help in maintaining his personal cleanliness. Very often the nurse will be required to give a total bed bath. If it is at all possible most patients prefer to be immersed in warm water to aid relief of their stiffness. A bath hoist should be used to help lift the patient into and out of the bath. A bath seat, nonslip mat and grab rails may also help the patient in the bath. Shower facilities in a ward may help the patient towards independence in bathing although elderly patients do not always like showering.
- Care must be taken, when drying the

patient, not to rub the patient's skin as this may cause it to chafe due to its fragility. If the patient is confined to bed and has to use a bed pan, he must never be left unsupported. Adjustments to his pillows must be such that he is safe and secure while using a bed pan.
- Rheumatoid arthritis may affect the cervical spine, therefore great care is necessary when washing the patient's hair. Long handled brushes and combs may help the patient to retain some independence.
- The patient's eyes require careful bathing and observation. Dry eyes and a dry mouth may indicate Sjögren's syndrome which occurs commonly in patients with rheumatoid arthritis. Artificial tears may be prescribed to relieve the symptoms in the eyes. Glycerine mouthwashes are helpful to relieve a dry mouth. The symptoms rarely become severe, but dry eyes are particularly vulnerable to wind and dry heat. Protective goggles or spectacles may be needed if this is the case.
- Normal fasteners on clothes may present a problem for the patient. 'Velcro' is used to replace normal fasteners.
- Aids such as help-hand devices will assist the patient to dress independently (see Figure 11.4). Further devices to aid putting on tights or stockings will also help the patient. Time to allow the patient to dress is important. He should not be hurried as success at dressing himself will show him that he is on the right road to recovery.

Eliminating

- Toiletting may present problems for the

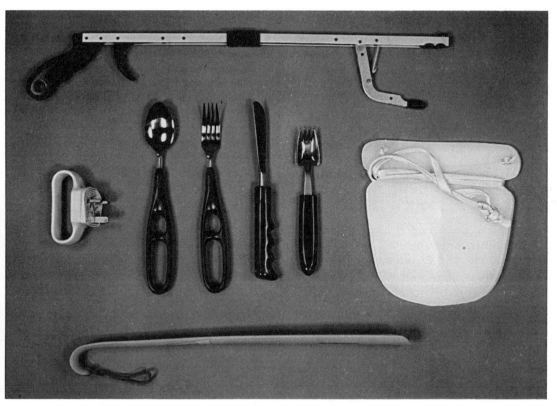

Fig. 11.4 Aids to help the patient remain independent.

patient with painful hips and knees. A raised toilet seat with grab rails around the toilet will help the patient.

Mobilizing

* Mobilizing the patient is taken slowly over a long period of time. Setting short, realistic goals to achieve in this area will help to boost the patient's morale. Wide space type shoes to accomodate painful feet will enable the patient to stand upright with the minimal amount of discomfort.

Working and playing

* The occupational therapist helps the patient to become familiar with the many aids available to help him in his daily life. She will make a careful assessment of the patient's requirements to enable him to retain maximum independence. The housewife with rheumatoid arthritis may need alterations to her kitchen and is often asked to cook a meal

in the occupational therapy kitchen to enable an assessment to be made.

* The disablement resettlement officer (DRO), is trained to advise people about returning to their employment. In some cases of rheumatoid arthritis this will be impossible and the patient then becomes a registered disabled person. The DRO may recommend retraining of the patient at an Employment Resettlement Centre to enable him to regain employment.

Expressing sexuality

* Sexuality, in the form of sexual difficulties and problems, may be raised by the patient. It may not be raised until a relationship has been established between the nurse and her patient. The medical social worker may be trained in sexual counselling or the nurse may be able to call on the services of a trained counsellor to deal with the problem as it arises.

The Arthritis and Rheumatism Council has produced a booklet called 'Marriage, Sex and Arthritis' which may be given to the patient to read.

The problem may be one of difficulty for the patient to accept an altered body image. Hand deformities in particular may cause great anxiety to a woman. Recognition of this anxiety by the nurse is important and attempts to talk the problem through with the patient should be made.

Sleeping

- A good night's sleep is important for the maintenance of health. Patients with rheumatoid arthritis often have difficulty in achieving a successful night's sleep. The patient's pain needs to be adequately controlled and a comfortable, well supported position assumed to enable sleep to be successful.

Rehabilitation is an ongoing process for the patient which starts as soon as the patient enters the hospital. Community support services, such as the primary health care team and social services, are employed to ensure the patient is able to maintain his daily life with maximum independence. Reassessment of the progress of the patient's disease and his needs is essential and is done on a regular basis. The nurse must liaise with the available community services to ensure continuity of care for the patient.

Specific nursing care for patients with rheumatoid arthritis undergoing surgery

Pre-operative nursing care

- Great care is necessary during shaving of the patient's skin. Rheumatoid patients have a low resistance to infection.
- A cervical collar is generally applied to the patient before going to the theatre. This acts as a warning to operating department staff that the patient could be a special risk.
- Patient education pre-operatively is important.

Practice, using one arm if upper limb surgery is to be undergone, will help to clarify the patient's needs at this point.

Postoperative nursing care

- Rheumatoid patients frequently have porotic bones due to their systemic illness. Careful handling of the patient's limbs postoperatively will prevent undue fractures of the bones.
- The skin touching aids, such as a Charnley wedge pillow used to maintain the patient's hips in abduction following a total hip replacement, are checked for signs of pressure and rubbing.
- Patients with rheumatoid arthritis suffer morning and inactivity stiffness. It is important, because of this feature, that the patient is confined to bed postoperatively for as short a time as possible.
- Healing of the patient's wound may take longer than the normal time. Sutures are often left in for a longer period than normal. The wound dressing should be left intact unless there are signs of infection.

JUVENILE RHEUMATOID ARTHRITIS

This rare type of rheumatoid arthritis (Still's disease, Juvenile chronic arthritis) is defined as arthritis starting below the age of sixteen years and involving four or more joints for a minimal period of three months (see Figure 11.5). The onset is usually between the ages of one to five years. Approximately one-quarter of the affected children will go on to develop a destructive type of arthritis which will leave them with permanently deformed joints which will affect them in adult life.

The medical management of these children closely follows that prescribed for an adult patient with rheumatoid arthritis.

Specific nursing care

Many of the features of the nursing care of adult patients apply to the children with this condition. There are differences and the specific nursing care is set out below.

- Steroid drugs, used in the medical management of juvenile rheumatoid arthritis, may suppress the growth hormone, stunting the growth of the child. This will lead to anxiety on the part of the parents and the child. There is a possibility that growth may catch

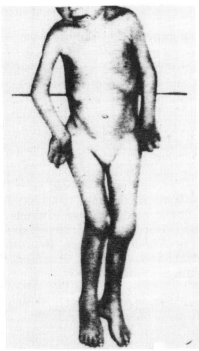

Fig. 11.5   Still's disease.

up during remission periods or at puberty. The nurse should take the optimistic view at all times with her patient and the parents, reassuring them that this may be the case. Aspirin in newly diagnosed cases is now not used in the light of recent research which revealed an association with Reyes syndrome (1) (2) (3).

- Exercise is very important for these children. Long periods of immobility, particularly in young joints, may lead to joint contractures and/or bony fusions. Exercise should be encouraged. It should become part of the daily nursing routine and play should become a part of exercise.
- The continuation of the child's education is vital. With the resulting joint deformities the child will seldom be able to seek employment of a physical nature. Intellectual development and stimulation is therefore important. A hospital school, visiting teacher or play leader may be available and the nurse has to arrange nursing care to allow for the child to attend school as normally as possible. Guidance on careers, advice and counselling about the child's life as an adult will be necessary.
- The child's parents and siblings may also

need a listening ear from the nurse. Anxiety about the child's future and his place in the family may be examples of the problems the nurse has to listen to. Parents are encouraged to work alongside the nurse and physiotherapist to learn how to handle the child's affected limbs and to encourage the child in exercising. Again, an optimistic view needs to be adopted by all members of the team who have dealings with the child and his parents.

OTHER TYPES OF DISEASE

There are several types of disease which imitate closely the clinical manifestations of rheumatoid arthritis. These include:

1. Other inflammatory types of arthritis such as:
   Systemic lupus erythematosus
   Polymyalgia rheumatica
   Systemic sclerosis.
2. Infective forms of arthritis such as:
   Pyogenic arthritis
   Tuberculous arthritis.
3. Metabolic bone disease such as:
   Osteomalacia
   Osteoporosis.
4. Haemophiliac arthritis.
5. Sickle cell disease.
6. Reiter's disease.
7. Psoriatic arthropathy.
8. Colitic arthritis.
9. Ankylosing spondylitis.

The nursing management of these conditions varies little from the nursing care offered to patients with rheumatoid arthritis. The nursing care of some of these conditions is explained in other chapters. One condition which is most commonly seen in the wards dealing with patients with rheumatoid arthritis is ankylosing spondylitis. Therefore the nursing management of this condition is included in this chapter.

ANKYLOSING SPONDYLITIS

Ankylosing spondylitis (Marie-Strumpell disease) is usually classified as a seronegative arthritis. It is a disease which affects predominantly young males. The patient presents with pain in his sacro-iliac joints which may go on to produce the classical bamboo or poker spine by progressive calcification of the spinal ligaments. If the thoracic vertebrae become involved, the patient's vital capacity will be reduced (see Figure 11.6).

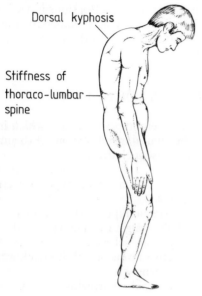

Fig. 11.6   Posture in ankylosing spondylitis.

Over 90 per cent of the patients with ankylosing spondylitis have an antigen, HLA B27. This is determined by genes present in a small part of one chromosome.

The patient is admitted to hospital for investigations, diagnosis and an intensive education programme.

Specific nursing care points

- The patient is nursed on a flat bed with only one pillow under his head if it is really required.
- Bed rest is positively harmful as it increases the risk of fusion of the spine. Therefore, in spite of some morning stiffness, the patient is encouraged to be up and active from first thing in the morning.
- Pain may be a prominent feature in the early stages of the condition. Phenylbutazone and indomethacin may be prescribed to control

pain and the nurse should note their effectiveness, advising the doctor if they do not control the pain.

- Hydrotherapy and physiotherapy form the major part of the patient's treatment. Back extension and chest expansion exercises are important to maintain an upright spine and an acceptable vital capacity. The nurse needs to be vigilant in observing that the patient adopts a good posture in all activities.

  Encouragement to develop a routine for exercise is important. Activities such as swimming, cycling and walking may be advised as being advantageous.
- The patient may need to change his employment, especially if it involves long periods of stooping or standing. Advice from the medical social worker and maybe the disablement resettlement officer may be sought.

Rheumatoid arthritis and its associated conditions continue to be the target for research. The Arthritis and Rheumatism Council and the British Rheumatism Association support much of this research. It is a condition which allows the orthopaedic nurse to practise a truly holistic approach to her nursing management both in the hospital setting and in the community.

REFERENCES

1. Snodgrass W.R. (1986) *Paediatric Clinics of North America.*
2. Hollister J.R. (1985) *American Journal of Diseases of Children.*
3. Committee on Safety of Medicines Update (1986) *British Medical Journal*, 14th June.

SUGGESTED FURTHER READING

Bird H.A., LeGallez P. & Hill J. (1985) *Combined Care of the Rheumatic Patient.* Springer-Verlag.
Currey H.L.F. (1983) *Essentials of Rheumatology.* London: Pitman.
Jayson M.I.V. (1976) *Stills Disease: Juvenile Chronic Polyarthritis.* London: Academic Press.
Panayi E.S. (1980) *Essential Rheumatology.* London: Baillière Tindall.
Swinson D.R. & Swinburn W.R. (1980) *Rheumatology.* London: Hodder and Stoughton.

12

NURSING CARE OF PATIENTS WITH TUMOURS OF THE MUSCULO-SKELETAL SYSTEM

Bone tumours, because of the tissue they attack, frequently lie undetected until they are well established. They are seldom palpable and are only diagnosed by x-ray examination. Bone tumours, like any other neoplasm, may be benign or malignant.

Many of the benign bone tumours are asymptomatic. Interference with joint function may be an early sign of these tumours. Malignant tumours may reveal themselves following a pathological fracture. Pain at the site of the tumour may only occur when the tumour is well established.

Benign tumours grow slowly, remain encapsulated and seldom destroy or invade other body tissues. They are relatively harmless neoplasms, but they may become malignant in the later stages of their development.

Table 12.1 provides a summary of the most commonly seen primary benign bone tumours.

Malignant bone tumours grow rapidly. Nearly all of them destroy the host bone. They produce soft tissue swelling. Pain is a predominant feature. They metastasize through the blood stream to other parts of the body; the brain and the lungs being the areas most commonly affected.

Table 12.2 provides a summary of the most commonly seen primary malignant bone tumours, and Figure 12.1 shows an x-ray of tibia, with osteosarcoma.

Secondary malignant tumours are those associated with a primary malignant tumour elsewhere in the body. The most common sites for the primary tumour to be located are the breast, the lung and the prostate gland. The

Table 12.1 Common benign musculo-skeletal tumours

Tumour	Cell of Origin	Incidence	Site Most Commonly Affected	Prognosis
Osteoblastoma	Osteoblasts	Males Children Young adults	Vertebral column Shoulder girdle bones Proximal extremity of humerus, femur and tibia Pelvic girdle bones	Good (rarely progresses to become malignant)
Giant cell tumour (osteoclastoma)	Osteoclasts	Young adults	Proximal extremity of humerus and tibia Distal extremity of radius, ulna and femur	Cure: 50 per cent (high degree of progression to malignancy May recur)
Osteoma	Osteoblasts	Any age	Anywhere in the bony skeleton except for the cervical and thoracic vertebrae	Excellent
Osteochondroma (most common of benign tumours)	Osteoblasts and chondroblasts	Children and adolescents	Proximal extremity of humerus and tibia Distal extremity of femur	Good (may progress to malignancy
Chondroblastoma	Chondroblasts	Adolescents	Proximal extremity of humerus and femur	Good

Table 12.2   Common malignant musculo-skeletal tumours

Tumour	Cell of Origin	Incidence	Site Most Commonly Affected	Prognosis
Osteosarcoma	Osteoblasts	Males, 10–30 years of age	Proximal extremity of humerus and tibia Distal extremity of femur	20 per cent: 1–5 years average: 18 months (lung metastases)
Chondrosarcoma (most common primary malignant tumour)	Chondroblasts	Males over 35 years of age	Vertebral column Bones of pelvic and shoulder girdles Proximal extremity of humerus, femur and tibia	May be good with treatment (recurs at site of treatment)
Fibrosarcoma	Fibroblasts	Middle age	Upper and lower jaw Proximal and distal extremities of humerus Whole length of femur and tibia	Better than osteosarcoma or chondrosarcoma
Ewing tumour (Sarcoma)	Unknown	10–20 years of age	Trunk area and bones of vertebral column Mid-third area of humerus, femur, tibia and fibula Bones of the foot	Mortality high Life expectancy approximately two years
Multiple myeloma	Plasma cell	Males, 40–60 years of age	Skull Vertebral column Shoulder and pelvic girdles	Poor prognosis Life expectancy 1–3 years

Fig. 12.1   An x-ray of tibia showing an osteosarcoma.

bony involvement may be from direct spread of the primary tumour or by invasion from the blood stream or lymphatic system.

Pathological fractures and pain are the commonest symptoms of secondary deposits in the bone. The metastatic tumours are generally of two types: those which destroy bone (osteolytic) and those which increase bone (osteoblastic).

There are two major age groups most commonly affected by bone tumours. The 60 years of age group is one, but adolescents and young adults form by far the largest group of people affected by bone tumours. This becomes a significant factor when considering the nursing care relevant to these patients.

The emotional upheaval of discovering a neoplasm during the stage of adolescence may have a devastating effect on the patient and his family. This is true whether the neoplasm is benign or malignant. Support for the parents and the patient in the form of giving time to allow them to express their feelings is an essential part of the nursing care. Careful explanations about treatments are very necessary to ensure full cooperation of all concerned.

The nurse caring for the terminally ill patient with a bone tumour needs to adopt a practical and encouraging attitude to her patient. Kindness and understanding are essential. Treating the patient as an intelligent adult is important to the patient.

The hospice movement has provided nursing with much needed advice on how to identify problems experienced by both the patient and the family and how these can be coped with.

Nursing care for a patient with a bone tumour

Maintaining a safe environment

- Fear of the unknown, of death and of the disease itself may be a symptom the nurse has to deal with. Careful explanation of all procedures and maintaining a safe environment can help to alleviate fear. Time for the patient to express his fears is important. Night nurses often find themselves forming a close bond with a patient as time seems more available to a patient at night.
- Pain associated with bone tumours may be acute or chronic and variable in intensity. Fear, depression and anxiety may all lead to an exacerbation of pain which analgesia will not relieve. It is not always the pain of the tumour which is causing distress to the patient.
- Careful assessment by the nurse of the location, pattern, intensity and duration of the pain may lead to methods other than the administration of analgesia being employed to relieve pain. Constipation, unrelieved pressure on a susceptible area or muscle pain should all be monitored.
- The patient's own past experiences and his expectation of pain may need to be taken into account. Margo McCaffrey says: 'Pain is whatever the experiencing person says it is and exists whenever he says it does' (1).
- When analgesia has been administered the nurse should monitor its effectiveness at regular intervals. How effective has it been in relieving pain? Is the patient ever totally pain free? The patient may be involved in monitoring his own pain levels by use of a scale to denote how intense the pain is and whether the analgesia given is effective.
- If there are secondary deposits in the brain, mental confusion may be a distressing symptom for the patient's family. The patient's

safety in this case is very important. Precautions must be taken to make sure the patient does not fall out of bed or injure himself or others.

Communicating

- Good communication between all the team caring for the patient is essential. Bad communication causes suffering.
- It is the surgeon's decision as to how much the patient and his relatives are to be told about his condition. The nurse must make sure she has the correct information about this to enable her to continue caring for her patient.
- Dr R. Twycross says, 'Communication is not just a matter of words. Holding a patient's hand while talking to him, or even an arm round his shoulder conveys a positive message: "No matter what happens I shall stand by you—I won't let you down"' (2).
- Communication with the patient's relatives is equally important. They, too, may need to come to terms with the patient's illness and work through their own stress.

Breathing

- Secondary deposits in the lung may lead to distressing symptoms for the patient. The patient should be nursed in the most comfortable position to enable him to breathe easily. Distressing symptoms such as dyspnoea and coughing may be relieved by inhalations or oxygen.

Eating and drinking

- Weight loss, particularly if the patient has a malignant tumour, may be a prominent feature. Patients are often anorexic and cachexia may be present.
- If the patient is receiving radiotherapy treatment, nausea may be present.
- Small, light, appetizing but nourishing meals should be offered to the patient. There are many commercially produced food supplements available and these should be used when necessary.
- There may come the time with a terminally ill patient when the need for food is minimal. Tube feeding may, at this stage, be inappropriate.

- Fluid intake should be encouraged and maintained, if possible, at between 2.5 and three litres daily.

Eliminating

- Urinary output should be monitored by recording the output on a fluid balance chart. Weekly urinalysis is performed. This is important if the patient is taking cytotoxic or corticosteroid drugs. Proteinuria and glucosuria in particular should be tested.
- Constipation and diarrhoea are two further distresssing symptoms which may be present. Constipation may be the cause of pain and may be due to the administration of narcotic analgesia. Steps such as the use of suppositories or laxatives may help to relieve the situation.
- The use of barrier creams to protect the skin around the anus and buttocks will prevent sores.

Personal cleansing and dressing

- It is important that the patient retains as much independence as possible for himself. Personal hygiene is maintained, whenever possible, by the patient himself. Relatives will be encouraged to help whenever necessary and if they wish to.

Mobilizing

- Mobility and activity should be encouraged whenever possible. The patient's joints should be put through a full range of activity each day. The patient is encouraged to perform these exercises himself until such times as it becomes impractical. At this stage passive movement is not so important if the patient's life-expectancy is poor. Comfort is important and, if the patient wishes his joints to be moved, this should be done gently.
- Massage performed expertly may help to retain muscle tone and relieve pain. It may cause further pain if performed inadequately.

Working and playing

- Diversional therapy plays an important part in relieving pain. Both attention and consciousness are essential to the perception of pain. If attention is directed towards another activity pain is often reduced.

Sleeping

- Sleeping may be fitful and not confined to the night time. The patient soon becomes accustomed to the sedative effect of analgesia. If the patient is pain free, comfortable and is not anxious, then it may be necessary to administer drugs to induce sleep.

Dying

- 'Death is the loneliest experience any of us will ever have to face.' (2) This is particularly true in an adolescent or young adult. Coming to terms with dying is difficult for any age but must be particularly harrowing for the young and their families. The patient should not be isolated in a corner of the ward unless he has other distressing symptoms. The patient's cooperation over procedures and his direct involvement with his care may help him come to terms with his illness. Support for the patient, time allowed for him to talk through his fears and continuity of management of his disease will help both the patient and his relatives to face reality.

Nonoperative treatments for patients with bone tumours

Radiotherapy

This may used for two reasons:

1. To control and halt the progression of the tumour. In an adolescent, whose life-expectancy is a few months or weeks, this treatment may be given instead of the trauma of an amputation.
2. As palliative treatment to control pain, bleeding or coughing.

Chemotherapy

1. *Cytotoxic drugs.* These may be used in combination with radiotherapy or operative measures. New drugs are constantly being discovered and produced. It is essential that all personnel involved with the administration of such drugs receive full instructions from a specialist oncologist on their use. The pharmacist may be

employed to help in this instruction with regard to the side-effects of the drugs and the observations which are necessary along with any precautions which should be taken. Patients are frequently admitted to a specialist centre for the period these drugs are to be administered.

2. *Corticosteroids.* These may help to reduce inflammation and therefore pain.
3. *Hormonal Therapy.*

Splints

These may be prescribed to support affected limbs or the spine.

Treatment

Treatment of such conditions as anaemia to improve general health is implemented.

Nursing care for patients receiving nonoperative treatments for bone tumours

As with any other orthopaedic patient, a high standard of nursing care is planned to meet the patient's individual need. Specific care is directed towards helping the patient to cope with the unpleasant side-effects of the treatment they are receiving. It is important that the patient is warned of the possible side-effects of treatment before it starts. Discussions with the doctor should facilitate this. However, the nurse must be aware of what the doctor has said so that she may reinforce those statements with the patient.

- Cytotoxic drug therapy causes bone marrow suppression. This leaves the patient liable to infections. Barrier nursing is used to lower the risk of infection for the patient.
- Meticulous personal hygiene will also help to prevent the onset of infection. Assisted bed baths and hair washing are carried out according to the patient's wishes.
- If radiotherapy is being used, the area to be irradiated is carefully marked by the radiologist. This area must never be washed until 7–10 days following completion of the treatment. Irradiation leaves the skin prone to breakdown. Rough handling, wetting the area or the application of cream or talcum powder may cause a skin breakdown.
- Nausea and vomiting are unpleasant side-

efects of both radiotherapy and chemotherapy. Anti-emetics are used to control these and should be given half-an-hour before food. A receptacle should be kept close at hand for the patient's use. Mouthwashes must be offered frequently. Oral hygiene is performed every 2–4 hours.

- Diarrhoea may be controlled by drugs. Use of a barrier cream may help the patient to feel more comfortable and avoid sores forming. A commode should be kept within easy reach for the patient.
- Mouth ulcers may form. The patient should be given oral toilet two-hourly to help these. Local applications of creams will help reduce discomfort in the patient's mouth.
- Alopecia is a recognized side-effect of chemotherapy. The patient and his relatives need to be warned about this problem before treatment commences. If the patient requests, a wig may be supplied. This should be discussed with the orthotist who will advise and help the patient with his selection.

Operative treatments for patients with bone tumours

1. *Local excision of the tumour mass with curettage.* Bone grafts may be employed to aid healing of the bone and to obliterate dead space. Prosthetic replacement of bones and joints is an expanding part of this approach. In some cases the whole length of the bone and its attendant joint are replaced. This avoids the necessity to amputate a limb. The long-term results of this type of replacement are not yet known.
2. *Amputation.* This is generally performed through a site well clear of the tumour. It may involve disarticulation of a limb or a hindquarter or forequarter amputation. Amputation is radical surgical intervention, sometimes with mutilating effects. However, it may be the only life-saving avenue left open the surgeon.
3. *Internal fixation of pathological fractures.* The aim of internally fixing these fractures is to reduce pain and to prevent further fractures occurring. The general health of the patient will largely direct whether internal fixation is a viable proce-

dure. This is particularly relevant when the fracture is as a result of metastatic deposits.

There is no specific nursing care for patients undergoing operative treatment for bone tumours. Routine pre-operative and postoperative nursing relating to the individual patient is planned according to his needs. Patients who are to have an amputation need special considerations as discussed later in this book.

However, it is well worth all personnel involved with the care of patients with bone tumours to read the following poem. It sums up the needs all patients with these types of disease have far better than anyone else could:

> I huddle warm inside my corner bed,
> Watching the other patients sipping tea.
> I wonder why I'm so long getting well,
> And why it is no-one will talk to me.
>
> The nurses are so kind. They brush my hair
> On days I feel too ill to read or sew.
> I smile and chat, try not to show my fear,
> They cannot tell me what I want to know.
>
> The visitors come in. I see their eyes
> Become embarrassed as they pass my bed.
> 'What lovely flowers' they say, then hurry on
> In case their faces show what can't be said.
>
> The Chaplain passes on his weekly round
> With friendly smile and calm, untroubled brow.
> He speaks with deep sincerity of Life.
> I'd like to speak of death, but don't know how.
>
> The Surgeon comes, with student retinue,
> Mutters to Sister, deaf to my silent plea.
> I want to tell this dread I feel inside,
> But they are all too kind to talk to me.

Reproduced by kind permission of Nursing Times, this poem first appeared in *Nursing Mirror* on 9th August, 1968.

REFERENCES

1. McCaffrey M. (1973) Intractable pain. *Journal of Nursing*: America.
2. Twycross R.G. (1975) *The Dying Patient*. London: Christian Medical Fellowship.

SUGGESTED FURTHER READING

Deeley T.S., Fish E.J. & Gough M.A. (1974) *A Guide to Oncological Nursing*. Edinburgh: Churchill Livingstone.
Saunders C.M. (1978) *The Management of Terminal Disease*. London: Edward Arnold.
Tiffany R. (1980) *Oncology for Nurses and Health Care Professionals*. Vols. 1 & 2. London: George Allen and Unwin.

13

NURSING CARE OF PATIENTS WITH TUBERCULOSIS OF BONES AND JOINTS

The incidence of tuberculosis, during recent years, has been greatly reduced by an increased understanding of how the disease spreads. Improvement to the standards of hygiene and the environment, less crowded living conditions and improved nutrition have all helped. Careful inspection and control of the cattle which produce milk and meat have helped to reduce the incidence of bovine tuberculosis.

Screening of all school children, and if necessary, vaccination by the BCG (Bacille Calmette Guérin), has acted as a preventative measure. Mass radiography has had a part to play, although the problems arising from frequent exposure to x-rays have led this method into disfavour. However, it is a fairly common disease in under developed countries, and with an increasing immigrant cosmopolitan population, the incidence of tuberculosis has shown an increase. Economic problems have caused many screening programmes to be curtailed. In the future these may need to be restarted. There is, equally, a concern that the incidence of the disease may increase due to a resistance to current antibiotic therapy and the current socioeconomic climate (1) (2).

The cause of tuberculosis is Koch's bacillus. The organism gains entry to the body through the nasopharynx or gastrointestinal tracts. The infection may be spread by direct or indirect contact. Thus overcrowded living conditions, with poor sanitary or hygiene arrangements, are prime areas to encourage the spread of the disease.

The main areas of the musculo-skeletal system affected by tuberculosis are the vertebral column (see Figure 13.1), the hip and the knee joint. Other joints are affected less often.

Tuberculosis of bones and joints is always secondary to a primary infection. The source of the primary focus is usually the lungs.

Nonoperative treatment of patients with tuberculosis

1. *Rest.* General rest of the patient's body and mind. Specific rest of the affected part by the application of traction, plasters or orthoses.
2. *Chemotherapy.* Antibiotic therapy has revolutionalized the treatment of tuberculosis. The introduction of streptomycin, combined with other drugs, has lessened the time patients spend in hospital and provided a means of curing the disease.

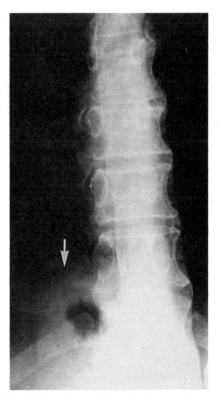

Fig. 13.1 Tuberculosis of the spine showing abscess.

There are side-effects to the commonly used drugs (see Table 13.1). The nurse must be aware of these and observe her patient for the onset of these.

Chemotherapy may be continued for a year or more, but is used by the patient as an outpatient rather than remaining in hospital.

Three drugs are given together during the initial phase. This is called 'Triple Therapy' and generally lasts for eight weeks. Two drugs are given during the continuation stage.

Operative treatments

1. *Incision and drainage of abscess formation.* Cold abscesses may form adjacent to an affected bone or joint, or track through soft tissue, including muscle, to the skin surface. A cold abscess contains pus. It appears as a fluctuant swelling, without local heat; thus the term 'cold' abscess. The patient may experience pain and demonstrate further signs of infection. Incision and drainage is undertaken to prevent a sinus forming or the abscess breaking down.
2. *Biopsy.* This may be undertaken to confirm a diagnosis.
3. *Osteotomy.* This may be used to realign a joint, thus increasing its stability.
4. *Arthrodesis.* A joint may be fused in a functional position. This will reduce pain in the joint and, although stiff, it will be stable and useful.

General nursing care of patients with tuberculosis

Tuberculosis is a chronic condition. The patient and his family require educating about the disease itself and the preventative measures they are able to adopt. Further, they require support of the medical, nursing and paramedical services over a long period of time.

Table 13.1 Drugs commonly used in the treatment of tuberculosis

Name	Administration	Side-effects	Comments	Information to be given to patients
Streptomycin	Intramuscular injection twice daily for up to three months	Damage to the 8th cranial nerve – tinnitus and headaches and giddiness, leading to deafness. Skin rashes. Gastrointestinal upsets	Nurse must protect her own skin during administration. Usually given with a second drug to prevent bacilli becoming resistant to it	Patients should be warned to report ringing in their ears
Streptomycin	Local injections into joint cavities or cerebrospinal fluid	As above	Scrupulous aseptic technique during all administrations of this drug	As above
Para-amino-salicylic acid (PAS)	Oral fluid, tablet or cachet, three or four times daily	Gastrointestinal upsets. Skin rashes	Given in conjunction with streptomycin to prevent bacilli becoming resistant to streptomycin	
Isonicotinic Acid Hydrazide (Isoniazid INH)	Oral fluid or tablet, three or four times daily	Peripheral neuropathy. Gastrointestinal upsets. Skin rashes	Also given in combination with streptomycin and/or PAS	
Rifampicin	Capsules or tablets, once daily before a meal	Gastrointestinal upsets. Peripheral neuropathy. Liver toxicity	Colours urine and saliva orange-red	Patient should report any influenzal, abdominal and respiratory change
Ethambutol	Tablets, once daily	Side-effects are rare. Blindness may occur	Used with rifampicin or isoniazid	Report any visual disturbances

Maintaining a safe environment

- One of the main components of the treatment plan is rest; therefore the nurse must ensure that the problems arising from long-term rest, as previously described, are avoided.
- Long term rest will also have social and economic implications for the patient. The medical social worker should be asked to help the patient identify and overcome such problems.
- The patient's family and close contacts need to be investigated to see whether they have contracted the disease.
- Fresh air, more particularly sun, still has a part to play in the treatment of tuberculosis. This helps to increase the patient's metabolism and improves his feeling of well being.
- If the patient has 'open' tuberculosis, i.e., when the bacillus is found to be present in sputum, urine or in exudate from a sinus, barrier nursing techniques may be employed to nurse the patient.

Communicating

- The patient needs to be given full knowledge of his condition and made aware of the possible length of his treatment.

Breathing

- Deep breathing and expectoration is encouraged. Usually the patient is asked to spend 5–10 minutes every hour taking deep breaths and expectorating. Any sputum obtained must be kept in a closed container. This is changed and sent for incineration every 8–10 hours or more frequently if necessary.
- If sputum is being expectorated, a specimen is sent to the laboratory for culture and sensitivity.

Eating and drinking

- A full, nourishing diet is provided for the patient. Milk drinks and milk products are a necessary part of the diet to increase the protein content. This will aid repair of damaged tissues and generally improve the patient's health.
- Fluid intake should be at least three pints in a 24 hour period. If the patient is able to tolerate more, then this should be encouraged. This will help to avoid the problems of immobilization.

Eliminating

- A fluid balance chart is maintained to record accurately the patient's daily fluid intake and output.
- The patient's urine is observed for colour, particularly if he is prescribed rifampicin drugs. Routine weekly urinalysis is performed to observe for any abnormalities; in particular, proteinuria may be present as a result of the chemotherapy.
- Laboratory examination of the patient's urine is carried out on a weekly basis.

Personal cleansing and dressing

- The patient is usually able to maintain all aspects of his personal hygiene. Night sweats are a feature of the disease. These are very distressing for the patient who will require a wash, sometimes a full bath and change of night clothes following one of these episodes. At the same time, the bed clothes will need to be changed as these often become wet and then cold.

Working and playing

- Future employment may appear to be an insoluble problem for the patient. The medical social worker will investigate the possibility of the patient's return to work. If this is not possible, retraining may be a necessary step to consider.
- Because the disease is long term, diversional therapy will be necessary to help the patient maintain an interest.

Dying

- In the days before antibiotics, death was the outcome for the majority of patients with this disease. The stigma of tuberculosis is still found today. The patient may well have a fear that death will be the outcome of his disease.
- Knowledge about the disease and its treatment will help to allay this fear. The patient may wish to see a priest and this can be arranged.

TUBERCULOSIS OF THE SPINE (POTT'S DISEASE)

The vertebral column may be affected by the tubercle bacillus at any point throughout its length. The most commonly affected areas are the vertebrae in the thoraco-lumbar regions (see Figure 13.2). Children are particularly prone to the disease in this region.

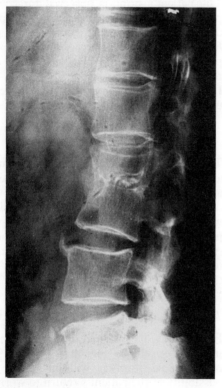

Fig. 13.2 Tuberculosis lesion of the lumbar spine showing affection of the disc and vertebral bodies.

Collapse of the vertebral bodies may produce protusion of the spinous processes (see Figure 13.3). This produces an acute 'hump' on the patient's back called a kyphos or gibbus.

As a result of the deformity or local abscess formation, pressure may be put on the spinal cord. This results in an increase of the tendon reflexes of the lower limbs with sensory changes occurring. This spastic lower limb paralysis is termed Pott's paraplegia. The paralysis may be partial or complete.

The patient's treatment follows the general pattern of treatment. Rest is achieved by nursing the patient in a plaster bed or on a Stryker frame. Both of these methods provide total rest

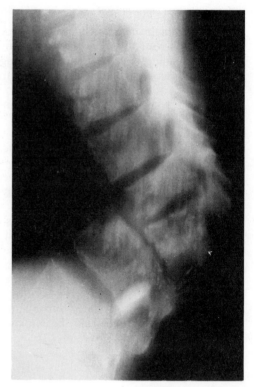

Fig. 13.3 Tuberculosis of the spine showing collapse of the vertebrae and the formation of a kyphos.

for the patient and immobilize the vertebral column.

Special intervention to decompress the spinal cord may be undertaken. If there is evidence of a local abscess an anterior approach may be used. This will involve a thoracotomy, and the patient is returned from surgery with a chest drainage system in place.

Nonoperative treatments

Immobilization

Total immobilization of the vertebral column by placing the patient on a plaster bed or Stryker frame.

Protective orthoses and plasters

These are used particularly when the patient is able to stand up and mobilize following treatment on a plaster bed.

1. Cervical lesions:
   A Minerva plaster jacket (see Figure 13.4).

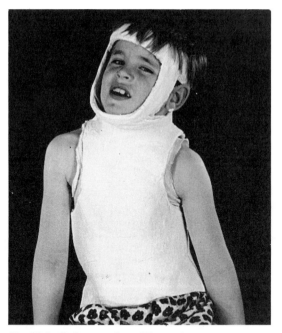

Fig. 13.4 Patient wearing a Minerva jacket.

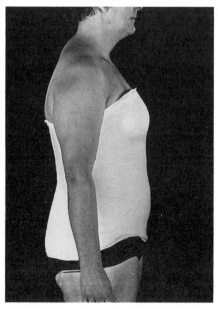

Fig. 13.5 A patient in a spinal jacket extending from the upper end of the sternum to the pubis.

A neck collar of leather, plastic or other firm material.
2. Thoracic lesions:
    A plaster jacket which may include a neck brace or collar if it is a high lesion.
    Spinal brace.
    Plaster, leather or plastic jacket (see Figure 13.5).
3. Lumbar lesions:
    Plaster spica.
    Goldthwaite belt.

THE PLASTER BED

The plaster bed is made in two halves; an anterior shell or turning case, and a posterior shell (see Figure 13.6). The posterior shell of the bed is made first. It is moulded around the contours of the body and around the kyphos, if there is one present. It is vital that the bed is an exact replica of the patient's back and it fits the patient like a second skin. If the bed is a perfect fit, there should be no need to line or pad it. However, some centres feel that by lining the bed the patient is warmer and more at ease. Gamgee tissue or Plastazote or some other thin material may be used to line the bed if it is felt necessary. If a lining is used it is essential that it

is not too thick or this will distort the bed and it must be kept wrinkle free.

Making a plaster bed

The patient will need a great deal of support during the procedure as he is usually frightened and apprehensive. A nurse must stay near to his head to talk to him and to tell him what is going on (see Figure 13.7). Occasionally a sedative is prescribed for the patient before the procedure starts. The making of a plaster bed is for an expert, but the nurse needs to know an outline of the procedure. This is set out below:

1. The patient lies prone on the table with his spine straight, head central, scapulae level, arms at his sides. His hips are extended and abducted sufficiently to allow normal use of a bed pan and to facilitate cleaning afterwards. If the legs are abducted too much the patient will feel spread-eagled. The knees are flexed to 5 degrees by putting a sandbag under the patient's ankles.
2. All of the patient's bony prominences, including the kyphos, are protected by pads of felt. The patient's hair is then

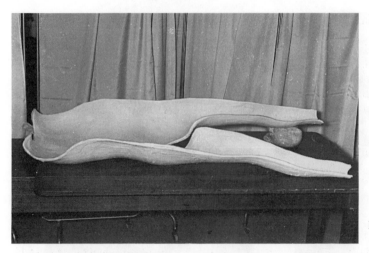

Fig. 13.6 Anterior shell for turning the patient.

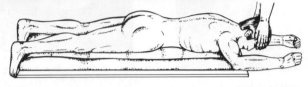

Fig. 13.7 Position of a patient for the application of plaster bed. The arms and head must be held or supported on a rest.

protected by a cover, and warm olive oil is poured over the patient's skin.

3. The bed extends from the seventh cervical vertebra to the tip of the coccyx. The leg pieces end just above the knee or above the malleoli (see Figure 13.8).

4. Prepared sheets of plaster are then quickly applied to the patient's back and legs. Layers are applied until the right thickness is achieved. No air is allowed between the layers or this will weaken the plaster shell.

5. The plaster is moulded to the patient's body contours. It is reinforced between the gluteal fold and upper thigh, as this is an area which takes a lot of stress.

6. When the plaster has set, it is marked for trimming and then carefully lifted off the patient. The shell is dried, usually in an oven. This will take from between two to

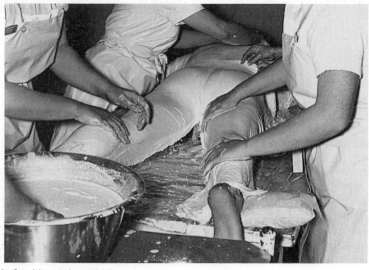

Fig. 13.8 Method of making a plaster bed.

three days. It is trimmed and the edges then smoothed.

7. Once the shell has been lifted off the patient his back is washed and dried. The patient is quickly covered as he will feel cold following removal of the warm plaster. The patient is then returned to his own bed.

8. A wooden frame is made to support the plaster bed and a turning case. The turning case is much lighter than the bed, but it is made by a similar method, often while the patient is lying in his plaster bed (see Figure 13.9).

The plaster bed may be suspended by a series of cords and pulleys from an overhead beam (see Figure 13.10). This method has the advantage of enabling the patient to learn to tilt himself from side to side or head to foot. By being able to do this the patient is able to see what is going on within his immediate vicinity. It is an aid to preventing renal complications and facilitates easier nursing by giving the nurse access to underneath the patient. The patient may also be able to feed himself with greater ease.

Specific nursing care for a patient in a plaster bed

Maintaining a safe environment

- The wooden frame with the plaster bed in place is placed on to a firm-based bed on top of the mattress. Foot stirrups are attached to the end of the leg pieces. Pillows are placed ready for the patient's head. A platform is often built on to the frame for this, or a stool may be used on which the pillows are placed. The frame will have pieces of wood down each side on which a pillow may be placed for the patient's arms. A tilting bed mirror is attached to the head of the bed.
- If it is at all possible the patient should be allowed to settle into the bed for a day or two. This may not be possible in an emergency situation.
- The patient is carefully lifted into the bed by a team of nurses. The patient's vertebral column must be kept straight. His legs and head must be supported throughout the procedure.
- The patient wears an open backed gown.

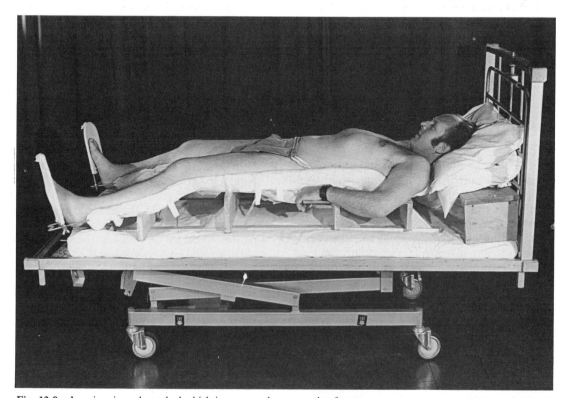

Fig. 13.9 A patient in a plaster bed which is supported on a wooden frame.

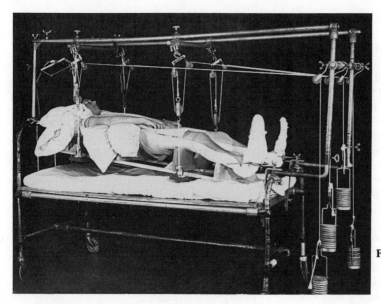

Fig. 13.10   A triple pulley attached to a plaster bed allows the patient to change position while retaining full immobilization of the spine.

This may be the patient's own nightdress, nightshirt or pyjama jacket put on back to front. Bed socks may be necessary to add extra warmth, as may a bed jacket or cardigan.

- Once the patient is in the bed, it is important to check that the bed is not causing undue pressure or discomfort. Each part of the patient should be inspected in turn. The patient's buttocks must not bulge through the cut away area, otherwise they will swell.
- The patient's locker and personal belongings are placed close at hand. It is sometimes possible to raise the patient's locker on a platform to provide easier access for the patient.
- The patient is instructed in the use of the overhead mirror and shown how to tilt it to the best advantage.
- The patient is not left unattended for long periods during the first two days. The nurse responsible for his care should constantly attend him to provide reassurance and respond to any complaint he may have quickly.
- Some patients complain of abdominal and thigh pain. This is due to stretching of the muscles in this region. It may be relieved by placing pillows on the leg pieces and flexing the patient's knees over them. This, however, must only be a very short-term measure.
- Vomiting may be a problem following the patient being put into the bed. This must not

be ignored as it may be the start of a paralytic ileus. The doctor must be informed and, if necessary, a gastric tube with suction passed. The patient is removed from the plaster bed and is fed through an intravenous route until the problem has resolved.

Breathing

- The normal activities of living may become difficult at first. Breathing needs to be monitored. The patient should be encouraged to breathe normally.

Eating and drinking

- Nutrition may be difficult at first. The patient is given small, light meals to start with. They are cut up as required. A large napkin is spread over the patient's chest, and with the help of the overhead mirror, the patient is encouraged to feed himself. Most patients manage this very well. A full nutritious diet may then be introduced.
- A high fluid intake is essential. This prevents the formation of renal calculi and subsequent infection. Some patients are happy to take fluid from a feeding cup, some manage better with an angled straw or glass rod.

Eliminating

- Elimination may prove both difficult and

embarrassing at first. Micturition may be easier for a male patient than a female patient. A female urinal may be used. The nurse will need to hold this for the patient during the first few days, but most patients manage to do this for themselves quite quickly. A female urinal has the advantage over a bed pan of reducing the risk of contamination of the plaster bed by urine. If all other remedies have been unsuccessful, as a last resort, catheterization may be used.

- For the patient to have his bowels open successfully, complete privacy is important. If necessary, a small enema or suppositories may be used to help the patient at first. It can be very embarrassing for an able-bodied adult to need cleaning following a bowel action. The nurse needs to be tactful and aware of this feeling when carrying this out.

Personal cleansing and dressing

- Personal hygiene needs to be assisted. The patient's legs are lifted gently by one nurse from the plaster bed to enable a second nurse to wash both the back and the front of the leg. Each is carefully dried and inspected for signs of pressure. The calves are gently massaged to encourage the flow of blood. Particular attention must be paid to the back of the heel, the malleoli and the area of skin around the head of the fibula. Some surgeons prefer the patient's knees to be bandaged into the bed. If this is the case, the bandage is removed, the patella gently mobilized after washing has taken place. The leg is then rebandaged into place.
- The patient's buttocks and anal region must be washed and dried daily. The area is inspected for signs of swelling and pressure.
- It is often difficult for a patient lying flat to reach the genital region. However, a long handled mop, or occasionally a soaped flannel, handed to the patient, may enable them to do this for themselves under the sheet.
- The patient's hair will need to be brushed or combed, particularly at the back. One nurse supports the patient's neck and head, while a second nurse brushes the patient's hair and turns the pillows.
- The patient may find it difficult to clean his teeth. The use of an electric toothbrush may help this. If this is not possible, once the patient has brushed his teeth, rinsing is

achieved by taking fluid via a straw and a receiver is held close to the patient's cheek to catch the fluid.

- A warm flannelette sheet is placed next to the patient and light, but warm, blankets placed over this. It is not necessary to use a bed cradle, as the foot stirrups should remove the weight of the bedclothes from the patient's feet. This should help to maintain the patient's warmth.

Mobilizing

- Physiotherapy is important. Passive exercises of the patient's lower limbs, particularly if they are paralysed, are performed at least twice daily. If the patient has no paralysis, then active exercises of his ankle and feet should be performed for five minutes every hour.
- Active arm exercises are encouraged. If the patient's plaster bed is suspended, this will automatically help exercise the patient's arms each time he tilts his bed.

Expressing sexuality

- Although the patient is lying flat and is heavily dependent on the nurse, he should be encouraged to retain his individuality and sexuality. Male patients should be encouraged to shave, unless they have, or wish to, grow a beard. Female patients should be encouraged to apply make-up as they would normally.

General care of the patient in a plaster bed

The patient is turned according to the policy set by the ward sister. This may be once a week, once a month or more frequently if specific procedures, such as the removal of sutures, are necessary.

Turning may be achieved manually or by the use of a turning machine. Whichever method is selected, the patient must be given complete confidence in the people turning him. Individualized care lends itself to building up a trusting relationship between the patient and the nurse.

The anterior turning case is placed over the patient and strapped securely into place. The patient's hands are held in front of the anterior case and he is turned (see Figure 13.11).

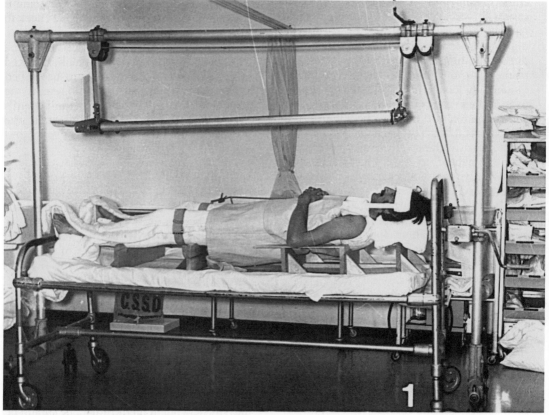

Fig. 13.11   Preparing to turn a patient using a turning frame. The anterior shell has been strapped in place.

Once the patient is turned prone, his back is inspected for signs of undue pressure. The skin is washed and dried and, at this time, the patient's hair may also be washed. The patient is covered and left for a short period of time. During this time the plaster bed is inspected for signs of wear or stress. Any rough edges are smoothed by applying waterproof adhesive tape. The lining, if one is used, is renewed.

When the patient is due to return, the bed is placed over the patient and the steps for turning are observed and carried out to return the patient back on to his frame in his own bed.

TUBERCULOSIS OF JOINTS

Muscle spasm and pain are prominent features of tuberculosis of joints. This is due to the destruction of the joint surface by the disease process. A synovial effusion, due to the thickened and inflamed synovium, may be another prominent feature. Joints will eventually fuse as a result of the bony destruction of joint surfaces.

Nonoperative treatments of tuberculosis of joints

General measures

These are as described on page 157.

Traction

Traction is used to rest the joint and to reduce muscle spasm:
1. Hip joint: a plaster bed may be used with leg skin traction and weight and pulley.
2. Knee joint: Thomas bed knee splint, with or without leg skin traction and weight and pulley.

Plaster fixation

1. Plaster bed: a plaster bed may be used

to immobilize both the hip and the knee joints.

2. Plaster spica: to immobilize the hip or knee joint.
3. Weight bearing plaster: a below knee weight bearing plaster will immobilize the ankle joint.
4. Infection: immobilization of an infection of the shoulder, elbow and wrist joints may be achieved by applying a plaster with the joint held in the position desired by the doctor.

Operative treatment

These are described under general treatments of tuberculosis (see page 158).

It is important that the nurse is familiar with the complications which may occur in patients as a result of a tuberculosis infection (see Table

Table 13.2   Complications which may occur in patients as a result of tuberculosis

Complication	General comments	Possible treatment or nursing care
Cold abscess	Cervical region: Paravertebral abscess which may track and eventually perforate into the pharynx and mouth (retropharyngeal abscess) Thoracic region: Paravertebral abscess which may remain localized or track through soft tissue to appear in the mid axilla. Lumbar region: Paravertebral abscess which may track through the iliopsoas muscle to appear in the groin (psoas abscess)	Evacuation of pus by aspiration under strict aseptic technique In some cases incision and drainage of the abscess may be carried out Postoperatively the nurse may have to include the care of chest drainage It is important to maintain strict observations of the patient's respiratory rate every fifteen minutes
Paraplegia		Extremes of temperature will aggravate muscle spasm and must be avoided A paralysed bladder is dealt with by a self-retaining catheter. Strict catheter care is maintained.
Muscle wastage	May occur as a result of joint destruction	Passive assisted and, whenever possible, active exercise is incorporated into a regime which the patient and nurse can carry out together
Sinus formation	A sinus provides a means of allowing other micro-organisms to gain entry into the body. This will mean the patient has two infections to combat	Strict aseptic technique is observed whenever dressing a sinus wound, however small the exit portal may be
Deformity of joints	These may be due to muscle spasm and destruction of joint surfaces	Great care is exercised when placing affected limbs in the bed. They must be supported in a functional position without muscles being left in a 'stretched' position
Tuberculous meningitis	Similar symptoms to general meningitis. The patient may eventually relapse into unconsciousness	Intrathecal injections of streptomycin are given daily. Nursing care is that of an unconcious patient
Amyloid disease	Associated with long standing infections. Waxy starch deposits are laid down in the vital organs. Metabolic processes then slow down. Death will eventually intercede It is rarely seen these days because of early detection of the disease and effective treatment by antibiotics	The patient exhibits symptoms of vomiting, diarrhoea or constipation. There is loss of weight and the patient becomes emaciated and exhausted

13.2). Her care may then be directed towards preventing the potential problems which may arise in her patient.

Tuberculosis is a chronic condition. As such it is important that the nurse teaches the patient all aspects of the disease. Any change in the patient's general health may indicate the possibility of a fresh lesion. Variations in temperature, a cough or complaints of pain in another joint should be reported. Loss of weight or anorexia are other signs which should alert the patient and his family to the possibility of recurrence of the problems.

The patient should be encouraged to have regular examinations by his general practitioner. The primary health care team are alerted to keep a watch on the patient's home circumstances.

Any orthoses used by the patient will require regular examination for wear and tear and replacement as necessary.

As mentioned, retraining of the patient into a suitable occupation may be necessary.

REFERENCES

1. Grenville-Mathers R. (1979) Tuberculosis in Britain today. *Midwife, Health Visitor and Community Nurse,* May, pp 79–81.
2. Rachmond I. (1979) Recent trends in pulmonary TB. *Nursing Times,* March 8th, pp 404–405.

SUGGESTED FURTHER READING

Girdlestone G.R., Somerville E.W. & Wilkinson M.C. (1965) *Tuberculosis of Bone and Joint,* 3rd Edn. Oxford: Oxford University Press.

Lobo E.H. de (1978) *Children of Immigrants to Britain: Their Health and Social Problems.* London: Hodder and Stoughton.

Powell M. (1986) *Orthopaedic Nursing and Rehabilitation,* 9th Edn. Edinburgh: Churchill Livingstone.

14

CARE OF PATIENTS WITH DISEASES OF THE NERVOUS SYSTEM

MANAGEMENT OF PATIENTS WITH CEREBRAL PALSY

Cerebral palsy was first described by Dr John Little in 1853. It was known as Little's disease for some time.

Cerebral palsy is a disorder of the brain, either from nondevelopment of the cells, or as a result of damage to the brain. It may develop at any period during life, but is most commonly seen in children as a result of anoxaemia at birth.

The child is left with a paralysis of part, or the whole of, the musculo-skeletal system. He may also have some degree of deafness, blindness and impaired mental capacity. It should be emphasized that not all cerebral palsy children are mentally subnormal. Some are very intelligent. Their inability to see, hear and to control their facial muscles may be regarded superficially as evidence of mental subnormality. It is important that accurate assessment of all of the child's abilities are made before conclusions are finalized.

There is no cure for cerebral palsy. The aim of treatment is to make the child as independent as possible and to develop and use as many of the unaffected muscles as possible. The Peto Institute in Hungary has developed a method of conductive education for these children. This involves intensive movement of the child's limbs. Dr Peto believes this will educate those parts of the brain which are unaffected by the lesion to take over the work of the affected parts. Long-term evaluation of this method is yet to be made.

The condition varies from very mild, when one group of muscles is affected, to very severe, where the child is totally helpless is every respect. Management of the child is a team effort involving the doctor, nurse, physiotherapist, occupational therapist, medical social worker, orthotist, the parents and, wherever possible, the child.

Orthopaedic nurses have a tendency to see these children only when they are admitted to hospital for a variety of treatments. A great deal of work with these children takes place in residential homes or special schools. Many successful attempts have been made to integrate them into the community and into normal school streams.

The main types of cerebral palsy are as follows:

1. *Spastic palsy* (20 per cent). This follows damage to the motor cortex. In untreated cases the classical deformity of 'scissor gait' may develop.
2. *Athetoid palsy* (20 per cent). This is caused by damage to the basal ganglia and the mid-brain. The child has no control over voluntary movement.
3. *Ataxia* (10 per cent). This is when the child has incoordination of his muscles.
4. *Rigid with tremors* (5 per cent). The lesion is believed to be in the mid-brain. This type is seldom seen.
5. *Mixed* (45 per cent). The child displays two or more signs of the previous types mentioned.

Treatment is begun as soon as the diagnosis is confirmed. Most of the time these children are healthy children.

Nursing care of the child with cerebral palsy

Any nursing plan can only be made on careful assessment of the individual patient's needs. All assessments must be continuous, as is evaluation of the outcome of nursing actions.

The nursing plan is a vital part of the care of

the child with cerebral palsy. It must be made with the multidisciplinary team. The actions planned should make full use of the child's abilities and potential.

The value of an ordered routine is explained to the parents where the child knows what is going to happen next.

Maintaining a safe environment

- A feeling of security is vital to these children who lose their balance easily. The first essential element is to gain the child's confidence by talking to him and showing him around the environment.
- Special equipment such as standing tables, which enable the child to stand supported and still use his arms, may be used. These need to be individually tailored for the child. Chairs are adapted to hold the child safely. All equipment is regularly checked to make sure it fits the child as he grows.
- Spastic limbs need to be handled gently. The child should never be forced into doing something. The child's limbs must be moved smoothly without abrupt jerky movements.
- The child must be encouraged at all stages. Patience and perseverence become the watchwords for the nurse.

Communicating

This may be difficult if the child has difficulties with speech and hearing. There are many devices which may introduce the child to accurate communication by using methods other than speech. Frustration at not being able to speak may lead the child to irrational and ill-tempered behaviour.

- Always tell the child what you are going to do and try to ascertain whether they have understood.
- Communication with the child's parents and siblings is essential. They must all be encouraged to participate in life with the affected child.

Breathing

Few problems arise with this activity of daily living.

- If possible, the child's head and shoulders should be raised and supported to help the child control his head. This will help respirations to be free.

Eating and drinking

- The child should be encouraged to feed himself. Protective clothing may be necessary for the child. It is important that sufficient time is allowed and the child is not hurried.
- Success in feeding themselves must be praised by the nurse to provide motivation for the child to continue.
- Careful observation of the amount the child actually eats and drinks is important. If the child is being encouraged to be independent, the nurse must know how much food and drink actually goes into the child and how much lands on the floor.
- Make sure food and drink is never boiling hot or the child may burn himself during feeding.
- Because the child is not always active, carbohydrate intake must be carefully assessed. Over indulgent parents are discouraged from providing the child with too many sweets.

Eliminating

Control of the bladder and bowels is learnt very slowly.

- Patience in teaching the child how to be successful at toileting themselves is important.
- Check that the child has cleaned themselves adequately following bowel evacuation.
- Make sure the child washes his hands each time he goes to the toilet.
- Carefully designed toilets will provide safety for the child during elimination.

Personal cleansing and dressing

- The bath must be prepared at a temperature not exceeding 38°C, otherwise the water will scald the child.
- There should be no running water and the child is washed with firm, even movements to prevent spasm occurring.
- The child is gradually introduced to independent washing and dressing, if possible.

- Clothes must be loose and easy for the child to handle. It is always tempting to help a struggling child, but in these cases it is detrimental. The child must be encouraged to succeed himself.
- Selection of clothes and aids, such as long handled combs and toothbrushes, to help the child are made by the occupational therapist in consultation with the parents and the rest of the team.

Controlling body temperature

- These children are susceptible to cold, which exacerbates their muscle spasms. Their environment should be maintained at an even temperature without excessive heat or cold.

Mobilizing

The physiotherapist has an important role in all mobility activities. The nurse cooperates with the physiotherapist to enable the child to gain maximum independence in this area.

- Relaxation techniques are taught to the child. These must be carried out regularly.
- Rhythmic movements and coordination exercises of affected limbs may help to control a spastic limb.
- Warm baths and hydrotherapy may help to exercise limbs.
- Play forms a valuable part in encouraging the child to move, but over tiredness and fatigue must be avoided.
- Extra rest periods are essential for the child.
- Passive movements are never performed as these will cause pain and increase spasm.
- Aids for walking and orthoses to aid stability are selected as appropriate for the individual child.

Working and playing

- Play is an important part of training the child and allowing him pleasure.
- Education is of vital importance. Careful assessment of the child's potential is necessary. Special equipment is used to enable the child to gain maximum education.
- Speech therapy is started as soon as is practical.

Expressing sexuality

Children with cerebral palsy have a warm, friendly nature. They have a desire to be recognized as equals among their peer group. Integration into such a group requires careful counselling of its members by the appropriate team member.

Operative measures

Surgical intervention is only undertaken in selective cases.

1. *Arthrodesis.* Once skeletal maturity has been attained, some joints may be fixed in a position of function and to improve the appearance of a limb.
2. *Osteotomy.* This may be used to improve the function of a joint.
3. *Tendon transfers.* The tendon of an overactive muscle is transposed to allow it to act as the opposing force; e.g., iliopsoas tendon may be taken from its insertion on the lesser trochanter and inserted on to the greater trochanter. This will help to overcome a flexion deformity of the hip joint.
4. *Tenotomy.* Division of the tendon of an over active muscle will help to lessen the deformity; e.g., an adductor tenotomy of the hip joint will help to overcome an adduction deformity.
5. *Neurectomy.* Division of a nerve to an over active muscle; e.g., an obturator neurectomy where the anterior branch of the obturator nerve is divided, will help to lessen an adduction deformity of the hip.

Postoperatively the nurse needs to be vigilant in her observations of any plasters or splints applied to the child's limbs to retain the position of the limb. Constant friction between the cast and the limb caused by spasms may result in sores forming.

The whole team need to provide constant support for the family. Local support groups are active in many areas for parents with children with this problem. Contact with other parents is important. Family involvement with the child is essential for the normal social and psychological and emotional growth of the affected child.

MANAGEMENT OF THE PATIENT WITH ANTERIOR POLIOMYELITIS

Poliomyelitis is a condition caused by a virus which infiltrates the motor cells in the anterior horn of the spinal cord. The resulting paralysis may be permanent or temporary, depending on how much of each motor cell is destroyed. There are two main types:

1. The bulbar type, which affects the brain stem.
2. The spinal type, which affects the spinal cord.

The incidence of anterior poliomyelitis in the Western World has been greatly reduced by the vaccination programmes set up by governments. However, in Third World countries it is still one of the frequently seen problems, in spite of the World Health Organization's attempts to secure a vaccination programme.

The Salk vaccine was introduced in 1954. This has been succeeded by the Sabin vaccine which is a live oral attenuated polio virus, usually given on a sugar cube.

Nursing care of a patient with anterior poliomyelitis

Nursing management depends on which stage of the disease process the patient has reached:

Stage I

This is the stage when the patient presents with a typical 'flu-like' illness. The patient may complain of a sore throat and muscle tenderness. If symptoms of meningitis, i.e., neck rigidity and photophobia develop, then medical advice is sought immediately.

Stage II

This is the time when paralysis is at its greatest. The paralysis is a lower motor neurone one. The muscles are flaccid. Respiratory complications may develop. The patient may need a positive pressure ventilator to assist breathing. Pooling of the patient's lung secretions and the inability to swallow fluids may lead to flooding of the lungs.

Stage III

This is the convalescent stage when there may be some recovery of power to some of the affected muscles. Those motor cells which have sustained only temporary damage now start to recover.

Stage IV

This is the residual stage when the patient is discharged from hospital. Residual paralysis at this stage is permanent.

Specific nursing care

Maintaining a safe environment

*   The patient should be constantly observed until the full extent of the paralysis is known in case respiratory complications occur. Observations of temperature, pulse and respirations are recorded. Any alteration in the rate and depth of the patient's respirations should be reported to the doctor straight away.
*   The time when the patient is infective is still undecided. Some centres may choose to barrier nurse the patient until the third stage of the disease is reached.
*   The patient must be nursed in a quiet part of the ward. During the acute stages of the disease he should be disturbed as little as possible. Any nursing procedures are performed with the minimal amount of fuss. Some doctors require the patient to be sedated.
*   Support for the parents, if the patient is a child, is important. The nurse must adopt a positive outlook, even when the prognosis is unsure.
*   The patient is nursed flat in bed with his trunk and limbs supported to prevent deformities occurring. His arms are supported on pillows, slightly abducted at the shoulder joint, with his hands and wrists placed in a functional position. His legs are supported by a small pillow placed behind the knee and his feet rested on a sandbag or footboard in a neutral position.
*   The patient is turned at regular intervals, two, four or six hourly according to the individual needs. Turns are from side to side, prone and supine. The patient may only tolerate very short periods lying prone.

Turning will help to prevent chest complications, the development of pressure sores and relieve pain.

- The patient frequently complains of pain, particularly in the small of his back. A small pillow placed there to support the back may also help to relieve this. Analgesia is only given in extreme cases as it may mask the symptoms of meningism which can arise.
- The environment should be kept at an even temperature. Extremes of temperature may increase the pain the patient experiences.

Breathing

- If bulbar poliomyelitis occurs, special care of the tracheostomy tubes and the ventilator is required.

Eating and drinking

- The patient generally has a poor appetite. Very small, frequent meals should be offered to the patient.
- Fluid intake is monitored carefully and recorded on a fluid balance chart. The use of straws or a feeding cup may enable the patient to take his fluids.

Eliminating

- Retention of urine may be present. The patient will require an indwelling catheter to be inserted. Careful toilet of the area should be carried out every four hours. Weekly specimens of urine are sent to the laboratory for culture and sensitivity.
- Constipation is another feature. The patient may have poor abdominal musculature which will contribute to this. It is important to establish a regular pattern for the patient's bowels at an early stage. Suppositories or a small enema are given every other day to establish this.
- The patient will require to be lifted on to a bed pan. Once on the pan, it is essential to retain a good position for the patient's trunk and limbs. Pillows must be placed strategically to support the patient.

Controlling body temperature

- The patient's limbs will have poor circulation which will lead to the patient feeling cold. The patient should be kept warm, but not overheated. Gentle massage of the limbs may help to stimulate circulation.

Personal cleansing and dressing

- Routine measures are carried out to maintain the patient's personal hygiene. Mouthwashes or oral toilet are given after every meal.

Mobilizing

- One of the main aims of treatment is to prevent deformity occurring. By the end of the first week of the disease, very gentle passive movements may be attempted of all the affected joints, once or twice daily, within the pain tolerance level of the patient. By the end of the third week, passive movements are usually pain free and can be more frequently performed for the patient.
- Physiotherapy and hydrotherapy become increasingly important as the acute stages of the disease are over. The nurse must learn all the techniques used for her particular patient to enable the exercises to be continued at regular intervals. It is important, in the early days, that paralysed muscles are not over used and thus fatigued and that they are maintained in an unstretched position. Mobility of all joints is maintained either by passive or assisted movement by the nurse for the patient, or actively by the patient himself.

Working and playing

- Aids to assist mobility and the activities of daily life are designed to meet the individual patient's needs.

A long term outlook is essential involving suitable education for the child. Vocational training and employment and a useful future for the patient are important parts of the care of the patient.

SUGGESTED FURTHER READING

Levitt S. (1984) *Treatment of Cerebral Palsy and Motor Delay*. London: Blackwell Scientific.
Samilson R.L. (1980) *Orthopaedic Aspects of Cerebral Palsy*. London: Heinemann Medical.

15

NURSING CARE OF THE AMPUTEE

Loss of part or all of a limb is an experience which few of us will ever have to face. It is a mutilation of the body and as such demands a great deal of understanding from the nurse and the team involved with the care of the patient. Amputation has been likened to the death of a close relative or friend. A period of 'mourning' for the loss is an essential part of recovery for the patient.

Amputation affects all age groups of people.

If the amputation is due to trauma there is little time for the nurse to prepare the patient and his family for the event. Patient and family education, because of the time factor, is limited. If the amputation is for elective reasons careful preparation of the patient, both physically and mentally, is possible. The final acceptance of an amputation needs courage from both the patient and his family.

Reasons for amputation

Peripheral vascular disease

This is the commonest cause of amputations. The patient is usually elderly and has intractable leg pain, often both at night and during the day. Sixty per cent of all amputees are over 60 years of age and their amputation is generally performed for ischaemia.

Trauma

Where there has been excessive tissue damage, particularly to the blood supply, amputation may be the only course left. Bomb blast injuries, frost bite and burns are also included in this category.

Malignant neoplasms

The problem of metastases (e.g., osteosarcoma) may make amputation necessary.

Infections

1. Acute infections, such as gas gangrene.

2. Chronic infections, such as chronic osteomyelitis.

Both situations may be life-threatening. With chronic infections long periods of incapacity and pain for the patient may be the prime considerations for amputation.

Deformity

For a patient with a deformity which is not correctable, amputation of the affected limb may enable them to lead an active life.

Paralysis

Particularly where there is loss of sensation, amputation, followed by the fitting of a useful prosthesis, will enable the patient to continue an active life.

Possible sites for amputation of the lower and upper limbs are illustrated in figures 15.1 and 15.2.

Pre-operative nursing care for a patient having amputation of a lower limb

The aim of surgery is to provide a functional, viable, well moulded stump that is able to take a prosthesis whenever possible. It is important for the patient to set himself realistic goals to achieve, both pre-operatively and postoperatively.

Physical preparation

- The skin of the affected limb is prepared as for any area where surgery is anticipated.
- The patient's toe nails are cleaned and cut. It may be necessary to ask the chiropodist to visit the patient.
- The patient is taught how to lift his buttocks free from the bed to prevent undue pressure.
- Exercises are taught to the patient by the physiotherapist to strengthen the patient's

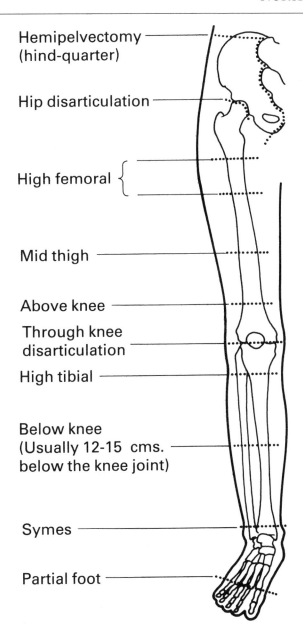

Hemipelvectomy
(hind-quarter)

Hip disarticulation

High femoral

Mid thigh

Above knee

Through knee
disarticulation

High tibial

Below knee
(Usually 12-15 cms.
below the knee joint)

Symes

Partial foot

Fig. 15.1   Possible sites for amputation of
a lower limb.

sound limbs. The affected limb's muscles above the line of expected surgery are also strengthened. If it is a lower limb amputation, the gluteal and quadricep muscles are particularly important.

- How to walk with crutches is practised by the patient. Explanations about the possible loss of a sense of balance are given to the patient.
- Any incorrect posture is corrected at this stage.
- Particular attention is given to the condition of the sound limb in a lower limb amputation to ensure the patient's mobilization following surgery is not hindered.

- The patient is taken to the artificial limb centre to enable him to become familiar with the prosthetist. Discussions on the type of prosthesis to be used will take place and the patient shown an example.
- The occupational therapist will make an assessment of the patient's potential capabilities for discharge. She may liaise with the social services department to enable altera-

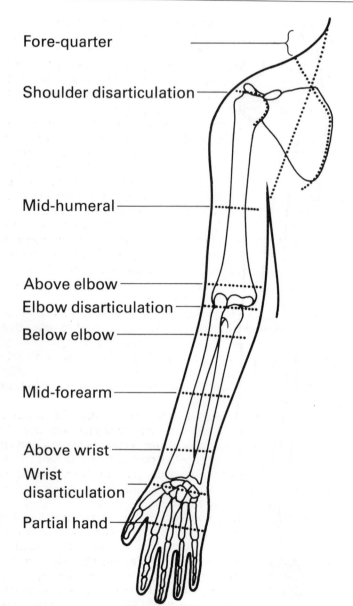

Fig. 15.2 Possible sites for amputation of an upper limb.

tions to the patient's home to be completed prior to discharge.

- The patient is encouraged to lie prone at least twice a day to become familiar with this position before surgery. Not all elderly patients are able to do this. This helps to prevent flexion contractures occurring at the hip joint of the stump.

Psychological care

- The patient will need time to adjust to the idea of an amputation. The doctor will have explained the reasons why surgery is necessary. The nurse must know these reasons to help her to aid the patient to an understanding of the proposed surgery.
- Family reactions and adjustment to the amputation will affect the patient. Time given to the family to talk about his fears, and understanding, will in the end benefit the patient.
- A full explanation of the postoperative regime is given to the patient.

- Some surgeons believe if the patient is warned of 'phantom limb' pains pre-operatively, they will experience these far worse postoperatively. The nurse will need to ascertain the doctor's feelings about this before talking to the patient.
- A visit from a similar, successful amputee may help the patient to accept the situation. The amputee must, however, be of similar age and sex and have received the amputation for a similar reason.
- Depression, a sense of defeat and loss of self-esteem are all phases the patient may experience prior to surgery. The nurse needs to be aware of these problems. She may need to allow the patient privacy for outbursts of anger or crying.

Specific postoperative nursing care of a patient following amputation of a limb

Maintaining a safe environment

Immediate fitting of a temporary prosthesis while the patient is still in the operating theatre is not often undertaken. The postoperative care described here is for the more common procedure of fitting the prosthesis once the postoperative period for the patient is complete.

- In the immediate postoperative phase observations of the patient's vital signs are very important to detect the onset of haemorrhage. These should be recorded at 15–30 minute intervals until the patient's condition is stable, then every 2–4 hours for the following 48 hours.
- The patient's stump is placed flat on the bed, never flexed over a pillow which may cause a flexion contracture to occur. It should be handled firmly but gently.
- To prevent abduction contractures occurring, the stump should also be placed near the sound limb in normal anatomical alignment.
- The foot of the bed may be elevated to prevent oedema occurring. Swelling may distort the shape of the stump creating a problem for an accurate prosthesis to be fitted.
- The wound dressing is observed for staining. Should any seepage occur the original dressing is left undisturbed. A thick, firm dressing is bandaged into place over it. Careful

bandaging of the stump is essential to retain it in functional shape. The stump is sometimes encased in a plaster of Paris cast following surgery. In this case the normal practice for drying plaster casts is observed.
- Any drains are removed at 48 hours, providing drainage has stopped.
- Sutures are removed at between twelve and fourteen days, providing the wound has healed. Careful bandaging of the stump is continued following removal of the sutures. The patient is taught how to do the bandaging as soon as it is realistically possible. Patients sometimes have great difficulty in looking at their stumps during the early postoperative days. This situation needs to be dealt with by a great deal of tact by the nurse. The stump should, if possible, not be hidden from view from the beginning of the postoperative care.
- The patient should be nursed in a bed where the top bedclothes are divided in order that the stump may be observed from the point of view of haemorrhage. This should also help the patient to view his loss as a socially acceptable proposition, not one to be hidden from view.
- Painful muscle spasms may be present. Frequent adequate analgesia will help to reduce this. Firm, gentle pressure to retain the stump flat on the bed may help. It is essential that the pressure is very gentle as excessive pressure may lead to swelling at the end of the stump.
- Pain may continue for some time after the stump has healed satisfactorily. It is necessary to provide the patient with adequate, effective analgesia during this period. Anxiety and pain have been shown to go together. The nurse who spends time listening to her patient will help to reduce his pain levels.
- Early physiotherapy to both the affected and sound limbs is given. A range of exercises, which have been taught pre-operatively, are started as soon as possible. The patient is turned prone, as described, when this is possible.

Communicating

- Communications between the patient and his family, and between the team and the family, are encouraged. The family need to be able to support the patient's acceptance of his stump by looking at it without showing horror or fear.

Breathing

- Deep breathing exercises are encouraged to aid circulation and are taught to the patient. The nurse may need to supervise such exercises to ensure they are carried out by the patient at predetermined intervals. The patient must maintain a good posture for breathing to help prevent a chest infection.

Personal cleansing and dressing

- Early independence in the activities of daily living will help the patient to accept his new body image. It is important to encourage the patient to maintain his former standards of personal cleansing. This will help him to think positively of his discharge and future.
- The prevention of pressure sores due to circulatory problems is important. Careful assessment of the patient's risk factor and appropriate nursing intervention is vital.

Eliminating

- Elimination may cause problems as the patient's centre of gravity is altered. Balancing on a bed pan may be difficult. To help overcome this a commode may be a safer way to successful elimination for the patient. A sliding board, placed alongside the patient, may help the transfer from his bed onto the commode during the early days.

Mobilizing

- Mobilization is started as soon as possible. The patient may sit out for short periods within three or four days of surgery. The short periods are necessary to prevent the patient's stump flexing for long periods. Within ten days of surgery the patient is mobilized in the gymnasium between parallel bars. Crutches or a frame may be used at this stage.
- Correct posture and balance need to be regained by the patient.
- Within fourteen days the patient will return to the 'Artificial Limb Application Centre' to be measured for a pylon or other walking device.

- Providing the patient's home circumstances are satisfactory he may be discharged at this stage. Liaison with community services is important. The patient will continue his treatment as an outpatient. The patient is usually fitted with his pylon within 28 days following surgery. Training continues either as an in-patient within the hospital or a special unit, if it is available. Once the patient is safe and managing his prosthesis he is discharged home once again. At about two to three months postoperatively the patient is reassessed by the limb fitting centre. If he is walking satisfactorily and the stump is well healed and moulded, a cast will be taken of the stump for a permanent artificial limb.

Care of the patient's stump is ongoing. The patient is taught to clean his stump as he would any other part of his body. Massaging and handling the stump is another way of encouraging the patient to accept the loss of his limb. Within four to six months the patient should have been fitted with his permanent limb. Training to enable him to regain his full independence is completed.

Reassessment throughout the remainder of his life may be necessary to accommodate the various changes which may take place within the stump.

Emotional support for the patient from the community services may be necessary over a long period. This support may be necessary for the family as well as for the patient.

Care of the patient's sound limb should be emphasized. Regular foot care, and if necessary, visits to a chiropodist are encouraged.

Care of patients following bilateral amputations

Double amputees require special consideration. Amputation of both lower limbs is a serious disability. The nurse needs to provide extra emotional support for the patient. Motivation is the prime factor in helping the patient towards success. Small, easily achievable, patient centred goals are set by the nurse for these patients. They can lead useful and active lives and are encouraged to be positive in their outlook.

Nursing care for a patient with amputation of an upper limb

Upper limb amputations are most commonly

traumatic or performed for malignant neoplasms.

The care for these patients follows closely that as described for the lower limb amputee. However, with traumatic amputations very little preparation can be carried out. Emotional support and psychological care are important areas for the nurse to deal with in these cases. If the patient has lost his dominant hand, he will require time to relearn many of his normal everyday activities such as writing, feeding, personal care and handling objects. Communication by touch and feel may be hampered. The nurse is required to give time to the patient as he tries to remaster these tasks.

Fitting of a prosthesis is carefully explained to the patient. The prosthesis will never totally replace a normal hand. Many activities are, however, reproduced by a successful prosthesis, but sensation will never be regained. The patient will take time to adjust to the loss of this sense.

SUGGESTED FURTHER READING

Humm W. & Rainey A.E.S. (1979) *Rehabilitation of the Lower Limb Amputee*, 3rd edn. London: Baillière Tindall.

16

THE MULTIDISCIPLINARY TEAM AND REHABILITATION

Although the term 'rehabilitation' has taken on many different meanings, it is seen as a process which begins when the person first suffers an acute illness or has an injury. It continues throughout each phase of care and may eventually need the individual to adapt to a new way of life. This has been reflected in all the previous chapters.

Rehabilitation will be needed by most persons at some time during their lifetime. With the increase of medical knowledge and treatments there is an increase in the number of children with chronic illnesses living into adult life. Likewise, the number of adults treated for conditions which would previously cause death have increased. As a consequence of the increased life expectancy of all age groups, rehabilitation services are required to deal with the increase in disabilities resulting from this. At the same time there has been an increase in the number of accidental injury cases and trauma to all age groups.

Rehabilitation is a team effort, the patient being an important member of the team. Philip Nichols (1) states: 'The secret of rehabilitation is the giving of the right help at the right time.' This applies as much to the nurse in the team approach to rehabilitation as it does to any other member. Communication between every member of the team and frequent case conferences with the patient and his family will ensure that everyone is aware of the various stages reached by the patient.

Most patients admitted to hospital will not require intensive rehabilitation programmes. Some patients do however require this. These patients are often admitted to a centre which is designed for such a purpose. At these centres the individual skills of a rehabilitation team are closely integrated to enable each patient to achieve maximum independence.

Ultimately the success of any rehabilitation programme will depend upon the cooperation of the patient and his family. The will to recover and succeed is within each one of us. The understanding the patient has of his disability and the acceptance of his limitations is important.

A rehabilitation centre should have a relaxed, informal atmosphere. There is no need for the centre to retain an acute hospital appearance. There should be ample room to allow for wheelchairs and mobility. The patients should be encouraged to be up and dressed each day. Rooms, where privacy can be achieved, are important. The patient's own room may contain familiar objects from home, personal photographs and plants which create a feeling of not being in an institution.

'Any rehabilitation programme, whether for child or adult, must be based on the belief that the individual with a disability is an individual first and foremost.' (2) With this concept in mind careful assessment, problem-solving and goal setting must involve the patient, his family and the whole team.

The nurse spends more time with the patient than anyone else. She needs to be aware of the role of other members of a rehabilitation team to enable her patient to resume his place in society. Rehabilitation requires the collaboration of all health care professionals and is the right of all disabled persons.

THE ROLE OF THE NURSE IN THE REHABILITATION TEAM

The nurse is an important member of any rehabilitation team as she is with the patient for many hours. The nurse needs to encourage the patient in his activities and allow the patient time to succeed and to talk. An encouraging word, approach or attitude does a lot to the success of any rehabilitation programme.

Bill Ellis (3) writing about his recovery from

total paralysis says: 'How important it is for those who are low to get words that will encourage and help raise them from depression.'

The nurse's role changes as the patient progresses. Total dependence of the patient on the nurse is rarely necessary once the acute stage of the disease has passed. The move towards self care by the patient is usually very gradual. If self care is never to be achieved by the patient then the caring aspect is gradually taken over by an outside agent, usually a relative. This allows the patient to become independent of institutional care.

Primary nursing is an ideal method of organizing nursing in a rehabilitation establishment. A close relationship can be established with the patient which will be of great benefit. The nurse will then be able to pass on information to other members of the team. The role of counsellor becomes easier in this situation and good communication with the patient is maintained on a personal basis. Dorethea Orem's model for nursing practice may be an appropriate tool on which to base nursing care in these departments.

Whilst retaining her own professional role the nurse needs an understanding of the role of other team members and of the facilities available to help these patients.

THE ROLE OF THE PHYSIOTHERAPIST

Physiotherapy is always an essential part of orthopaedic treatment. 'Physiotherapists are concerned with the maintenance of total body function during acute illness, as well as the maintenance of joint range, and muscle power of the limbs.' (1) Their activities are aimed at achieving early mobilization and rehabilitation following acute illness or injury. For those patients with a long-term disability they are involved in the assessment and use of many aids and appliances. They are often required to adapt standard wheelchairs, hoists and splints to the requirement of the individual.

Physiotherapy techniques can be broadly divided into those in which the patient takes a passive role and those in which the patient has an active part.

Passive treatments

These treatments include the use of heat, electrical current, manipulations and massage. Passive movement of a joint is performed by the physiotherapist on the patient. They are used when control of the joint is affected by disease or injury such as is seen in poliomyelitis or peripheral nerve lesions. The joint is gently put through a full range of movement to prevent stiffness and soft tissue contractures occurring. Passive movement cannot be used for stiff joints, only those joints in which muscle control has been interfered with.

Active movements

These movements are a series of exercises performed by the patient. The exercises are taught by the physiotherapist and changed as the patient's muscles begin to gain power. The aims of active exercises are as set out below:

1. Conserve the function of joints and muscles during periods of immobilization or bed rest.
2. Strengthen weak muscles.
3. Restore mobility in joints following manipulation by a surgeon.
4. Re-educate neuromuscular control in order to walk following a period of immobilization or bed rest.
5. Aid the prevention of the complications of bed rest, e.g., deep venous thrombosis or chest problems.

Active assisted exercises

These are performed by the patient with the assistance of another person or by a piece of apparatus. The apparatus may be a polished board, water, suspended slings or weights and pulleys.

Resisted movements

These movements occur when the patient exercises against resistance supplied by another person, gravity or apparatus, such as springs or pulleys and weights.

Treatment by heat or cold

Heat has been used as a treatment for musculoskeletal pain and stiffness for many years. It may be applied to the body surface by radiation of energy into the body, warm water compresses, warm baths and wax baths.

Ultrasound, sound waves with a high frequency, have been shown to accelerate the healing processes of tissues.

Ice may also relieve pain and stiffness and reduce oedema. It is particularly valuable for patients who have had knee surgery or for those patients who have painful spasm associated with spinal cord lesions.

Hydrotherapy

Hydrotherapy is treatment in a pool where the water is maintained at blood temperature. The buoyancy and warmth of the water enables active and passive exercises to be achieved (see Figure 16.1).

THE ROLE OF THE OCCUPATIONAL THERAPIST

Occupational therapy has a traditional picture of providing diversional therapy for the long-stay patient in a hospital setting. This type of therapy still retains an important role within many settings, but with the advent of increased knowledge and treatments, there are fewer long-stay patients. The work undertaken by the occupational therapist is now one based mainly on assessment of the patient's actual and poten-

tial functional capabilities. She has an increasing part to play in assisting the patient to return to his fullest possible physical, psychological and social competence. This will include assessing the patient's domestic circumstances, his former occupation and his customary role in life.

The patient's activities with which the occupational therapist is mainly concerned are:

1. *Mobility:*
    Transfer from bed to chair, toilet and bath.
    Need for transport, and if it is available.
    Type of residence.
    Access to house or flat (whether there are steps and stairs).
    Use of wheelchair.
    Use of walking aids and appliances.
2. *Personal care*:
    Personal hygiene.
    Feeding (see Figures 16.2 and 16.3), and whether there is a need for meals on wheels.
    Dressing.
    Communication (speech, telephone, writing, typing, reading, shopping).
3. *Domestic activities*:
    Housework.
    Meal preparation and cooking.
    Laundry.
    Ability to manage small children at home.

Fig. 16.1 Hydrotherapy (by courtesy of The Spastics Society).

Fig. 16.2 Training a patient with an upper limb prosthesis.

4. *Employment*:
    Problems with previous job.
    Schooling and education of children.
    Retraining and training of older children.
5. *Leisure activities*:
    Games and hobbies (such as gardening).

Much of the occupational therapist's work is done in a community setting. In the patient's home she becomes closely involved with the patient and his daily life. Eventually she is often able to provide a counselling service enabling the patient to discuss his problems as they arise. The therapist is then able to alert other members of the team involved with the patient to these problems.

Assessment is an ongoing process and, as such, the occupational therapist is involved in a continual reappraisal of the patient's needs to enable him to live his life to the fullest (see Figure 16.4). Long-term planning of resettlement in the home and at work are a great stimulant to active recovery (see Figure 16.5).

THE ROLE OF THE MEDICAL SOCIAL WORKER

The medical social worker is involved with the social or psychological difficulties which are caused by illness or accident and which are likely to interfere with resettlement into the family, community or employment. Part of her work will be concerned with social conditions, income, housing, transport and retraining when necessary.

In the outpatient department the social worker is able to help the patient prior to admission to hospital. She will provide information on the services available to the patient and his family to enable him to overcome difficulties prior to and during his admission, such as payment for visits to the hospital.

During the time the patient is in hospital her help continues to make sure the patient's personal problems, such as finance, are not causing undue worry to the patient. She will also start to encourage the patient and his family to accept his altered social role and monitor his progress in this context, if appropriate.

The social worker's part in preparing the patient for discharge is to make sure the patient is prepared mentally for his return home. She will alert the patient to the benefits to which he is entitled.

These benefits include:

Family income supplement.
Sickness and invalidity benefit.
Industrial injury and disablement benefits.
Attendance allowance.
Mobility allowance.
Heating allowance.

Fig. 16.3   Training the flail limb in bilateral activities using ball-bearing supports.

She will coordinate the community services and agencies necessary to help the patient return home. These are available through the Social Services Department and include:

Meals on wheels.
Home help.
Help in obtaining a telephone.
Day care.
Car invalid badge.
Home adaptation grants, to enable the patient to manage such things as a wheelchair in the home.

Aids to help with the normal activities of daily living, e.g., raised toilet seats.

Once the patient has been discharged the medical social worker will continue to give support to the patient and his family. It is sometimes necessary for long-term social care to be given to the patient. This will enable them to lessen the dependence on others and to live their own lives as normally as possible within their own homes.

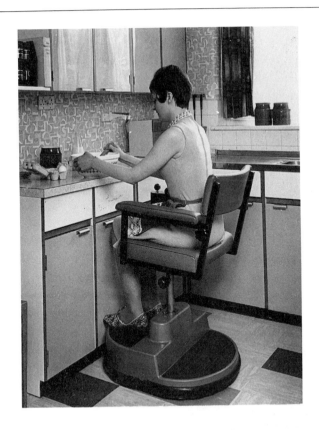

Fig. 16.4 Assessment of a disabled person in the working kitchen (by courtesy of Newton Aids Ltd).

THE ROLE OF THE DISABLEMENT RESETTLEMENT OFFICER

The disablement resettlement officer's (DRO) role in the rehabilitation of the patient is to provide retraining and job placement, when appropriate, and he works closely with the patient's occupational therapist. He assesses the patient's potential ability for work and may need to negotiate with an employer for the patient to return to part-time employment at first. If the patient is unable to return to a previous occupation, retraining may be necessary. The DRO is able to place the patient within specialized centres to enable this process to be completed.

THE ROLE OF THE SEXUAL COUNSELLOR

Everyone has the need to love and be loved and to express some form of sexual image. Many disabled people feel they are unable to fulfil either of these roles. The sexual counsellor is a very necessary member of the rehabilitation team. The sexual counsellor works with the patients gradually to allow them the realization that they can achieve a full sexual life within the limits of their disabilities.

Such organizations as the Committee on Sexual and Personal Relationships of the Disabled (SPOD) and the Family Planning Association are setting up counselling services in many areas. This is an important area of rehabilitation of the disabled which has for too long been ignored.

REFERENCES

1. Nichols P.J.R. (1980) *Rehabilitation Medicine*. London: Butterworth and Co.
2. Ince L.P. (1974) *The Rehabilitation Medicine Services*. Springfield, Illinois: Charles C. Thomas.
3. Ellis B. (1981) *The Long Road Back*, edited by Mary Kenny. Great Britain: Mayhew-McCrimmon Ltd.

SUGGESTED FURTHER READING

Davies B.M. (1982) *The Disabled Child and Adult*. London: Baillière Tindall.

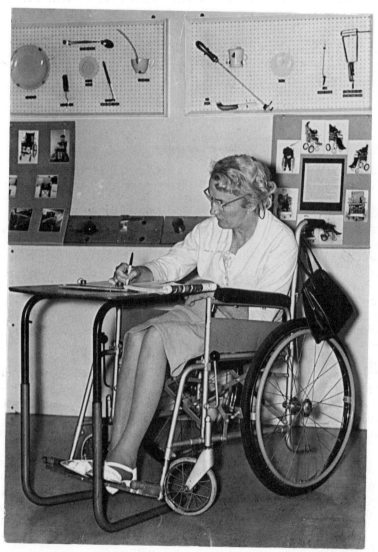

Fig. 16.5   Assessment room in the disabled living research unit.

Macdonald E.M. (1985) *Occupational Therapy in Rehabilitation*, 4th edn. London: Baillière Tindall.

Nichols P.J.R. (1980) *Rehabilitation Medicine*, 2nd edn. London: Butterworth & Co.

Nichols P.J.R., with Haworth R. & Hopkins J. (1981) *An Illustrated Manual of Self Help*. London: David & Charles.

GLOSSARY OF ORTHOPAEDIC TERMS

Active movement: Movement of a joint performed by the person's own efforts.

Adhesion: Abnormal attachment between two structures normally separated.

Ankylosis: Spontaneous fusion of a joint by either fibrous or bony tissue.

Arthrodesis: Surgical fusion of a joint.

Arthroplasty: Remodelling or reorganization of a joint.

Arthrotomy: Surgical opening of a joint.

Atrophy: Wasting, usually of muscle.

Avulsion: Forcible separation.

Brodie's abscess: An abscess of bone due to chronic infection.

Bursitis: Inflammation of a bursa.

Carpal: Relating to the wrist.

Charcot's joint: A neuropathic joint with osteoarthrosis.

Chondromalacia: Erosion of articular cartilage.

Clonus: Spasmodic movement of a muscle.

Cold abscess: An abscess caused by a tubercular infection with few if any signs of inflammation.

Coxa: Relating to the hip.

Cubitus: Relating to the elbow.

Diaphysis: Shaft of a long bone.

Dislocation: Displacement of joint surfaces.

Distraction: Excessive pulling on a broken bone.

Dorsal: Relating to the back of the trunk.

Dorsiflexion: Bringing the foot and toes upwards.

Dupuytren's contracture: Contracture of the palmar fascia.

Dysplasia: Disordered growth.

Dystrophy: Disorder of a muscle or organ caused by faulty nutrition of the part.

Eburnation: Dense bone formed when cartilage is worn away.

Effusion: An increase of synovial fluid within a joint causing swelling.

Epiphysis: Growth nucleus at bone ends.

Equinus: Plantar flexion of the foot.

Exostosis: A bony outgrowth.

Extracapsular: Outside the joint capsule.

Fascia: A sheath of connective tissue enclosing muscles.

Flexor: Any muscle causing flexion of a limb.

Ganglion: A small cystic swelling near a joint.

Gibbus: An acute angling of the vertebral spinous processes causing a hump.

Haemarthrosis: A collection of blood in a joint.

Haemophilia: A familial disease characterized by absence of some degree of the clotting factor in the blood.

Hallux: The big toe.

Hemiplegia: Paralysis of one half of the body.

Hyperextension: The forcible extension of a limb beyond the normal position.

Idiopathic: Cause unknown.

Involucrum: New bone laid down outside of existing bone.

Ischaemia: Inadequate or deficient blood supply to a part of the body.

Isometric: The contraction and relaxation of muscles without producing movement.

Kyphosis: Posterior curvature of the spine.

Lordosis: Abnormal forward curve of the spine.

Lower motor neurone: Motor cells in the anterior horn of the spinal cord whose axons transmit to the periphery.

Ligament: A band of fibrous tissue connecting a bone to a bone.

Meniscus: A semilunar cartilage in the knee.

Metatarsalgia: Pain in the metatarsal bones.

Monoplegia: Paralysis of one limb, a single muscle or a group of muscles.

Myelogram: Injection of a radio-opaque dye into the subarachnoid space to examine the spinal cord.

Myositis: Inflammation of muscle tissue.

Neurectomy: Surgical division of a nerve.

Optimum: Most favourable.

Orthosis: Splint or surgical appliance.

Osteoarthrosis: A degenerative 'wear and

tear' disease affecting the weight bearing joints.

Osteochondritis: Inflammation of cartilage and bone.

Osteophytes: New bone spurs found at the joint margins in a joint affected by osteoarthrosis.

Osteoporosis: Rarefaction of bone.

Osteotomy: Surgical division of a bone.

Passive movement: Movement of a joint performed by someone other than by the patient's own efforts.

Plantar flexion: Bringing the foot and toes downwards.

Prosthesis: An artificial part fitted to the body to replace a diseased or damaged part.

Pseudarthrosis: A false joint.

Radiculogram: An injection of radio-opaque dye into the subarachnoid space used to outline the nerve roots.

Reye's disease: Acute disease of childhood where there is fatty degeneration of the liver and other organs.

Scoliosis: Lateral curvature of the spine.

Spondylosis: Disease of the spine.

Subluxation: Partial dislocation of two surfaces normally in contact with each other.

Synovitis: Inflammation of the synovial membrane of a joint.

Tendon: A band of fibrous tissue attaching a muscle to a bone.

Tenosynovitis: Inflammation of a tendon sheath.

Tenotomy: Surgical division of a tendon.

Torticollis: Drawing of the head to one side.

Ultrasound: Sound waves used to examine the interior organs of the body.

Upper motor neurone: Motor cells whose axons extend from the cerebral cortex to end in the anterior horn of the spinal cord.

Valgus: The bone beyond the joint which qualifies the term is directed away from the midline of the body.

Varus: The bone beyond the joint which qualifies the term is directed towards the midline.

INDEX